Open Skies for Africa

Open Skies for Africa
Implementing the Yamoussoukro Decision

Charles E. Schlumberger

THE WORLD BANK
Washington, D.C.

© 2010 The International Bank for Reconstruction and Development / The World Bank

1818 H Street, NW
Washington, DC 20433
Telephone 202-473-1000
Internet www.worldbank.org
E-mail feedback@worldbank.org

All rights reserved.

1 2 3 4 :: 13 12 11 10

This volume is a product of the staff of the International Bank for Reconstruction and Development / The World Bank. The findings, interpretations, and conclusions expressed in this volume do not necessarily reflect the views of the Executive Directors of The World Bank or the governments they represent.

The World Bank does not guarantee the accuracy of the data included in this work. The boundaries, colors, denominations, and other information shown on any map in this work do not imply any judgment on the part of The World Bank concerning the legal status of any territory or the endorsement or acceptance of such boundaries.

Rights and Permissions

The material in this publication is copyrighted. Copying and/or transmitting portions or all of this work without permission may be a violation of applicable law. The International Bank for Reconstruction and Development / The World Bank encourages dissemination of its work and will normally grant permission to reproduce portions of the work promptly.

For permission to photocopy or reprint any part of this work, please send a request with complete information to the Copyright Clearance Center Inc., 222 Rosewood Drive, Danvers, MA 01923, USA; telephone: 978-750-8400; fax: 978-750-4470; Internet: www.copyright.com.

All other queries on rights and licenses, including subsidiary rights, should be addressed to the Office of the Publisher, The World Bank, 1818 H Street NW, Washington, DC 20433, USA; fax: 202-522-2422; e-mail: pubrights@worldbank.org.

ISBN: 978-0-8213-8205-9
eISBN: 978-0-8213-8206-6
DOI: 10.1596/978-0-8213-8205-9

Cover photo: Charles E. Schlumberger.

Cataloging-in-Publication data is available from the Library of Congress.

This book is dedicated to the many African men and women who, every day, fulfill their duties as pilots and flight attendants to the best of their abilities to ensure safe air travel, while sometimes facing difficult and exceptional challenges.

Contents

Foreword xi
Acknowledgments xiii
About the Author xv
Abbreviations xvii

| Chapter 1 | Introduction | 1 |
| | Notes | 7 |

Chapter 2	Elements and Entry into Force of the Yamoussoukro Decision	9
	The Yamoussoukro Declaration	9
	The Yamoussoukro Decision	10
	The Abuja Treaty and Its Entry into Force	16
	Entry into Force of the Yamoussoukro Decision	20
	Conclusion	27
	Notes	27

| Chapter 3 | Status Quo of the Implementation of the Yamoussoukro Decision | 29 |
| | Policy Implementation | 31 |

	Operational Implementation	37
	The African Air Transport Industry and Liberalization	41
	Safety and Security Requirements	42
	Implementation: Condition Precedent or Subsequent?	52
	Notes	57
Chapter 4	**Regional Implementation of the Yamoussoukro Decision**	**61**
	North Africa	62
	West Africa	72
	Central Africa	86
	Southern and East Africa	92
	Conclusion	110
	Notes	112
Chapter 5	**Impact of Liberalization**	**115**
	Data Sources and Methodology	115
	General Traffic Analysis	119
	General Fleet Analysis	121
	Effects of Liberalization on Traffic and Air Carriers by Region	124
	Conclusions	146
	Notes	148
Chapter 6	**Economic Aspects of Liberalizing Air Services in Africa**	**149**
	Economic Benefits of the Air Transport Sector	150
	Potential Impact of Liberalizing of Air Transport Services	157
	Economic Significance of Liberalizing African Air Transport Services	165
	Conclusion	168
	Notes	170
Chapter 7	**Conclusions and Policy Recommendations**	**171**
Appendix A	Ethiopian Air Service Agreements with Other African States	177

Appendix B	African Country Overview of Air Transport and the Yamoussoukro Decision	191
Appendix C	Safety Review and Rating of African States	199
Appendix D	Aviation Laws and Regulations Adopted and Enacted by the West African Economic and Monetary Union	207

References 215

Index 229

Boxes

1.1	Freedoms of the Air	4
3.1	Duties and Responsibilities of the Monitoring Body	56

Tables

3.1	Major Accidents of African Carriers Operating Western-Built Aircraft, October 1998–June 2008	45
3.2	Accidents of African Carriers Operating Western- or Eastern-Built Older Aircraft, February 1998–October 2007	49
3.3	Quality and Progress of Safety Oversight by RECs as of 2009	53
5.1	Grading of RECs on Their Liberalization of Air Services as of 30 June 2009	120
5.2	Estimated Number of Seats on International Flights within and between RECs, Selected Years	121
5.3	International Flights, REC City Pairs, Selected Years	122
5.4	Changes in Fleet Composition by REC, 2001–07	123
5.5	Fleet Analysis, Africa, Selected Years	125
5.6	Changes in the Number of Seats by REC	126
5.7	Fifth Freedom Flights by Carriers of Each REC, Selected Years	127
5.8	Fifth Freedom Flights by African Carriers of Other RECs, Selected Years	128
5.9	Fifth Freedom Flights by Non-African Carriers, Selected Years	128
5.10	Fleet Analysis, North Africa, Selected Years	129

5.11	Fleet Analysis, West Africa, Selected Years	131
5.12	Fleet Analysis, Central Africa, Selected Years	135
5.13	Out of Region Carriers Providing Intraregional Service in CEMAC, 2007	136
5.14	Fleet Analysis, East Africa, Selected Years	138
5.15	Fleet Analysis, Southern Africa, Selected Years	141
5.16	Fleet Evolution of Major South African Carriers, Selected Years	142
5.17	Fleet Analysis, Indian Ocean Island Countries, Selected Years	145
A.1	Bilateral Air Service Agreements Concluded by Ethiopia with Other African States as of October 2006	178
A.2	Summary of Intra-African Bilateral Air Service Agreements Concluded by Ethiopia in Conformity with the Yamoussoukro Decision and Actual Routes Flown	188

Foreword

It gives me much pleasure to write this foreword for the publication of Dr. Charles E. Schlumberger's research on the implementation of the Yamoussoukro Decision. Dr. Schlumberger, a scholar and professional who has made a significant contribution to civil aviation in Africa through his position at the World Bank, has written a penetrating book on a subject that profoundly affects African aviation, addressing numerous issues and providing an impressive spectrum of facts and creative thoughts on the Decision's current and future relevance.

Dr. Schlumberger analyzes in depth the major elements and objectives of the Yamoussoukro Declaration, adopted by the African Union states in 1999, which calls for gradual transition toward the multiple designation of airlines; the free grant of third, fourth, and fifth freedom traffic rights; no regulation of capacity and tariffs; and complete liberalization of non-scheduled and air cargo operations. He discusses the relationship between the Declaration and the Yamoussoukro Decision, explaining the enduring relationship between the two documents and ensuring a credible link between them.

Dr. Schlumberger goes on to discuss conditions and requirements for implementation of the Decision on a regional basis against the backdrop of liberalization of air services in Africa. He concludes with several policy recommendations for the implementation of the Yamoussoukro Decision within a robust and sustained safety and security oversight regime.

Many of the subjects treated in this work require a mastery of multiple disciplines such as law, economics, and management, all of which have required the application of the range of Dr. Schlumberger's knowledge to the depths of his curiosity. This comprehensive survey of the field by an able scholar and competent professional, whose specialization in African aviation has already earned him considerable attention, will be a leading contribution to the literature on the subject and will promote a better understanding of the manner in which the problems attendant on civil aviation in Africa can be addressed and overcome.

I commend this book to all those who are interested in aviation in Africa and wish it the success it deserves.

Raymond Benjamin
Secretary General
International Civil Aviation Organization

Acknowledgments

The research for this book would not have been possible without the consent and support of my employer, the World Bank. I am especially grateful to Maryvonne Plessis-Fraissard, former director of the Transport and Urban Development Unit; Jamal Saghir, current director of the Energy, Water, and Transport Department; and Marc H. Juhel, sector manager, Transport, for actively supporting my research by recognizing that it serves the interests of the World Bank and of its client countries in Africa. I also want to recognize two colleagues at the World Bank, Michel J. Iches, senior air transport economist, and Heinrich C. Bofinger, air transport consultant, for their dedication and efforts in supporting my research at Bank headquarters and in the field.

In addition, I would like to express my gratitude and thanks to Paul S. Dempsey, director of the Institute of Air and Space Law, McGill University, for motivating me to initiate this research and for providing me with excellent guidance and enlightening suggestions throughout the preparation of this book. His academic excellence and detailed knowledge in the field of air transport policy were essential elements for the successful conduct of this research. Also at the Institute of Air and Space Law, I want to give special thanks to my colleague Yaw Otu Mankata Nyampong, doctor of civil law candidate, for his continued support and advice during the preparation of this book.

This research would not have been possible without the willingness of numerous African government officials, airline executives and staff, and other persons engaged in air transportation in Africa to open their books and databases or to provide background information sometimes considered confidential. A warm and collective expression of thanks and appreciation goes to them.

This research is supported in part by a World Bank research project on trade in services which is partially financed by the governments of Norway, Sweden, and the United Kingdom through the Multidonor Trust Fund for Trade and Development.

Finally, I want to thank my wife, Maria Teresa Villanueva de Schlumberger, and our two children, Ana Cristina and Eric Manuel, for their understanding and sacrifice during the many nights and weekends I spent researching and writing this book. Without their support, my work would certainly not have been so fruitful. I have promised to stay home and dedicate more time to them in the future.

About the Author

Charles E. Schlumberger is the principal air transport specialist of the World Bank in Washington, DC. In this function he is responsible for the Bank's policy and development priorities in the field of air transportation. Prior to his appointment to the World Bank he held the position of vice president at the Union Bank of Switzerland, was the chief executive officer of the Steinbeck Global Logistics Group in France, and has worked as a lawyer on aviation-related matters in Switzerland. Schlumberger holds a law degree from Basel Law School in Switzerland, an MBA from Harvard Business School in the United States, and a doctorate in civil law from the Institute of Air and Space Law of McGill University in Canada.

Abbreviations

AEC	African Economic Community
AFCAC	African Civil Aviation Commission
AFRAA	African Airlines Association
AMU	Arab Maghreb Union
BAG	Banjul Accord Group
CEMAC	Communauté Économique et Monétaire de l'Afrique Centrale (Central African Economic and Monetary Community)
CFA	Communauté Financière Africaine
COMESA	Common Market for Eastern and Southern Africa
COSCAP	Cooperative Development of Operational Safety and Continued Airworthiness Program
EAC	East African Community
ECOWAS	Economic Community of West African States
EU	European Union
FAA	Federal Aviation Administration (United States)
GDP	gross domestic product
IATA	International Air Transport Association
ICAO	International Civil Aviation Organization
km	kilometer

MASA	Multilateral Air Services Agreement
OAU	Organisation of African Unity
PTA	Preferential Trade Area
REC	regional economic community
SADC	Southern African Development Community
SARP	standards and recommended practices
UNECA	United Nations Economic Commission for Africa
WAEMU	West African Economic and Monetary Union
WAMU	West African Monetary Union

CHAPTER 1

Introduction

In Africa, where poor road, port, and railway infrastructure often constrain the rapid and efficient transportation of both goods earmarked for export and passengers, air transport offers potential for growth and for economic development by fostering trade and foreign investment. However, Africa's air transport industry has always been a relatively small player compared with the global industry. In terms of revenue passenger-kilometers flown (1 revenue passenger-kilometer is defined as 1 fair-paying passenger transported 1 kilometer [km]), the intra-African market represents less than 1 percent of the global market and total African revenue passenger-kilometers (intra African and intercontinental traffic) account for only 4.12 percent of global revenue passenger-kilometers (Boeing Company 2006, p. 37). Given a potential market of more than 12 percent of the world's population, African air traffic is expected to grow at 5.7 percent, per year, which is considerably faster than the world average of 4.9 percent (Boeing Company 2006, p. 35). However, despite strong expected growth, intra-African markets in particular are still thin and most regions lack a true competitive environment.

Prior to gaining independence, most African countries had air services that were primarily based on European relationships and agreements. Only in the early 1960s, when many colonies became independent countries, did

African states begin to negotiate and conclude their own air services agreements. During that time, most of the newly independent African states also created their own, mostly government-owned, national air carriers, many of which failed (Guttery 1998).[1] Most of these African national carriers pursued a business model that consisted of using profitable international routes to and from the territories of their former colonial masters to cross-subsidize their costly, yet extensive, domestic route networks (Guttery 1998, p. 1). This often resulted in the maintenance of strict bilateral relationships for intercontinental routes, where capacity was limited and controlled to maximize profitability. Governments tended to view the development of regional air services as secondary, especially when they had to maintain a costly domestic network.

Nevertheless, following the international example pertaining at the time, intra-African air transport services also became regulated by the traditional framework of bilateral air service agreements (bilaterals). The typical bilaterals of the 1960s were based on the traditional predetermination model, under which market access and capacity were predetermined (Doganis 2001, p. 19).[2] This model controlled the market by effectively restricting competition. However, whereas liberalization of air services has been actively pursued in the United States since the late 1970s (see the details of the 1978 U.S. Airline Deregulation Act in Dempsey and Gesell 2004, p. 192) and in Europe since the late 1980s, African air services have remained generally restrictive, costly, and inefficient.[3]

In the early days of independence, air transportation came to be recognized as "both far-reaching and essential for the development of Inter-African trade and for the improvement of the economic, social and cultural conditions of the African peoples" (OAU 1973, p. 39). The main reason was that countries' road and highway networks, which existed prior to their independence, tended to serve only their own territories and were not interconnected. The road network was mainly designed to move raw materials from the interior to seaports rather than to link countries. At the same time, African politicians considered African air transport to be threatened by dominating carriers from Europe and especially the United States (OAU 1973, p. 39). This was because the main focus of African carriers in international air transport remained on intercontinental traffic, while the intra-African network remained far less developed. (As late as 1990, 249 bilaterals were still in place between Sub-Saharan African and other countries for intercontinental traffic versus only 57 bilaterals among African states for intra-Africa traffic [Institute of Air Transport 1990, p. 8].) In 1979, the threat of liberalization was seen as being driven by the "United States, which wished to export its deregulation throughout the world" (Institute of Air Transport 1990, p. 5) when it organized a conference on air transport in Nairobi. However, African states themselves also began to realize that "Europe itself, the buffer zone which could have protected Africa from the new policy's direct effects, has now joined the liberalization bandwagon, and Africa can no longer afford to be the odd man out" (Institute of Air Transport 1990, p. 5).

The Economic Commission for Africa of the United Nations Economic and Social Council (UNECA) had also recognized early on that a new policy was needed to support the development of Africa's air transport sector (UNECA 2004, p. 31).[4] UNECA's inspiration came from several declarations and resolutions that eventually resulted in the Lagos Plan of Action, all of which addressed the declining economic environment and the role of the air transport sector in Africa (UNECA 1988, Preamble). The Lagos Plan of Action aimed at promoting the integration of transport and communication infrastructure to increase intra-African trade and open up landlocked countries and isolated regions (OAU 1980, p. 58). It was the outcome of many discussions and consultations among African states that focused primarily on how to eliminate the physical and nonphysical barriers that hindered the development of intra-African air services (UNECA 2004, p. 31). The initiative, which was led by UNECA, considered intercontinental air service to be the prime instrument for Africa's integration and development. Consequently, intercontinental air service was only discussed in relation to its competitive aspects as posed by overseas operators. It was understood that African carriers first had to grow (and merge) before they could successfully enter the markets between Africa and Europe and the United States.

In November 1984, UNECA organized a conference in Mbabane, Swaziland, to discuss why African carriers faced difficulties in obtaining traffic rights in other African states. The conference ended with the Declaration of Mbabane, which called for the creation of a technical committee that would develop "a common African approach for the exchange of third and fourth freedom rights" and "encourage the exchange of fifth freedom rights" (UNECA 1988, p. 1) (box 1.1). It further proposed an additional set of measures that focused primarily on closer cooperation between African carriers. These measures, which later became the core of the Yamoussoukro Declaration, included a joint financing mechanism, a means of coordination for scheduling air services, a centralized databank and research program, and the promotion of the creation of subregional

Box 1.1

Freedoms of the Air

The freedoms of the air are defined as follows:

- *First freedom of the air.* The right or privilege, with respect to scheduled international air services, granted by one state to another state or states to fly across its territory without landing (also known as a first freedom right).
- *Second freedom of the air.* The right or privilege, with respect to scheduled international air services, granted by one state to another state or states to land in its territory for nontraffic purposes (also known as a second freedom right).
- *Third freedom of the air.* The right or privilege, with respect to scheduled international air services, granted by one state to another state to put down, in the territory of the first state, traffic coming from the home state of the carrier (also known as a third freedom right).
- *Fourth freedom of the air.* The right or privilege, with respect to scheduled international air services, granted by one state to another state to take on, in the territory of the first state, traffic destined for the home state of the carrier (also known as a fourth freedom right).
- *Fifth freedom of the air.* The right or privilege, with respect to scheduled international air services, granted by one state to another state to put down and to take on, in the territory of the first state, traffic coming from or destined to a third state (also known as a fifth freedom right).
- *Sixth freedom of the air.* The right or privilege, with respect to scheduled international air services, of transporting, via the home state of the carrier, traffic moving between two other states (also known as a sixth freedom right). The so-called sixth freedom of the air, unlike the first five freedoms, is not incorporated as such into any widely recognized air service agreements such as the Five Freedoms Agreement.
- *Seventh freedom of the air.* The right or privilege, with respect to scheduled international air services, granted by one state to another state, of transporting traffic between the territory of the granting state and any third state with no requirement to include on such operation any point in the territory of the recipient state, that is, the service need not connect to or be an extension of any service to and/or from the home state of the carrier.
- *Eighth freedom of the air.* The right or privilege, with respect to scheduled international air services, of transporting cabotage [trade] traffic between two points

(continued)

> **Box 1.1** *(continued)*
>
> in the territory of the granting state on a service that originates or terminates in the home country of the foreign carrier or (in connection with the so-called seventh freedom of the air) outside the territory of the granting state (also known as an eighth freedom right or consecutive cabotage).
> - *Ninth freedom of the air.* The right or privilege of transporting cabotage traffic of the granting state on a service performed entirely within the territory of the granting state (also known as a ninth freedom right or stand alone cabotage).
>
> *Source:* ICAO 2004b, part 4, p. 793.
> *Note:* The International Civil Aviation Organization characterizes all freedoms beyond the fifth as so-called, because only the first five freedoms have been officially recognized as such by international treaty.

carriers. However, the focus on liberalization quickly degraded, and in the Yamoussoukro Declaration it was only envisaged in the form of gradual elimination of traffic rights (UNECA 1988, Preamble). It was only a decade later, when the Yamoussoukro Decision was reached, that the policy focus shifted primarily to liberalizing access to intra-African air service markets.

In addition, the airlines themselves wanted to liberalize access to develop new markets. Represented by the African Airlines Association (AFRAA), the African airline industry proposed a set of rules and conditions to liberalize the granting of first to fifth freedom rights. In 1984, AFRAA proposed that all African carriers receive unrestricted first and second freedom rights, third and fourth freedom rights (limited to three a week) on certain defined corridors, and fifth freedom rights on multiple leg flights that had to be negotiated and agreed upon. Fifth freedom rights were to be given to carriers with multiple destinations in the hope of building a network, and sixth freedom rights were to be given to all North African carriers with Sub-Saharan destinations (UNECA 2004, pp. 33, 35).

Until 1991, nearly all African carriers were state owned. These carriers were mostly run as government entities and lacked the necessary economic and commercial focus to ensure market-based profitability. Their main means of operating with some profitability was to control income effectively, using restrictions provided by the framework of bilaterals. This allowed them to control the market and restrict the entrance of new carriers. In some cases, certain states even refused to grant traffic rights to foreign carriers even though their own carriers lacked the technical, human, and/or financial means to develop a proposed new route. Sometimes, however, they obtained fifth freedom rights by paying "royalties" or commissions (UNECA 2004, p. 33). As a result, intra-African air traffic remained costly and inefficient, especially in those cases where the bilaterals protected a state-owned carrier.

To address these shortcomings, on 14 November 1999, African ministers responsible for civil aviation adopted the Yamoussoukro Decision on the liberalization of access to air transport markets in Africa (UNECA 1999). In essence, the Yamoussoukro Decision is a multilateral agreement among most of the 54 African states.[5] It allows the multilateral exchange of up to fifth freedom air traffic rights between any African Yamoussoukro Decision party state using a simple notification procedure.[6] The Yamoussoukro Decision became fully binding on 12 August 2002, following its endorsement by heads of states and governments of the Organisation of African Unity (OAU) in July 2000. However, 20 years after the initial Yamoussoukro Declaration of 1988 and more than 5 years after the Yamoussoukro Decision became fully binding, only a few cases of the exercise of new air traffic rights granted by applying the principles and mechanism of the Yamoussoukro Decision have been observed. The reasons for not applying the Yamoussoukro Decision range from non-implementation of certain elements of the decision, for example, establishing competition rules, a dispute settlement mechanism, and an operational monitoring body, to simply ignoring it by continuing to agree to traditional restrictive bilaterals (see the example of Zambia discussed later).

For the purposes of this book, "open skies" refers to a bilateral or multilateral air service agreement that liberalizes the rules for international aviation markets and minimizes government intervention. It can apply to passenger or cargo services or both, for both scheduled and charter air services. This book evaluates Africa's progress toward liberalizing air services. It specifically examines what the term implementation means in the context of applying the principles of one of the major pan-African multilateral agreements, the Yamoussoukro Decision. It also highlights the shortcomings of the 20-year-old effort toward liberalizing air services in Africa by analyzing pending or completed implementation steps both on a pan-Africa level and within various regions. The book focuses on the challenges posed by the poor aviation safety and security standards in most African countries. Finally, the sector work measures the impact of certain policy steps of the decision and evaluates the economic significance of air transportation and its full liberalization in Africa. It concludes with policy recommendations that aim at completing implementation to fully liberalize Africa's air services.

Notes

1. Examples include Botswana National Airlines (1966–69); Air Burkina (1984); Royal Air Burundi (1960–63); Air Tchad (1966); Air Congo–Brazzaville (1961–65); Air Congo, later Air Zaire (1961–95); Air Djibouti (1963–70); Líneas Aéreas de Guinea Ecuatorial (1969); Gambia Airways (1964); Ghana Airways (1958); Air Guinée (1960); Air Bissau (1960); Lesotho Airways (1967–70); Libyan Arab Airlines (1964); Air Malawi (1964); Air Mali (1960); Air Mauritanie (1962); Air Mauritius (1967); Royal Air Maroc (1957); Air Namibia (1991); Air Niger (1966–93); Nigeria Airways (1958–2003); Air Rwanda (1975–96); Air Senegal (1962); Sierra Leone Airways (1958–87); Somali Airlines (1964); Royal Swazi National Airways (1978); Tunis Air (1948); Uganda Airlines (1976–2001); Zambia Airways (1963–94); and Air Zimbabwe (1980).
2. Doganis refers to the preliberalization types of bilateral air service agreements, which emerged in the aftermath of World War II with the prime purpose of controlling market access (points served and traffic rights), market entry (designation of airlines), capacity, and frequencies. This was the outcome after a failed attempt, spearheaded by the United States, to create a competitive regime for international air transport with minimal regulation at an intergovernmental conference held in Chicago in 1944.
3. A World Bank study (1998, p. 30) states that reasons for this are high operating and capital costs, which include 40 percent higher airline insurance premiums, 50 percent higher fuel costs, 15 to 30 percent higher lease rates for equipment, and 100 percent higher air navigation fees (compared with South America); high handling and maintenance costs; and difficulties in obtaining necessary working capital.
4. UNECA recognized air transportation as one of the most important modes of transportation for the physical integration of Africa. To examine and discuss its development, in 1964 UNECA organized the first conference on African continental air transportation in cooperation with the Organization for African Unity and the International Civil Aviation Organization.
5. Africa has 53 internationally recognized states; however, the African Union has granted membership to the Saharawi Arab Democratic Republic (better known as the Western Sahara), the territory of the former Spanish Sahara,

which proclaimed itself a country despite territorial claims by Morocco. This study will therefore assume a total of 54 states in Africa.

6. The five freedoms derive from negotiations during the International Civil Aviation Conference in Chicago in November 1944 (United Nations Information Organization 1944, pp. 1, 4, 31).

CHAPTER 2

Elements and Entry into Force of the Yamoussoukro Decision

The Yamoussoukro Declaration

On 17 October 1988, the ministers in charge of civil aviation of 40 African states met in Yamoussoukro, Côte d'Ivoire, and announced a new African air transport policy that was subsequently named the Yamoussoukro Declaration (UNECA 1988, p. 7).[1] Even though the Yamoussoukro Declaration is seen as the origin of the later Yamoussoukro Decision, it focused primarily on airline cooperation and integration. It stated a commitment by the governments represented to make all necessary efforts to integrate their airlines within eight years (UNECA 1988, p. 2). The eight-year period was subdivided into three phases. In the first phase (two years) the focus was to be on maximizing capacity usage between carriers. This was to be achieved by exchanging technical and capacity data, preparing for the designation of gateway airports, and promoting cooperation among national carriers in order to eventually merge them into larger and more competitive airlines. The second phase (three years) would have committed the airlines to joint operations on international routes. In addition, certain airline operations would have been conducted jointly to achieve better economies of scale and deeper integration, for example, instituting a common insurance mechanism and computer reservation system, purchasing spare parts and aircraft, undertaking promotion and marketing, providing training, and maintaining equipment (UNECA 1988, p. 3). The last phase (three years) was to be used to strive toward achieving the complete integration of airlines by establishing joint airline operations or entities (UNECA 1988, p. 4).

The stated strategy of cooperation and integration of African carriers seemed to be driven more by the need for pan-African cooperation than by the objective of creating a more competitive market environment. Nevertheless, the Yamoussoukro Declaration also foresaw the gradual elimination of traffic restrictions. Specifically, the granting of fifth freedom rights to African airlines during the implementation period was a declared necessary measure to achieve flexibility. However, the stated objectives and schemes aimed at full integration of the African air transport market, comprising at least 40 of the 53 African states, within eight years were overly ambitious. In addition, as its denotation indicated, the Yamoussoukro Declaration was widely understood to be a general, nonbinding expression of strategy (interviews with Jorge Lima Delgado Lopes, minister of infrastructure and transport of Cape Verde, on 13 May 2002; Sama Juma Ignatius, director general of the Cameroon Civil Aviation Authority on 27 August 2003; and António Pinto, director general of the Instituto De Aviação Civil de Moçambique on 30 March 2004).

Despite its too ambitious objectives and its weak likelihood of implementation, the Yamoussoukro Declaration set in motion further initiatives aimed at liberalizing the African air transport market. In 1994, having evaluated the steps required to implement the Yamoussoukro Declaration, the African ministers in charge of civil aviation met in Mauritius and agreed on a set of measures to facilitate the granting of third, fourth, and fifth freedom rights to African carriers. Most remarkable was the understanding that fifth freedom rights should be granted on routes where third and fourth freedom flights did not exist (UNECA 2004, p. 32).[2] Significant also was the fact that the Yamoussoukro Declaration enforced the notion that the air transport sector in Africa primarily needed to be liberalized.

This led UNECA to include the liberalization of air services in its work program. Furthermore, it was UNECA that, in November 1999, initiated the conference in Yamoussoukro that resulted in the Yamoussoukro Decision, the historic agreement to liberalize pan-African air services.

The Yamoussoukro Decision

On 13–14 November 1999, African ministers in charge of civil aviation met in Yamoussoukro, Côte d'Ivoire, to discuss the liberalization of air services. Their mandate was based mainly on the objectives of the

Yamoussoukro Declaration and on their previous decision adopted in Mauritius in September 1994 aimed at accelerating implementation of the Yamoussoukro Declaration. In addition, the recommendation of the 11th Conference of African Ministers Responsible for Transport and Communications held in Cairo in November 1997 called for a regional meeting of African ministers to find ways to implement the Yamoussoukro Declaration (UNECA 1999). The conference in Yamoussoukro ended with the adoption of the Decision Relating to the Implementation of the Yamoussoukro Declaration concerning the Liberalization of Access to Air Transport Markets in Africa, which became known as the Yamoussoukro Decision. The Yamoussoukro Decision was then formally adopted during the Assembly of Heads of State held in Lomé, Togo, on 10–12 July 2000.

The objective of the Yamoussoukro Decision is defined under Article 2, Scope of Application, as the gradual liberalization of scheduled and nonscheduled intra-African air transport services. The main elements are the granting to all state parties to the decision the free exercise of first, second, third, fourth, and fifth freedom rights on both scheduled and nonscheduled passenger and freight (cargo and mail) air services performed by an eligible airline. The granting of fifth freedom rights was initially limited in Article 3 by the possibility for a state to grant these rights only in specific circumstances.[3] However, this limitation was set for a transitional period of two years and expired on 12 August 2002. The Yamoussoukro Decision came into force on 12 August 2000, 30 days after its signature by the chair of the Assembly of the African Economic Community (AEC).

Article 4 of the Yamoussoukro Decision liberalizes tariffs to the extent that the aeronautical authorities of state parties do not require approval for any increases. An increase in tariffs has to be filed with the appropriate authorities only 30 working days before it enters into effect, while a lowering of tariffs takes effect immediately. As the Yamoussoukro Decision liberalizes only international air services, the tariff liberalization regime thereby established only applies to international air traffic.

In relation to capacity and frequency, Article 5 stipulates that frequencies and capacity offered on air services linking any city pair combination shall not be limited by either of the state parties concerned. It specifies this by providing that no state party shall unilaterally limit the volume of traffic, the type of aircraft to be operated, or the number of flights per week. However, the same article stipulates that for environmental, safety, technical, or other special considerations, states may limit traffic. While limitation or refusal of air services for environmental, safety or technical reasons are standard practices in traditional air service agreements (see, for example, the 1997 Air Transport Agreement between the United States of America and Singapore[4]), "other special considerations" needed further clarification.

The monitoring body, which was established in accordance with Article 9 of the Yamoussoukro Decision, issued a directive clarifying that other special considerations are primarily of a technical nature, such as fuel shortages, runway repairs in progress, or security issues (UNECA 2004, p. 89). These considerations should not be driven by commercial considerations in favor of any particular airline. Article 9 further sets out conditions applicable to any limitation of capacity and frequencies. The limitation must

- be nondiscriminatory to any carrier,
- be of limited duration,
- not affect the objectives of the Yamoussoukro Decision excessively,
- not distort competitive forces among carriers,
- not be too restrictive to tackle the problem and not be more restrictive than that applied to a party state and to the Yamoussoukro Decision.

In addition, a state party may refuse to authorize an increase in capacity if such additional capacity is not in compliance with the provisions of the rules of fair competition as set forth in Article 7.

Article 6 outlines the procedure for designating and authorizing an airline. Each state party can designate in writing at least one airline to operate intra-African air transport services. The notification to the other state party, or in fifth freedom cases, to two other state parties, must be done in writing through diplomatic channels. According to the directive of the monitoring body, a copy of the notification should be transmitted to the regional economic organizations concerned. The state party that grants the operational permit must in turn notify the monitoring body and the regional economic organization (UNECA 2004, p. 90). A state can designate any eligible airline from another state party to operate air services on its behalf, including an eligible African multinational airline in which it is a stakeholder. There is no limitation to the number of carriers a state party can designate, as long as they meet the eligibility criteria. The notification obligates the other state party to initiate the process of authorization and licensing of the designated airline to operate the services in accordance with its national laws. The authorization must be granted within 30 days, and the airline must submit its proposed schedule of flights to the appropriate authorities for approval.

The eligibility criteria, set forth in Article 6.9, aim at ensuring that the designated airline meets minimum standards with regard to its legal and physical establishment, its licensing and operating capacity, its insurance coverage, and its capacity to maintain international standards. The carrier must, therefore, be legally established in accordance with the regulations applicable in the relevant state party and have its headquarters, central administration, and principal place of business physically located in that same country. It must also be effectively controlled by the nationals of one, or in the case of multinational airlines, several, state parties. The airline (a) must be duly licensed by a state party as per the requirements of annex 6 of the 1944 Convention on International Civil Aviation;[5] (b) must fully own or have a long-term lease exceeding six months on an aircraft for which it has technical supervision; (c) must be adequately insured with regard to passengers, cargo, mail, baggage, and third parties; and (d) must be capable of demonstrating its ability to maintain standards equal at least to those set by the International Civil Aviation Organization (ICAO). If an airline fails to meet the eligibility criteria, a state party may revoke, suspend, or limit its operating authorization by informing the carrier at least 30 days before the measure enters into force (UNECA 2004, Article 6.10).

One of the strong elements of the Yamoussoukro Decision is its focus on safety and security. Not only must an airline meet the standards defined by ICAO, but the state parties explicitly reaffirm in Article 6.12 their obligation to comply with established civil aviation safety and security standards and practices. A state party must also recognize air operating certificates, certificates of airworthiness, certificates of competency, and the personnel licenses issued or validated by other state parties and still in force provided that the requirements for issuing such certificates or licenses are at least equal to the minimum standards set by ICAO. Although justified, the strong focus on safety and security has become the main obstacle to timely implementation, as many African states do not, or only marginally, comply with ICAO's safety and security standards and recommended practices (SARP).[6]

Another perceived obstacle to the implementation of the Yamoussoukro Decision is the issue of unfair competitive behavior when the decision is applied. Smaller African carriers in particular fear unfair competitive practices such as price dumping, when competing with larger established airlines (Macdonald 2006). Article 7 of the decision obligates state parties to "ensure fair opportunity on non-discriminatory basis for the designated African airline to effectively compete in providing air transport services within their respective territory." While this implies that certain common competition rules should be established, the Yamoussoukro Decision falls short of further defining this requirement. It does, nevertheless, refer in Article 8 to arbitration procedures, which are set forth in annex 2 of the decision. The latter primarily defines the duties and responsibilities of the monitoring body, which is established in Article 9. It does not make particular reference to competition rules or arbitration procedures except the duty of the monitoring body to prepare the relevant annexes to the Yamoussoukro Decision for adoption by the Subcommittee on Air Transport. The assumption is therefore that arbitration procedures, still missing from annex 2, are one of the tasks that must be performed by the monitoring body in order to implement the Yamoussoukro Decision. Another indication in annex 2 (g) is the monitoring body's obligation to state, at the request of state parties, its views on predatory and unfair competition practices.

The monitoring body is established in Article 9.1. Its principal responsibility is the overall supervision, follow-up, and implementation of the decision. It is composed of representatives of UNECA, the OAU, the African Civil Aviation Commission (AFCAC) (founded on 17 January 1969 as a specialized agency what was then the OAU, now the African Union, in the field of civil aviation, with headquarters in Dakar, Senegal), and AFRAA, who shall be assisted by representatives of subregional organizations. As defined in Article 9.2, the monitoring body's main purpose is to assist the Subcommittee on Air Transport, composed of African ministers responsible for civil aviation, to follow up on implementation of the decision. Article 9.3 refers to annex 3 of the decision for an outline of the monitoring body's overall duties and responsibilities, but as annex 3 does not exist, it presumably refers to annex 2, "Duties and Responsibilities of the Monitoring Body." As annex 3 became annex 2, the arbitration procedures referred to in Article 8 that were supposed to be spelled out in annex 2 were never prepared.

In addition to the monitoring body, an African air transport executing agency shall be established. Article 9.4 defines the principal responsibilities of this agency to be the supervision and management of Africa's liberalized air transport industry to ensure successful implementation of the Yamoussoukro Decision. Article 9.5 stipulates that it shall have "sufficient powers to formulate and enforce appropriate rules and regulations that give fair and equal opportunities to all players and promote healthy competition." In addition, in Article 9.6 the executing agency is also mandated to protect consumers' rights. In other words, it is the executing agency that is in charge of assuring fair competition and consumer protection once the appropriate rules have been drafted and adopted.

As a transitional measure, Article 10 (1) of the Yamoussoukro Decision provides the option for state parties not to grant and receive the rights and obligations envisaged in Articles 3 and 4, that is, up to unrestricted fifth freedom rights and a liberal tariff regime. This option is limited to a maximum transitional period of two years, which expired when the Yamoussoukro Decision became fully binding on 12 August 2002. Given that implementation of the Yamoussoukro Decision was considered pending for the past five years, the transitional measures remain theoretical and were never applied. According to the African Union (2005b, p. 11) reasons for the slow implementation of the Yamoussoukro Decision include the lack of tools and funds for monitoring implementation of the decision, the lack of clear and independent responsibilities assigned to the regional economic communities (RECs), the establishment of the monitoring mechanism without any clearly defined powers to prescribe rules, and the negative implications of the position and policy of the European Union (EU) on an open aviation area.

Finally, Article 11 of the Yamoussoukro Decision addresses some commercial and operational issues. In Article 11.1, certain commercial aspects are provided for on a reciprocal basis, such as (a) the right of the designated airline to establish offices in the territory of the other state party, (b) the right to convert and remit revenues in local currency without restrictions, (c) the option to pay for local expenses such as handling and fuel costs in local currency, and (d) the possibility of employing and bringing into the territory employees to perform various tasks. Article 11.2 allows the designated carrier certain operational flexibility, such as the use of one-way or return service on the concerned segments, the use of code sharing arrangements, and the right to serve additional points as well as to omit certain stops. The cooperative arrangements, first mentioned under operational flexibility by "the use of the same flight number," are further defined in Article 11.3 as marketing arrangements such as blocked space, code sharing, franchising, or leasing arrangements among state party airlines.

In addition to these operational issues, Article 11.4 provides the possibility for a state party to request consultations with respect to the interpretation or application of the Yamoussoukro Decision. This is enhanced by the mandate given in Article 11.5 to the Air Transport Subcommittee to review the decision every two years or earlier if requested by two-thirds of the state parties. The main purpose of the review is for the monitoring body to propose measures to further eliminate existing restrictions.

The Abuja Treaty and Its Entry into Force
Origins of the Treaty of Abuja
On 3 June 1991, an international treaty was signed in Abuja, Nigeria, that established the AEC. The Treaty Establishing the African Economic Community, commonly known as the Abuja Treaty, was the culmination of more than 30 years of initiatives all aimed at achieving greater economic, social, and cultural integration among African countries. The origin of these initiatives was the establishment of the OAU on 25 May 1963, in Addis Ababa, Ethiopia, by signature of the OAU Charter by the representatives of 32 governments (Charter of the Organization of African Unity [OAU Charter], Article XXXIII).[7] Subsequently, a further 21 African states joined the OAU, with South Africa becoming its 53rd member on 23 May 1994.

The main purpose of the OAU was to promote unity and solidarity among African states, coordinate efforts to improve living standards, defend the sovereignty and independence of African states, eradicate all forms of colonialism, and, promote international cooperation with due regard to the Charter of the United Nations and the Universal Declaration of Human Rights (OAU Charter, Article II). The OAU's initial purpose and mission were greatly influenced by a period of intense political struggle during 1960–63, with the "main preoccupation on an accelerated liberation process" (El-Ayouty and Zartman 1984, p. 4). Subsequently, during its initial decade, the OAU was primarily seen as a political organization that focused on the liberation struggle through both peaceful means, such as working through the United Nations, and nonpeaceful means, such as training freedom fighters and engaging in trade boycotts (OAU 1973, p. 28); the settlement of disputes, for instance, border disputes; and the continued decolonization efforts of territories under British, French, Portuguese, and Spanish domination and of Namibia and South Africa.

However, at its 10th Summit Anniversary in 1973 the OAU recognized that the First Assembly of Heads of State and Government of the OAU, held in Cairo on 21 July 1964, had specified that the OAU had a basic role in planning and direction in relation to economic and social matters in Africa (OAU 1973, p. 36). This included intensifying regional cooperation, accelerating industrial development with an emphasis on multinational projects, increasing inter-African trade, harmonizing customs procedures, promoting cooperation between African air transport companies to increase trade and promote tourism, and harmonizing social and labor legislation.

After a series of international meetings at different levels and on various issues, the heads of states met again in Lagos on 28–29 April 1980, under the auspices of the OAU. (From 1963 until 1980, the OAU held more than 66 documented meetings in various locations in Africa; see El-Avourty and Zartman 1984.) The objective was to take stock of the declining economic situation of many member states and to prepare an action plan to address the then prevailing deficiencies. The result was the adoption of a plan of action aimed at overcoming problems in various fields. The so-called Lagos Plan of Action retained a broad, state-led model of actions that were considered necessary given the past 20 years of disappointing economic performance (OAU 1980). The OAU's adoption of the Lagos Plan of Action and of an agenda for creating an African economic community by 2000 was the culmination of the initiative for change in the international economic order launched by the United Nations in 1974–75. The states committed themselves to promoting economic and social development and to integrating their economies (OAU 1980, Preamble). The actions and objectives focusing on industrial development were grouped into short-term (until 1985), medium-term (1990), and long-term actions (2000) that were supposed to significantly improve Africa's economic and social situation. However, while the need for integration was clearly stipulated, the Lagos Plan of Action did not include liberalization of trade or services as a declared objective.

The transport and communications sector was recognized as most important for all sectors and for socioeconomic development (OAU 1980, p. 58). However, the actions proposed were based on UN resolution 32/160 (19 December 1977) declaring 1978–88 as the Transport and Communications Decade for Africa, which was focused mainly on infrastructure improvements.[8] In the field of air transport, the plan mentioned the development of air transport infrastructure, the extension and modernization or airports, and technical assistance for better air transport integration (OAU 1980, p. 61).[9]

Overall, the 1980 Lagos Plan of Action was an attempt to gradually strengthen economic and cultural relationships between states and its ultimate goal was the establishment of an African common market by 2000. Achievement of these goals was impeded by the failure of the numerous conferences of independent African states held between 1958 and 1968, which aimed at establishing a universal African organization, coupled with the failure of regional initiatives, such as the collapse of the East African

Community (EAC) in 1977. However, there was also an opposing viewpoint that continental unity could only be achieved through political integration (M'buyinga 1982).

Establishment of the African Economic Community

The establishment of the AEC was a clear sign of a new philosophy of regional economic cooperation that would eventually lead to full economic integration. The preamble of the Abuja Treaty lists the various conferences at which declarations and resolutions paved the way for consensus by the governments of the various African states. Among them were the OAU Summit in Algiers in 1968, the Monrovia Summit of 1979 (resulting in the Monrovia Declaration), and the Lagos Economic Summit of 1980, where the Lagos Plan of Action was formulated and the Final Act of Lagos adopted.

Article 2 of the treaty provides for the establishment of the community, while Article 4 (1) lists its objectives in four paragraphs that cover (a) the promotion of economic, social, and cultural development and the integration of African economies; (b) the establishment of a framework for the development, mobilization, and utilization of human and material resources; (c) the promotion of cooperation in all fields of human endeavor; and (d) the coordination and harmonization of policies among existing and future economic communities to foster the gradual establishment of the AEC.

Article 4 (2) then itemizes 15 actions that the community is expected to implement to achieve the stated objectives. Some have seen this itemization of actions as a somewhat worrisome approach (Akanle 1993, p. 10). Akanle (1993, p. 10) suggested that an omnibus provision that granted the power to take whatever action necessary to the attainment of its objectives would have been more suitable. However, the focus on economic integration in Africa is further emphasized in Article 88 (3), which states that the treaty shall coordinate, harmonize, and evaluate the activities of existing and future regional economic bodies.

Article 6 (1) defines the modalities for the establishment of the community, which shall be gradual over a transitional period not exceeding 34 years. This period is subdivided into six stages of different durations. The initial stages focus primarily on regional activities and initial steps toward sectoral integration, while the final phase is aimed at reaching a full union, including a monetary union and a pan-African parliament. Article 98 (1) then provides that the community shall be an integral part of the OAU, which implies that the community has priority over regional economic bodies and is expected to streamline its activities with the general objectives of the OAU as stipulated in the OAU's Charter of 1963.

Article 3 (5) provides the principle that the parties to the treaty shall observe the legal system of the community. This implies that the legal system of the treaty, which is separate and distinct from those of the member states of the community, will apply throughout the community in each of the member states (Akanle 1993, p. 12). There will be a duality of legal systems: the national legal system and the community's legal system. Article 5 (2) obligates member states to ensure the enactment and dissemination of such legislation as necessary to implement the provisions of the treaty.

The institutions of the community are provided for in Article 7 (10). The supreme organ of the community is the Assembly of the Heads of State. Article 8 (2) states that the assembly's main responsibility is to implement the objectives of the AEC. In Article 8 (3), the assembly is further directly responsible for 12 specific tasks ranging from determining general policy to coordinating and harmonizing various policies of member states to undertaking certain organizational matters and, finally, to taking "any action, under this Treaty, to attain the objectives of the community." Article 9 (1) mandates the assembly to meet once every year for a regular session and also empowers the chair to convene extraordinary sessions at the request of a member state provided that such a request is supported by two-thirds of assembly members. However, for a legislative organ of an economic community to meet only once a year is rather inappropriate. A better option would have been to limit the assembly's role to solving political problems (Akanle 1993, p. 31).

Finally, the most significant rule for the implementation of the Yamoussoukro Decision is Article 10. In this article, the assembly is empowered to act by decision (on any subject according to Article 8), which if reached by consensus or two-thirds majority, becomes binding for all member states, other organs of the community, and the RECs. Decisions shall become automatically enforceable 30 days after the date of their signature by the chair of the assembly.

Ratification and Entry into Force of the Abuja Treaty

For the provisions of the Abuja Treaty to be binding, Article 100 requires that the high contracting parties (the representatives of states that have signed or ratified a treaty) must sign and ratify the treaty and the protocols thereto in accordance with their respective constitutional procedures. The article further stipulates that the instruments of ratification shall be deposited with the secretary-general of the OAU. Article 101 stipulates that the treaty shall enter into force 30 days after the deposit of the instruments of ratification by two-thirds of the member states of the OAU.

The Abuja Treaty entered into force on 12 May 1994, after two-thirds of the member states of the OAU had deposited their instruments of ratification (African Union 2006b, p. 2). The ratification process continued and, as of 22 June 2004, 48 of the 54 African states had signed and ratified the treaty. However, four of those ratifications and/or deposits of the ratification instruments were done when the Abuja Treaty had been replaced by the African Union framework (the ratification period for the treaty establishing the AEC ended on 26 May 2001, when the treaty establishing the African Union came into force). Four states (Djibouti, Gabon, Madagascar, and Somalia) have signed, but not ratified, the treaty, and Eritrea and Morocco were never signatories to the treaty.

Entry into Force of the Yamoussoukro Decision

The Abuja Treaty as the Legal Basis of the Yamoussoukro Decision

African ministers in charge of civil aviation from 40 African states convened in Yamoussoukro, Côte d'Ivoire, on 13–14 November 1999 to discuss and adopt a new framework for liberalized air transport on the African continent. The basis of the discussions was the Yamoussoukro Declaration (UNECA 1988), which aimed at integrating African carriers, gradually eliminating traffic rights, and reducing tariffs. The meeting resulted in the adoption of the Yamoussoukro Decision, which focused primarily on full liberalization of traffic rights up to the fifth freedom.

The Yamoussoukro Decision has its legal basis in Article 10 of the Abuja Treaty, which states that the decisions of the Assembly of the AEC shall be binding on member states and organs of the community as well as on RECs. The assembly, however, is defined in Article 8 as the Assembly of Heads of State, while the meeting in Yamoussoukro was attended by the African ministers in charge of civil aviation. The formal adoption of the Yamoussoukro Decision on the basis of the Abuja Treaty took place during the Assembly of the Heads of State on 10–12 July 2000, in Lomé, Togo (UNECA 2004, p. 63).

It is generally assumed that the legal basis of the Yamoussoukro Decision is the formal decision of the Assembly of the AEC, which was taken on 12 July 2000. If this assumption is correct, the Yamoussoukro Decision then becomes an obligation of the Abuja Treaty, and is thus a legally binding instrument. However, this is only the case for those countries that signed and ratified the treaty and its protocols and deposited the instruments of ratification with the secretary-general of the OAU (Article 100). For states that did not sign the treaty, formal acceptance through accession, acceptance, and approval remains a valid path for the treaty to become binding (Brownlie 2003, p. 583).

Several states signed, ratified, and/or deposited their instruments of ratification after the treaty came into force. As none of the ratifying state parties have expressed any reservations or consent to be bound by part of the treaty only (See Vienna Convention on the Law of Treaties, 1969, Articles 17, 19 [Vienna Convention]), all state parties that later succeeded to member states are therefore bound to all the prior decisions taken by the AEC, that is, decisions taken on the basis of Article 10 of the treaty. The only such significant decision taken by the AEC was the Yamoussoukro Decision.

Establishment of the African Union

At the Fourth Extraordinary Session of the AEC in Sirte, Libya, on 9 September 1999, the assembly decided to establish a new organization called the African Union, which would be in conformity with "the ultimate objectives of the Charter of our Continental Organization and the Treaty establishing the African Economic Community" (African Union 2000, Preamble). The decision was based on the need to "accelerate the process of implementing the Treaty establishing the AEC in order to promote the socio-economic development of Africa and to face more effectively the challenges posed by globalization" (African Union 2000, Preamble). The formal constitutive Act establishing the African Union was adopted in Togo on 11 July 2000. Initially, 27 states signed the act (African Union 2006b, p. 2), which formally entered into force on 26 May 2001. By July 2003, all African countries except Morocco had adopted and ratified the act (Institute for Security Studies 2007a). (Morocco withdrew from the OAU in 1985 after it admitted the Saharawi Arab Democratic Republic [West Sahara], which Morocco did not recognize as a legitimate signatory member of the act. Later, Morocco refused to sign the act creating the African Union for the same reason.)

Similar to the AEC, the constitutive act of the African Union established several organs. Article 5 stipulates that these organs are (a) the Assembly of the African Union; (b) the Executive Council; (c) the Pan-African Parliament; (d) the Court of Justice; (e) the Commission; (f) the Permanent Representative Committee; (g) the specialized technical committees; (h) the Economic, Social, and Cultural Council; and (i) the financial institutions. Despite some slight changes in their titles, the organs of the African Union are similar to the organs of the AEC. The only exceptions are the financial institutions to be created (African Union 2000, Article 19, provides for the establishment of the African Central Bank, the African Monetary Union, and the African Investment Bank).

The main, and the most relevant for the Yamoussoukro Decision, difference between the AEC and the African Union is that the constitutive act of the African Union does not provide for the assembly's decisions to be automatically binding and enforceable on member states and organs of the community. Instead, Article 9 of the act limits the assembly's powers and functions to policy decisions, to membership and financial issues, to directions to the Executive Council on issues concerning war or emergencies, and to the appointment of judges and commissioners. The functions and powers of the various other organs are also limited to policy recommendations (Article 13 for the Executive Council) or to project preparation and supervision (Article 15 for the technical committees) or are left to be determined in future acts, such as the creation of a Pan-African parliament (Article 17). (The Pan-African Parliament was established by the adoption of the Treaty Establishing the African Economic Community Relating to the Pan-African Parliament on 30 July 2003.)

Article 33 (1) of the constitutive act of the African Union stipulates that the act shall replace the Charter of the OAU after a transitional period of one year or such further period as determined by the assembly. It further provides in Article 33 (2) that the act shall take precedence over and supersede any inconsistent or contrary provision of the treaty establishing the AEC. In essence, the constitutive act of the African Union replaced the Abuja Treaty,[10] and especially canceled those provisions that had not been carried over into the African Union framework.

For purposes of the Yamoussoukro Decision, the most relevant provision that was not carried over into the new treaty establishing the African Union was Article 10 of the Abuja Treaty. This meant that from the day the constitutive act of the African Union entered into force, decisions taken by the assembly would no longer become automatically binding for all member states. Under Article 7 of the constitutive act, decision making of the Assembly of the African Union requires consensus or a two-thirds majority of the member states. However, the words "automatically binding" were omitted. It can thus be assumed that the member states of the constitutive act of the African Union wanted to preserve their rights to ratify major decisions taken in the future by the Assembly of the African Union.

Ratification Period of the Yamoussoukro Decision Based on the Abuja Treaty

The entry into force of the African Union on 26 May 2001 terminated the ratification period of the Abuja Treaty, which included accession to the Yamoussoukro Decision as a binding element of the Abuja Treaty. Thus, even though the constitutive act of the African Union provides for a transitional period of one year or such further period as may be necessary (African Union 2000, Article 33), it does so solely for the purpose of enabling the OAU to undertake measures for the devolution of its assets and liabilities to the union.

The question of whether the constitutive act of the African Union can be seen as a successor of the Abuja Treaty with regard to the Yamoussoukro Decision can be answered by referring to Article 12 of the Yamoussoukro Decision. This article declares Article 10 of the Abuja Treaty as the basis for entry into force of the Yamoussoukro Decision by stating that "in accordance with Article 10 of the Abuja Treaty, this Decision shall automatically enter into force thirty days after the date of its signature by the Chairman of the Assembly of Heads of State and Government at which this Decision was adopted." This is the provision that provides for the prime difference between the Abuja Treaty, where decisions of the assembly become automatically binding on member states, and the act of the African Union, which does not include this mechanism. In other words, if the Yamoussoukro Decision would have been agreed upon when the African Union was established (and the Abuja Treaty replaced), its entry into force would have depended on the ratification of the decision by each state, because the African Union treaty does not include the provision that decisions are automatically binding on member states.

The day that the African Union framework came into force by replacing the Abuja Treaty therefore marks the end of the mechanism (automatic binding for member states) of Article 10 of the Abuja Treaty. Consequently, the ratification period of the Abuja Treaty (which also constituted membership of the Yamoussoukro Decision), which includes accession, acceptance, and approval of the treaty, started when the treaty was signed on 3 June 1991, and ended on 26 May 2001.

Status of the Non-Abuja Treaty States

Of the 54 African states, 10 must be considered to be non-Abuja Treaty states. These 10 states can be grouped into three categories: (a) states that never signed the Abuja Treaty (Eritrea and Morocco); (b) states that signed, but never ratified, the treaty (Djibouti, Gabon, Madagascar, and Somalia); and (c) states that ratified and/or deposited the instruments of ratification after the African Union entered into force (Equatorial Guinea, Mauritania, South Africa, and Swaziland).

Those states that never signed or ratified the Abuja Treaty can clearly be described as nontreaty states. They are not part of the Yamoussoukro Decision framework. The status of states that ratified and/or deposited the instruments of ratification after the African Union entered into force can be examined from different perspectives. A first lead can be found in paragraph 1 of Article 33 of the constitutive act of the African Union, which stipulates that this act shall replace the Charter of the OAU, and a second in paragraph 2, which states that the act takes precedence over and supersedes any inconsistent or contrary provision of the AEC Treaty.

The main provision concerning the Yamoussoukro Decision that was superseded in the constitutive act of the African Union was Article 10 of the Abuja Treaty, which provides that the decisions of the Assembly of the AEC shall be binding on member states and organs of the Community, as well as on RECs. The argument that the provisions of Article 10 were terminated when the constitutive act of the African Union came into force can also be made with Article 59 of the Vienna Convention. This article stipulates that a treaty shall be considered to be terminated if all the parties to it conclude a later treaty relating to the same subject matter and the provisions of the later treaty are so far incompatible with those of the earlier one that the two treaties are not capable of being applied at the same time. As all four parties concerned (Equatorial Guinea, Mauritania, South Africa, and Swaziland) have signed, and two (Equatorial Guinea and South Africa) even ratified, the constitutive act of the African Union before its entry into force, one can conclude that these parties knew and agreed to the new framework of the African Union. It is nevertheless remarkable that all four of these states also ratified the Abuja Treaty and deposited their instruments of ratification after 26 May 2001, the date on which the African Union came into force and replaced the Abuja Treaty framework. This is even more astonishing when considering that three of the states (Equatorial Guinea, South Africa, and Swaziland) actually deposited their instruments of ratification of the Abuja Treaty much later than they did the same instruments for the constitutive act of the African Union, which replaced the Abuja Treaty.

The key question to analyze before we can conclude that states that did not sign the Abuja Treaty during its legal existence are not parties to the Yamoussoukro Decision is whether decisions of the African Union are automatically binding for all its member states without any further ratification. Article 10 of the Abuja Treaty is clear on this issue. It provides that the decisions of the Assembly of the AEC shall be binding on member states and organs of the community, as well as on RECs. The constitutive act of the African Union is less clear on this question. Article 6 stipulates that the assembly shall be the supreme organ of the union, and Article 7 states that the assembly shall take its decisions by consensus or, failing which, by a two-thirds majority of the member states of the union. However, the constitutive act of the African Union does not explicitly state that the decisions of the assembly are binding on all member states, but at the same time it provides in Article 23 (2) for the imposition of sanctions against a member state that fails to comply with the decisions and policies of the union, such as the denial of transport and communication links with other member states, and other measures of a political and economic nature to be determined by the assembly.

One strong indication about the nature and scope of applicability of decisions of the African Union on a member state can be found in Article 33 of the *Rules of Procedure of the Assembly of the Union* (African Union 2002). Article 33 states that decisions of the assembly shall be issued as (a) regulations; (b) directives; and (c) recommendations, declarations, resolutions, and opinions. Regulations are applicable in all member states, which "shall take all necessary measures to implement them." The question here is whether "all measures to implement them" means formal adoption or ratification in each member state. Article 34 (1) states that regulations and directives shall be automatically enforceable 30 days after the date of publication in the *Official Journal of the African Union* or as specified in the decision. Furthermore, Article 34 (2) provides that regulations and decisions shall be binding on member states, organs of the union, and RECs. Before we conclude that Article 34 does indeed render any decision of the assembly automatically enforceable after publication, we need to examine two issues, namely: (a) can the adoption of rules of procedure of the assembly by the assembly overcome the fact that the constitutive act of the African Union did not provide for the powers of automatic enforceability after publication, and (b) what is the demonstrated practice of the assembly in this matter?

The first question is relatively easy to answer. The constitutive act of the African Union needed ratification by all member states. One of the major provisions, the power of automatic enforceability on member states, was not included in the act. However, in 2002, the assembly adopted its own rules of procedure and gave itself the power of automatic enforceability on member states. As member states never ratified this significant rule, and as the assembly did not have these powers in the constitutive act, the new provision cannot be deemed to be an expressed or implied amendment of the constitutive act. The rules of procedure that gave the Assembly of the African Union the power of enforceability of decisions on member states must be considered an amendment of the original treaty. According to Article 40 of the Vienna Convention, any proposal to amend a multilateral treaty must be notified to all the contracting states. Each state has the right to take part in (a) the decision to be taken in regard to such a proposal, and (b) the negotiation and conclusion of any agreement to amend the treaty. Article 32 of the constitutive act of the African Union provides that amendments shall be adopted by the assembly by consensus or, failing which, by a two-thirds majority and submitted for ratification by all member states in accordance with their respective constitutional procedures. The second question, the practice of the assembly, is less clear. The African Union has taken several decisions during its assemblies, but little evidence of automatic enforcement in member states is apparent. A concrete lead came during the Sixth Assembly of the African Union, at which the assembly took notice of Libya's intervention concerning nonsubmission of decisions of the African Union to the ratification mechanism of African Union member states. Libya called upon all member states "to sign and ratify the Treaties, Charters, Conventions and Protocols adopted by the Assembly and requests national parliaments to hold, if necessary, extraordinary sessions for their ratification" (African Union 2006a, p. 5).

Finally, the evidence is strong that the African Union does not enjoy the same automatic enforcement mechanism as provided in the Abuja Treaty for the AEC, another factor underlining the argument that certain states that ratified the Abuja Treaty after 26 May 2001 are not bound by the Yamoussoukro Decision. If we assume that the Assembly of the African Union was empowered to grant itself the power of automatic enforceability in Article 33 of its rules of procedure, we need to review the date of effectiveness of this decision. The assembly's rules of procedure were adopted during the First Ordinary Session of the African Union on 10 July 2002. According to Article 34 of the rules of procedure, decisions become enforceable 30 days after the date of their publication in the *Official Journal of the African Union*. However, three of the four states that ratified the Abuja Treaty after it was replaced by the constitutive act of the African Union on 26 May 2001 did so before the new rule would have taken effect in August 2002 (South Africa ratified on 31 May 2001, Swaziland on 6 June 2001, and Mauritania on 20 November 2001). Only

Equatorial Guinea could claim that its ratification of the Abuja Treaty on 20 December 2002 would have benefited from the same automatic enforcement mechanism as Article 10 of the Abuja Treaty should the assembly's rules of procedure be recognized as binding.

As outlined earlier, the Assembly of the African Union does not enjoy the same power as provided for in Article 10 of the Abuja Treaty. Therefore, all four states (Equatorial Guinea, Mauritania, South Africa, and Swaziland) that ratified and/or deposited their instruments of ratification after the African Union entered into force cannot be considered Yamoussoukro Decision party states. Concluding that the late ratification of the Abuja Treaty by certain states indicates that those states primarily intended to join the Yamoussoukro Decision framework would also be inappropriate. The Yamoussoukro Decision provides for a much simpler procedure for nontreaty states that wish to be parties to the decision (UNECA 2002, Annex 1 [a]). The late and obsolete ratification was much more likely to have been caused by administrative delays.

Conclusion

The Abuja Treaty, which formally entered into force on 12 May 1994, can be recognized as the legal basis for the Yamoussoukro Decision. All states that signed and formally ratified the Abuja Treaty during its legal existence from the date of initial signing on 3 June 1991 to the date of its replacement on 26 May 2001 have also adhered to the Yamoussoukro Decision, which became fully binding on 12 August 2002.

Of the 54 African states, 44 have signed and formally ratified the Abuja Treaty. Those states became parties to the Yamoussoukro Decision. The other 10 states (Djibouti, Equatorial Guinea, Eritrea, Gabon, Madagascar, Mauritania, Morocco, Somalia, South Africa, and Swaziland) cannot be considered parties to the Yamoussoukro Decision.

Notes

1. The states represented at the conference were Algeria, Benin, Botswana, Burkina Faso, Burundi, Cameroon, Cape-Verde, Central African Republic, Chad, Congo, Côte d'Ivoire, the Arab Republic of Egypt, Equatorial Guinea, Ethiopia, Gabon, The Gambia, Ghana, Guinea, Guinea Bissau, Kenya, Liberia, Libya, Madagascar, Mali, Morocco, Mauritius, Mauritania, Niger, Nigeria, Rwanda, Senegal, Sierra Leone, Somalia, Swaziland, Tanzania, Togo, Tunisia, Uganda, Zaire (today, the Democratic Republic of Congo), and Zimbabwe.

2. The ministers decided that states would grant the fifth freedom no later than 1 November 1997 as follows:
   - Where no other airlines are operating under the third and fourth freedoms, fifth freedom rights should be unconditional.
   - Where airlines are operating the third and fourth freedoms, up to 20 percent of the traffic (based on the total volume of traffic in the preceding year) or of the number of seats available on the route shall be reserved for operation under the fifth freedom, provided that 80 percent of the total traffic or number of seats available on the route are reserved for airlines operating the third and fourth freedoms.
   - Where airlines are operating the third, fourth, and fifth freedoms, fifth freedom rights should be granted to non-African operators on a reciprocal basis after due consultation with concerned operators in the subregion for the benefit of the Economic Community of West African States subregion.
3. Article 3.2 limits the obligation to grant and receive unrestricted fifth freedom rights to (a) sectors where, for economic reasons, no third and fourth freedom operators exist; and (b) up to a minimum of 20 percent of the capacity offered on the route concerned during any given period of time with respect to any sector where third and fourth freedom operators exist.
4. As an example see Air Transport Agreement between the United States of America and Singapore (31 March 1978).
5. Convention on International Civil Aviation, signed at Chicago on 7 December 1944, 61 Stat. 1180 (1944), [Chicago Convention].
6. African ministers responsible for air transport discussed the safety-related challenges of African carriers at a conference in Gabon in May 2006. They recognized that capacity building in safety oversight must be addressed on a regional level and aircraft that do not meet basic airworthiness criteria must be banned (African Union 2006c, pp. 6–8).
7. The governments represented were Algeria, Burundi, Cameroon, Central African Republic, Chad, the Republic of Congo, Côte d'Ivoire, Dahomey (today, Benin), Ethiopia, Gabon, Ghana, Guinea, Liberia, Libya, Madagascar, Mali, Mauritania, Morocco, Niger, Nigeria, Rwanda, Senegal, Sierra Leone, Somalia, Sudan, Tanganyika (today, Tanzania), Togo, Tunisia, Uganda, United Arab Republic (today, the Arab Republic of Egypt), Upper Volta (today, Burkina Faso), and Zaire (today, the Democratic Republic of Congo).
8. See Resolution by the Economic Commission for Africa Conference of Ministers held in March 1977, which was endorsed by the Economic and Social Council and, subsequently, by the General Assembly of the UN.
9. Lagos Plan, supra note 3, at 61.
10. The adoption by a two-thirds majority of the constitutive act of the African Union is a major amendment of the Abuja Treaty in accordance with the principle in Article 103.

CHAPTER 3

Status Quo of the Implementation of the Yamoussoukro Decision

Since its enactment by heads of state in 1999, the central theme of the Yamoussoukro Decision has been its implementation across the continent. According to the African Union (2005a, p.1), the Yamoussoukro Decision is a "landmark initiative to develop the industry through the removal of barriers by promoting the liberalisation of the industry." However, as the complete title of the decision is the "Decision Relating to the Implementation of the Yamoussoukro Declaration Concerning the Liberalization of Access to Air Transport Markets in Africa" (UNECA 1999), the question arises as to what implementation actually means in the context of the Yamoussoukro Decision. This is relevant, because one could easily conclude that the Yamoussoukro Decision of 1999 is actually the legally binding framework for implementing the former Yamoussoukro Declaration. If this were the case, no further legal action would be necessary and the Yamoussoukro Decision would become applicable after the transition period provided for in Article 10.

Yet many African politicians, representatives of economic organizations, and members of the aviation industry refer to the pending implementation of the Yamoussoukro Decision. Numerous conferences, studies, papers, and initiatives present a set of actions that has been developed to implement the Yamoussoukro Decision, which is commonly seen as the most important measure for developing the African aviation sector (African Union 2006c). However, one could conclude that using the term *implementation* in relation to the Yamoussoukro Decision is a pleonasm (the use of more words than necessary, that is, a form of redundancy), because the Yamoussoukro Decision itself is the decision to implement the Yamoussoukro Declaration of 1988. Alternatively, one could also state that implementation stands for applying the Yamoussoukro Decision framework, because its legal implementation was achieved at the time of its adoption by heads of state in 1999.

The question arises regarding what is actually meant in a legal and political sense by the term implementation of a treaty, which in this case is implementation of a declaration or intent to liberalize air services. A definition of the word implementation can be found in the popular online encyclopedia Wikipedia: "In political science, implementation refers to the carrying out of public policy. Legislatures pass laws that are then carried out by public servants working in bureaucratic agencies. This process consists of rule-making, rule-administration and rule-adjudication. Factors impacting implementation include the legislative intent, the administrative capacity of the implementing bureaucracy, interest group activity and opposition, and presidential or executive support."[1]

In analyzing the implementation of the Yamoussoukro Decision as the carrying out of public policy based on a law or treaty, we need to review which elements have been formally created by the decision itself and which elements of the decision are to be established. The entity that is explicitly created in Article 9 of the Yamoussoukro Decision is the monitoring body. Its duties are defined in annex 3, which at publication became annex 2. While this body was created by the Yamoussoukro Decision, Article 9.4 mentions the African Air Transport executing agency, which needs to be created for the "successful implementation of the Decision." This indicates that implementation of the Yamoussoukro Decision is indeed understood as an administrative procedure that will be carried out by a specialized agency.

Finally, implementation of the Yamoussoukro Decision could also be understood as the application of its operational principles. These operational principles are defined in Article 3.1 as granting free exercise of the rights of the first, second, third, fourth, and fifth freedoms of the air on scheduled and nonscheduled passenger, cargo, and/or mail flights performed by an eligible airline to and/or from their respective territories. The application mechanism is defined in Article 6.1. Each state party has the right to designate in writing at least one airline to operate in accordance with the principles of the Yamoussoukro Decision, and the designation should be notified to the other state party in writing through diplomatic channels. Article 6.4 obliges the other state party to initiate the process of authorization and licensing of the designated airline to operate the services. The authorization should be granted in 30 days.

A supplementary application can be found in Article 2, which states that the Yamoussoukro Decision has precedence over any multilateral or bilateral agreements on air services between state parties that are incompatible with the decision. However, it also states that provisions of such agreements that are not incompatible with the Yamoussoukro Decision remain valid and supplementary to the Yamoussoukro Decision. Even though the formal application mechanism of the Yamoussoukro Decision as defined in Article 6.1 is clear, one could conclude that agreeing on a bilateral that complies fully with the provisions of the Yamoussoukro Decision is a valid application mechanism. This is especially important as long as many elements of implementation in the sense of carrying out of public policy remain pending.

One can conclude that implementation of the Yamoussoukro Decision is widely understood as the carrying out of public policy based on a law or treaty. This entails several additional steps, such as setting up specialized agencies and defining competition regulation. However, the key question is whether the absence of implementation in the sense of public policy suspends the application of the operational principles of the Yamoussoukro Decision. With reference to the various interpretations of the word implementation discussed earlier, the status quo must be analyzed both as policy implementation and as operational implementation. In addition, probably, the most challenging hurdle for the development of liberalized air services in Africa regardless of the stage or the degree of liberalization is meeting safety and security requirements.

Policy Implementation

As seen earlier, the Yamoussoukro Decision implements the Yamoussoukro Declaration. It provides the following main elements of implementation:

- The competition rules (Article 7) state that "state parties shall ensure fair opportunity on non-discriminatory basis for the designated African airline, to effectively compete in providing air transport services within their respective territories." There are no further provisions for competition rules other than in Article 9.5, which states that the executing agency shall have sufficient powers to formulate and enforce appropriate rules and regulations that give fair and equal opportunities to all players and promote healthy competition.

- The arbitration procedure (Article 8) encourages state parties to settle disputes by negotiation. Failing that, either party may submit the dispute to arbitration in accordance with the procedures set forth in appendix 2. However, appendix 2, which is actually annex 2, does not include any arbitration procedure but describes the duties and responsibilities of the monitoring body.
- The monitoring body (Articles 9.1–9.3) is the only element that is formally created ("hereby established") by the Yamoussoukro Decision. It takes the form of the Subcommittee on Air Transport of the Committee on Transport, Communications, and Tourism of the former African Economic Community (now the African Union), which is responsible for the overall supervision, follow-up, and implementation of the Yamoussoukro Decision.
- The executing agency (Articles 9.4–9.6) shall be created to ensure successful implementation of the Yamoussoukro Decision, which includes the supervision and management of Africa's liberalized air transport industry. To this end the executing agency shall formulate and enforce appropriate competition rules and regulations and ensure that consumer rights are protected.

Based on the foregoing elements of implementation of the Yamoussoukro Decision, the following four main components must be completed: (a) developing competition rules and consumer protection rights; (b) implementing formal arbitration procedures; (c) assuring that the monitoring body, which has already been created, starts functioning by meeting regularly to supervise and follow up on implementation of the Yamoussoukro Decision; and (d) establishing an executing agency.

Developing Competition Rules
Article 7 of the Yamoussoukro Decision provides that state parties must "ensure fair opportunity on non-discriminatory basis for the designated African airline, to effectively compete in providing air transport services within their respective territory." This provision of fair opportunity and antidiscrimination is kept extremely marginal, and Article 7 does not provide any further principles or rules that would better define fair and unfair competition between operators. The absence of any competition rules can therefore be seen as a missing element in the implementation of the Yamoussoukro Decision.

The First Ordinary Session of the Ministers Responsible for Air Transport, held by the African Union in Sun City, South Africa, in May 2005 concluded that harmonization of the rules for liberalizing air transport was necessary, as different rules in different subregions were hindering full implementation of the decision (African Union 2005a, para. 5.2.8). This conclusion was primarily based on the fact that joint draft regulations for competition in air transport services within the Common Market for Eastern and Southern Africa (COMESA), the EAC, and the Southern African Development Community (SADC) had already been prepared and discussed (Council of Ministers of COMESA and EAC Responsible for Civil Aviation and the Committee of Ministers of Transport and Communications of SADC 2004). However, the Council of Ministers of COMESA, the EAC, and SADC had not yet adopted these competition rules. Mauritius had even informally indicated that it was withdrawing from the Yamoussoukro Decision because of the failure of SADC countries to adopt the competition rules relating to the full liberalization of air transport.[2]

During the Second Session of African Union Ministers Responsible for Air Transport, held in Libreville, Gabon, in May 2006, the experts' meeting positively recognized the aforementioned joint elaboration of competition regulations by COMESA, the EAC, and SADC. It also became evident that no progress had been made in having all the RECs adopt these regulations (African Union 2005b, para. 63).

Finally, in 2007 the African Union drafted its own common competition rules, including special provisions on air transportation (African Union 2007b). These competition rules, which are similar to the draft regulations for competition in air transport services within COMESA, the EAC, and SADC, prohibit engaging in anticompetitive agreements and practices, abusing a dominant position, and having any member state grant any subsidy that distorts or threatens to distort competition. At the Third Session of African Union Ministers Responsible for Air Transport, held in Addis Ababa, Ethiopia, in May 2007, the ministers noted the preparation of draft texts concerning the harmonization of common competition rules. These were prepared based on a conclusion and recommendation of a meeting of African Union air transport experts that called for harmonizing competition rules on the basis of regulations developed by the RECs (African Union 2007c, paras. 31–36). Accordingly, the ministers asked the African Union Commission to proceed with the process of validation and finalization (African Union 2007c, para. 45). The objective was to have the heads of state formally adopt these rules at the Ninth Ordinary Session of the Assembly of the African Union, which was held in Accra, Ghana, on 1–3 July 2007. However, the matter remains pending.

Implementing Arbitration Procedures

In addition to ensuring fair competition, Article 8 of the Yamoussoukro Decision addresses dispute settlement. While it encourages state parties to settle any dispute by negotiation, it also refers to arbitration procedures, which are provided for in annex 2 of the Yamoussoukro Decision. However, annex 2 of the decision makes no reference to arbitration procedures, but defines the duties and responsibilities of the monitoring body established by Article 9 of the decision.

The First Ordinary Session of African Union Ministers Responsible for Air Transport, held in Sun City, South Africa, did not elaborate on the issue of missing arbitration procedures in the Yamoussoukro Decision. It did, however, consider a first apparent dispute, which arose between the Arab Republic of Egypt and Nigeria in relation to operational difficulties. The ministers did not deal with the case directly, but recommended that the president of the monitoring body contact the Economic Community of West African States (ECOWAS) and COMESA to clarify the nature of the dispute between the two countries' civil aviation authorities to find an amicable solution (African Union 2005a).

As with the issue of competition regulation, the experts recognized the work done by COMESA, the EAC, and SADC to elaborate a dispute settlement mechanism during the Second Session of the Ministers Responsible for Air Transport held in Libreville, Gabon. They linked the implementation of a dispute settlement mechanism to the outcome of a study on the creation of the pending executing agency (African Union 2005b, para. 63). The executing agency was finally created in 2007 during the Third Session of African Union Ministers Responsible for Air Transport, held in Addis Ababa, by assigning its responsibilities and duties to AFCAC, a specialized institution of the African Union (African Union 2007a, p. 2). The arbitration procedures of the dispute settlement mechanism remain pending for the time being. However, one can expect that AFCAC, as the executing agency, will play a leading role in establishing this mechanism.

Assuring Functioning of the Monitoring Body

Article 9.1 of the Yamoussoukro Decision established the monitoring body. Its main task is the overall supervision, follow-up, and implementation of the Yamoussoukro Decision. The initial plan was to empanel the monitoring body with representatives of UNECA, the OAU, AFCAC, and AFRAA assisted by representatives of subregional organizations. Annex 2 (not annex 3 as referred to in Article 9.3), which is adequately titled "Duties and Responsibilities of the Monitoring Body," details the monitoring body's overall duties and responsibilities.

The first meeting of the monitoring body was held in Addis Ababa, Ethiopia, in November 2000. Representatives of several agencies, including the OAU, AFCAC, AFRAA, the Intergovernmental Agency on Development, COMESA, and UNECA attended the meeting.[3] The meeting took note of several reports by individual organizations on their experience and ideas on rules, procedures, and a proposed timetable for implementation of the Yamoussoukro Decision. In addition, it examined and approved the versions of annex 1 (a), (b), and (c) and annex 2 (formerly annex 3) of the Yamoussoukro Decision. It also set the deadline of 31 March 2001 for states to submit their declaration to limit, for a period not exceeding two years, their obligations and rights provided for in Articles 3 and 4 of the Yamoussoukro Decision (UNECA 2000).

The monitoring body held a few additional meetings in subsequent years. At its fourth meeting, held in Sun City, South Africa, in March 2005, participants included representatives from the African Union, COMESA, AFRAA, the African Development Bank, and the New Partnership for African Development (NEPAD). The meeting reviewed an evaluation of the progress made on implementation of the Yamoussoukro Decision and discussed an action plan for the way forward. The participants noted in particular that RECs such as COMESA had made good progress with respect to coming up with a common, liberalized air transport policy; harmonizing civil aviation regulations, and coordinating safety oversight and security programs. However, one of the main concerns was that the monitoring body lacked sufficient resources to secure financing for the many proposed activities (African Union 2005a, pp. 5–6).

Nevertheless, and even though the monitoring body has met only a few times since its legal creation, we can conclude that it was established and is indeed functioning. Its responsibilities, as set forth in Article 9 of the Yamoussoukro Decision, namely, overall supervision, follow-up, and implementation of the decision to assist the Subcommittee on Air Transport, composed of African ministers responsible for civil aviation, are quite well served. However, the infrequent meetings of the monitoring body are one indication of the overall slow pace of implementation of the Yamoussoukro Decision.

Establishing an Executing Agency

To ensure successful implementation of the Yamoussoukro Decision, Article 9.4 provides that an African air transport executing agency should be established as soon as possible. The same article defines the principal responsibility of the executing agency as supervising and managing Africa's liberalized air transport industry. Article 9.5 stipulates that the executing agency should have "sufficient powers for [sic] formulate and enforce appropriate rules and regulations that give fair and equal opportunities to all players and promote healthy competition." In addition, Article 9.6 mandates the executing agency to ensure consumer protection.

The creation of the executing agency was discussed and delayed at several meetings of the ministers responsible for air transport (African Union 2005b, para. 61; 2006c, para. 63). Finally, having prepared a detailed study on the creation of the agency, the Third African Union Conference of Ministers Responsible for Air Transport decided in Addis Ababa in May 2007 that AFCAC would be entrusted with the functions of the executing agency as set forth in Article 9.4 (African Union 2007a, p. 2). However, the experts noted two issues concerning this decision. First, even though AFCAC is a specialized institution of the African Union, eight member states of the African Union are not also members of AFCAC. Second, the integration of the executing agency into a specialized institution of the African Union does not comply entirely with the wording of Articles 9.4 to 9.6, which call for a powerful and mostly independent agency. The failure to create an independent agency stems from the experts' rejection of a proposal to fund the agency at least partially by collecting community aviation charges (African Union 2005b). This was reflected by the ministers, who concluded that AFCAC needed to be strengthened by entrusting it with the responsibilities of the executing agency. To address the funding issues, they called for financial support from the African Union and from African Union member states, as well as for the secondment of national experts and for the organization of meetings (African Union 2007a, p. 2).

The formal creation of the executing agency by assignment of its responsibilities to AFCAC must be evaluated by examining its achievements. AFCAC has had a history extending over 40 years, with a mandate of encouraging cooperation in all civil aviation activities throughout Africa. It further aims to promote the coordination and improved utilization and development of African air transport systems and the standardization of aircraft, flight equipment, and training programs for pilots and mechanics. Finally, it has organized some working groups and seminars and compiled statistics (OAU 2000, para. 6.7.3).

Africa's civil aviation sector has performed somewhat poorly over the last 40 years. In particular, attempts to improve cooperation and consolidation have failed and the standardization of aircraft, flight equipment, and training programs has never been addressed, with the most prominent example of a failed attempt at airline cooperation being the bankruptcy of Air Afrique (UNECA 2004, p. 95). However, if the assignment of the executing agency is considered under AFCAC's current objectives, which include promoting the development of the civil aviation industry in Africa to fulfill the objectives of the African Union Charter of 1963 and the Abuja Treaty of 1991, the compatibility is far greater (AFCAC 1969). The wide recognition that the development of air transport in Africa depends on liberalizing intra-African markets supports AFCAC's new role of supervising and managing Africa's liberalized air transport sector under the Yamoussoukro framework.

However, the newly designated executing agency will need to be given sufficient powers to enforce competition rules and regulations and to successfully arbitrate and settle disputes arising from unfair competition. Currently, neither the rules and regulations nor the arbitration procedures and the dispute settlement mechanism have been elaborated. Finally, not all Yamoussoukro Decision party states would be equally bound by AFCAC's rulings, as only 46 of the 54 Yamoussoukro Decision party states are currently members of AFCAC.[4] The following eight states, six of which are full party states of the Yamoussoukro Decision, should join AFCAC: Cape Verde, Comoros, Djibouti, Equatorial Guinea, Liberia, the Saharawi Arab Democratic Republic (better known as the Western Sahara), the Seychelles, and Zimbabwe.

In summary, the policy implementation of the Yamoussoukro Decision has made little progress over the past eight years. However, the outcome of the most recent meeting of ministers responsible for air transport indicates some enhanced political will to move ahead with the required policy implementation of the Yamoussoukro Decision (African Union 2007c).

Operational Implementation

At the operational level, the current situation in Africa concerning the liberalization of intra-African air services reflects a heterogeneous picture. On the one side are those states that typically maintain a small, often struggling, state-owned carrier and that generally remain very protective in their bilaterals. By not applying the principles of the Yamoussoukro

Decision, they aim at regulating access, capacity, and frequency to limit competition, which maintains tariffs at high levels.

On the other side are two groups of countries that actively support the liberalization of air services. The first group of states consists of those that have strong, and often market–dominant, air carriers. These states are typically able to compete on an operational, as well as on a financial, level. Their main challenge, however, is access to adequate markets, as intra-African air service markets remain generally thin, fragmented, and underdeveloped. To support the development of new markets, states with strong carriers therefore aim at opening up to achieve free access on a bilateral basis. The second group consists of states that have lost or never had a significant national carrier. These states are typically keen to attract more flights to serve their country and do not mind foreign domination of the airline industry. Both types of states with a liberal air service policy have begun to agree to bilaterals, which are mostly in line with the principles of the Yamoussoukro Decision.

The Cases of Ethiopia, Uganda, and Zambia

An interesting case of a special form of protectionist policy is Zambia, which liquidated its national airline, Zambia Airways, in 1994. Even though Zambia does not currently have a recognized national carrier,[5] and even though it is unlikely that a national carrier could be operated successfully on the proposed network, which includes transcontinental flights to Europe, the government of Zambia continues to plan for the re-establishment of such a carrier (SH&E Ltd. and Ernst and Young 2005, p. 8). This has resulted in a continued policy of protectionism when negotiating international air service agreements. The government of Zambia has signed a total of 72 bilaterals, but of these only the following eight are currently in use: Angola, the Democratic Republic of Congo, Ethiopia, Kenya, Malawi, South Africa, the United Kingdom, and Zimbabwe. The most important bilateral air service relationship is with South Africa, for which traffic between five city pairs was agreed: Johannesburg to Lusaka (3,000 seats per week each party), to Ndola (2,700 seats), to Livingstone (2,200 seats), and to Mfuwe (400 seats) and from Pilanesberg to Livingstone (400 seats).

The capacity of these traffic rights was initially only partially used, because Zambia did not designate a qualified operator. Eventually, the Zambian traffic rights on the Lusaka–Johannesburg segment were assigned to a South African low-cost carrier that operated under a Zambian operator's certificate. However, further liberalization has been constrained because of continued resistance by both the South African and the

Zambian governments. Both countries have repeatedly refused to grant fifth freedom rights, which were requested on the basis of the Yamoussoukro Decision: Egypt (Cairo–Lusaka–Johannesburg) was refused by South Africa in 2001, Libya (Tripoli–Lusaka–Johannesburg) was refused by Zambia in 2001, Ethiopia (Addis Ababa–Lusaka–Johannesburg) was refused by Zambia in 2005, Nigeria (Lagos–Lusaka–Johannesburg) was refused by Zambia in 2006 during bilateral negotiations, and a request by Kenya (Nairobi–Lusaka–Harare) was refused by Zambia in 2005 (Schlumberger 2007, p. 192). Clearly Zambia's protectionism policy is geared at protecting a future national carrier. This is especially obvious on the most lucrative routes, where even existing Zambian operators have been refused traffic rights.

The stark contrast to Zambia is Ethiopia, which for more than 60 years has operated Ethiopian Airlines, its strong national carrier. For many years Ethiopia pursued an aggressive open skies policy that aimed at granting liberal air service rights on a reciprocal basis to states both within and outside Africa.[6] As an airline, Ethiopian Airlines recognizes access to new markets, especially in Africa, as a strategic opportunity that clearly outweighs possible fare reductions resulting from a more competitive environment (interview with Girma Wake, chief executive officer of Ethiopian Airlines, 25 April 2007, Addis Ababa). As of October 2006, Ethiopia had concluded a total of 84 bilaterals. Of these, 46 bilaterals had been undertaken with African states,[7] 13 with European states, and 25 with other states (Strategic Planning Consulting 2006). Of the 46 bilaterals with African states, 19 can be considered to be in accordance with the Yamoussoukro Decision, of which 6 were concluded before the Yamoussoukro Decision came into force and 13 were signed after the Yamoussoukro Decision was adopted.

An analysis of Ethiopian Airlines' current network provides an interesting picture:

- Of the 19 bilaterals that conform to the Yamoussoukro Decision, 13 are regularly served by Ethiopian Airlines with third, fourth, and fifth freedom traffic. Six have no traffic.
- Of the 27 bilaterals that do not conform to the Yamoussoukro Decision, 10 are regularly served by Ethiopian Airlines with third, fourth, and fifth freedom traffic. Seventeen have no traffic.

The analysis of the bilaterals of Ethiopia with the current network flown by its designated carrier indicates that two-thirds of these bilaterals result in regular third, fourth, and fifth freedom traffic, while only two exclude fifth freedom operations. At the same time, of the 27 bilaterals that do not conform to the Yamoussoukro Decision, only about one-third results in regular third, fourth, and fifth freedom traffic, while two exclude fifth freedom operations and most result in no traffic at all (see appendix I).

The example of Ethiopia demonstrates that implementation, when understood as application of the principles of the Yamoussoukro Decision, can be done successfully on a purely operational basis. This is important, because it supports the statement that implementation of the Yamoussoukro Decision does not depend primarily on carrying out public policy based on a law or treaty. In other words, even if certain elements of the Yamoussoukro Decision such as the executing agency are absent, implementation can be achieved between two or more states on a bilateral basis. This also implies that certain elements of the Yamoussoukro Decision that are considered crucial for implementation, for example, competition regulation, could be substituted by a bilateral understanding. Therefore, should a conflict arise in the application of a bilateral that conforms with the Yamoussoukro Decision, a solution would most likely be sought in negotiations rather than by calling upon a third party institution such as the executing agency or the monitoring body.[8]

A country that has developed an open skies policy without having a strong carrier to benefit from liberalization is Uganda. Uganda's national carrier, Air Uganda, was liquidated in 2001 after it had declared bankruptcy. In the absence of a significant national carrier, Uganda began opening up its air service market by agreeing to bilaterals that have no restrictions in terms of access, capacity, or frequency. These bilaterals conform fully to the Yamoussoukro Decision. The government's objective was to allow the foreign private sector to develop the air transport market, recognizing that Uganda had insufficient private capital to support the start-up of an operator that could compete successfully (interview with Zephaniah M. Baliddawa, chair of the board of directors of the Civil Aviation Authority of Uganda, 24 April 2007, Addis Ababa). This open policy has resulted in the continued growth of air services expressed in passengers and cargo carried. According to Ugandan Civil Aviation Authority statistics, the flow of international passengers grew by an average of 11 percent per year from 2002 to 2006 while cargo grew at a rate of 7.9 percent. In 2001, when the Ugandan national carrier was liquidated, international passenger flows stagnated, but air cargo experienced a significant increase of 42.7 percent.

The African Air Transport Industry and Liberalization

AFRAA has also recognized the opportunities that liberalization of air transportation in Africa provides. AFRAA expressed its concerns about the lack of progress in the liberalization of market access within Africa at its 38th Annual General Assembly held in 2006. It stated that procrastination in implementation was inhibiting the growth and competitiveness of African carriers. However, it also recognized that full implementation by all states at the same time was not feasible because of the great disparity in air transport development and level of preparedness of many African countries. To support implementation by certain member states and the African Union, AFRAA decided to establish a core group of states that were like-minded, ready, and willing to spearhead implementation of the Yamoussoukro Decision on a multilateral basis without waiting for implementation by all other countries (AFRAA 2006, p. 2). This group, referred to by AFRAA and subsequently by the press and others, as the club of the ready and willing, does not carry any legal weight, because it was initiated by AFRAA, a private association of African carriers, without any official endorsement by the states that are party to the Yamoussoukro Decision. However, it signifies an important political factor, namely, while many states are still procrastinating, implementation of the Yamoussoukro Decision is indeed supported by the industry.

Finally, when assessing the current situation in Africa in terms of operational implementation, one needs to review the air transport sector by breaking it down on a country-by-country basis according to the type of national carrier operated. This results in an extremely fragmented picture (see appendix B for a complete analysis):

- Five countries have dominating state-owned carriers: Egypt, Ethiopia, Kenya, Morocco, and South Africa.
- Twenty countries have weak or small state-owned carriers: Algeria, Angola, Botswana, Cameroon, Cape Verde, Comoros, Djibouti, Libya, Madagascar, Malawi, Mali, Mauritania, Mauritius, Mozambique, Namibia, Seychelles, Sudan, Tanzania, Tunisia, and Zimbabwe. (Weakness is defined as either maintaining a heavily subsidized air carrier with public funds or providing other government-directed advantages, for instance, airport privileges, to the flag carrier.)
- Twenty-five countries have only private operators: Botswana, Burkina Faso, Burundi, Chad, the Democratic Republic of Congo, the Republic of Congo, Côte d'Ivoire, Equatorial Guinea, Eritrea, Gabon, The Gambia, Ghana, Guinea, Guinea-Bissau, Liberia, Nigeria, Rwanda,

São Tomé and Principe, Senegal, Sierra Leone, Somalia, Swaziland, Togo, Uganda, and Zambia.
- Four countries have no known operators: the Central African Republic, Niger, Lesotho, and the Western Sahara.

When evaluating the status quo of the ready and willing countries, which are applying or will apply the Yamoussoukro Decision, one can assume that all 5 countries with dominating state-owned carriers, most of the 25 countries with private operators, and all 4 countries with no operators would be included. These 34 countries represent a clear majority compared with the 20 countries that maintain weak or small state-owned carriers and that are procrastinating in opening up their air service markets.

Safety and Security Requirements

Several articles of the Yamoussoukro Decision address safety and security directly and indirectly. Article 5.1 notes that a state party may unilaterally limit the volume of traffic, the types of aircraft to be operated, or the number of flights per week for environmental, safety, technical, or other special considerations. Article 6.9 declares that the eligibility criteria for a designated airline to operate under the Yamoussoukro Decision framework are that the airline must be capable of demonstrating its ability to maintain standards at least equal to those set by ICAO and to respond to any query from any state to which it provides air services. Article 6.10 cites that a state party may revoke, suspend, or limit the operating authorization of a designated airline of the other state party if the airline fails to meet the eligibility criteria. Article 6.11 notes that state parties must recognize air operators certificates, certificates of airworthiness, certificates of competency, and personnel licenses issued or validated by the other state parties that are still in force provided that the requirements for issuing such certificates or licenses are at least equal to the minimum standards set by ICAO. Finally, Article 6.12 addresses security by setting out that state parties explicitly reaffirm their obligation to comply with civil aviation safety and security standards and practices.

ICAO regularly assesses the degree of states' compliance with its safety and security oversight requirements. In 1994, the ICAO General Assembly established ICAO's Safety Oversight Programme, a voluntary assessment of states' compliance with SARP, which included assistance to states whose compliance was deficient. In 1999, ICAO commuted this program to the mandatory Universal Safety Oversight Audit

Programme, which consisted of a well-structured and in-depth evaluation of each ICAO contracting state's compliance with annexes 1, 6, and 8 (ICAO 2000). In 2002, ICAO launched its Universal Security Audit Programme, which assesses compliance with annex 17, "Security: Safeguarding International Civil Aviation against Acts of Unlawful Interference," to promote global aviation security. While the safety audits are shared between contracting states and became public as of March 2008, the security audits remain strictly confidential. Finally, in 2005, ICAO extended the scope of its Universal Safety Oversight Audit Programme to a much more detailed audit that includes all annexes except annex 17.[9]

Several other sources of information for assessing Africa's current aviation safety and security situation are also available in addition to ICAO's safety and security audit programs. In 1991, the U.S. Federal Aviation Administration (FAA) launched the International Aviation Safety Assessment Program. This mandatory audit program of foreign states by FAA inspectors assesses the compliance of countries that currently operate flights to the United States on aircraft registered in that state or will do so in the near future. This came about after a series of accidents and incidents in the United States involving foreign carriers, often from developing countries (Dempsey 2004). However, as the International Aviation Safety Assessment Program only assesses countries that have currently or will have future flights by foreign-registered operators into the United States, the program has only evaluated 10 African countries, half of which are considered to be compliant with IACO's SARP (FAA 2007).

Another useful tool for assessing states' safety standards is the Operational Safety Audit Program of the International Air Transport Association (IATA). The program's aim is to be "an internationally recognized and accepted evaluation system designed to assess the operational management and control systems of an airline." It claims to provide a "degree of quality, integrity and security such that mutually interested airlines and regulators can all comfortably accept IOSA [the program's] audit reports" (IATA 2007b). Each member airline of IATA had to become certified by the program by the end of 2007 or risk losing its IATA membership. Currently, only nine certified carriers are registered in seven African countries (Egypt, Ethiopia, Kenya, Mauritius, Morocco, South Africa, and Tanzania [IATA 2007b]).

The most recent source of information on air carrier safety is the EU's blacklist of certain airlines. After a series of accidents in 2004 and 2005, the European Commission decided, in consultation with member states' aviation safety authorities, to ban airlines found to be unsafe from operating in European airspace.[10] The EU published its first list on 22 March 2006, and it included 50 carriers, mostly from Africa (Dempsey 2006, p. 61). The two-part list is updated regularly and published in the *Official Journal of the European Union* as annexes A and B to the Commission Regulation. The first list includes all airlines banned from operating in Europe. The second list includes airlines whose operations in Europe are restricted under specific conditions.[11] The 4 July 2007 list contains 156 airlines from 17 countries. Of these, 74 airlines (47 percent) and 9 countries (53 percent) are in Africa.

Another approach to assessing the overall safety situation in Africa could be to compare Africa's accident statistics with those of other regions. According to IATA, Africa has the worst accident statistics. In 2004, African airlines accounted for 23 of the total of 103 accidents worldwide, or 22 percent of all accidents. However, Africa accounts for only 4.5 percent of all flights flown globally for all fleets (Eastern- and Western-built aircraft) (IATA 2006, p. 23). Expressed in hull losses per million sectors flown, African carriers lost an average of 6.3 aircraft per million departures in 2004 compared with 0.78 aircraft per million departures worldwide (IATA 2006, p. ix). This rate improved slightly in 2006, when African carriers lost 4.31 aircraft per million departures compared with 0.65 aircraft per million departures worldwide (IATA 2006, p. 7). This still represents an accident rate 6.6 times higher than the worldwide average. When compared with Europe (0.32 losses), the accident rate in Africa is 13.5 times higher, and when compared with North America (0.49 losses), it is 8.8 times higher.

When analyzing the cause of the high accident rates in Africa one needs to look at three distinct groups of carriers. The first group is the major intercontinental carriers that operate between the African continent and Europe, Asia, and the Americas. Most of these carriers are registered in Europe, North America, or Asia and have an excellent safety record.[12] Indeed, none of these carriers had any major accidents on intercontinental operations to and from Africa during 1998–2007 except for one crash of a Spanish-registered regional flight between Spain and Morocco. (On 25 September 1998, a BAe-146 of the Spanish operator Paukn Air crashed near Boumahfouda, Morocco, claiming 38 lives [Flight Safety Foundation 2007]).The second group involves operators that are registered in an African country and that operate Western-built air transport category aircraft that are currently still in use in most developed countries.[13] Table 3.1 summarizes all major accidents of this group from

Table 3.1 Major Accidents of African Carriers Operating Western-Built Aircraft, October 1998–June 2008

Date	Type of aircraft	Operator	Number of deaths	Crash location
10 October 1998	Boeing 727	Congo Airlines	41	Kindu, Democratic Republic of Congo
7 August 1999	Dornier Do-228	Transportes Aéreos de Cabo Verde	18	Santo Antão, Cape Verde
31 October 1999	Boeing 767	EgyptAir	217	Nantucket, United States
30 January 2000	Airbus A310	Kenya Airways	169	Abidjan, Côte d'Ivoire
17 March 2001	Beech 1900	SAL Express	16	Quilemba, Angola
7 May 2002	Boeing 737-500	EgyptAir	14	Tunis, Tunisia
4 July 2002	Boeing 707	New Gomair	28	Bangui, Central African Republic
6 March 2003	Boeing 737-200	Air Algérie	102	Tamanrasset, Algeria
8 July 2003	Boeing 737-200	Sudan Airways	116	Port Sudan, Sudan
19 July 2003	Metroliner	Ryan Blake Charter	14	Mount Kenya, Tanzania
25 December 2003	Boeing 727	Union des Transports Africains	151	Cotonou, Benin
3 January 2004	Boeing 737-300	Flash Airlines	148	Sharm el Sheikh, Arab Republic of Egypt
22 October 2005	Boeing 737-200	Bellview Airlines	117	Lisa, Nigeria
10 December 2005	DC9-30	Sosoliso Airlines	108	Port Harcourt, Nigeria
29 October 2006	Boeing 737-200	ADC Airlines	97	Abuja, Nigeria
5 May 2007	Boeing 737-800	Kenya Airways	114	Douala, Cameroon
15 April 2008	DC9-51	Hewa Bora	48	Goma, Democratic Republic of Congo
2 May 2008	Beechcraft 1900C	Flex Air	23	Rumbek, Sudan
10 June 2008	Airbus A310-324	Sudan Airways	30	Khartoum, Sudan

Source: Flight Safety Foundation 2007.

October 1998 through June 2008. Note that this report defines a major accident as a full hull loss with 10 or more fatalities (Flight Safety Foundation 2007).

The most accurate source for researching the causes of aircraft accidents are the official accident reports that each state of occurrence must initiate provided that it is an ICAO contracting state. Annex 13 of the Chicago Convention specifies the requirements for the notification and reporting of certain incidents and accidents (ICAO 2001). The following accident reports are available and provide a clear overall picture of the causes:

- On 31 October 1999, EgyptAir Flight 990 dove into the Atlantic Ocean about 60 miles south of Nantucket, Massachusetts, in international waters, killing all 217 people on board. At the request of the Egyptian government, the U.S. National Transportation Safety Board took the lead in this investigation, with the Egyptian Civil Aviation Authority participating. The board determined that the probable cause of the accident was the airplane's departure from normal cruise flight and subsequent impact with the Atlantic Ocean as a result of the relief first officer's flight control inputs. The reason for his actions was not determined (National Transportation Safety Board 2002, p. 67).

- Kenya Airways Flight 481 crashed into the sea on 30 January 2000, shortly after it took off from Abidjan en route for Lagos. Of the 179 people on board the Airbus A310 aircraft, only 10 passengers survived the crash. The investigation determined that the cause of the accident was the pilot's action to put the aircraft into a descent after a faulty stall warning sounded immediately after takeoff (Bureau d'Enquêtes et d'Analyses pour la Sécurité de l'Aviation Civile 2002, p. 73).

- On 19 July 2003, a Fairchild Metroliner II (SW4) of the South African operator Ryan Blake Air Charter collided with terrain a few hundred feet below the peak of Mount Kenya. All 12 passengers and 2 crew members perished on impact. The probable cause of the accident was the pilot's failure to maintain situational awareness of the aircraft's proximity to the surrounding terrain, resulting in controlled flight into terrain. Contributing factors were inadequate flight planning, poor pilot briefing by air traffic control personnel in Nairobi, poor communication between air traffic control units, and failure of the radar controller to advise the pilot of termination of radar service (Ministry of Transport Department of Air Accident Investigation 2003, p. 69).

- Air Algérie Flight 6289 crashed shortly after liftoff on 6 March 2003, killing 96 of the 97 passengers and all 6 crew members. The investigation determinate that the probable cause of the accident was a combination of loss of an engine during the critical phase of the flight, followed by the nonretraction of the landing gear after the engine failure, and the captain as the nonflying pilot taking over control of the airplane before having clearly identified the problem (National Commission of Inquiry 2004, p. 40).

- On 25 December 2003, Flight 141 of the charter company Union des Transports Africains crashed on takeoff at Cotonou Cadjèhoun Airport in Benin killing 151 of the 163 people on board. The accident was a result of the aircraft being severely overloaded (the exact number of passengers could never be completely determined, but the overload was estimated at around 8 tonnes or 10 percent of the total weight) and the aircraft's centre of gravity was affected (Bureau d'Enquêtes et d'Analyses pour la Sécurité de l'Aviation Civile 2004, p. 63).

- On 3 January 2004, Flash Airlines Flight 604 crashed into the Red Sea shortly after takeoff from Sharm el-Sheikh International Airport killing all 135 passengers and 13 crew. The National Transportation Safety Board and the French Bureau d'Enquêtes et d'Analyses pour la Sécurité de l'Aviation Civile conducted a joint investigation in support of the Egyptian authorities. Their conclusion was that the pilot had suffered spatial disorientation and that the copilot was unwilling to challenge his more experienced superior, plus both pilots were insufficiently trained (Ministry of Civil Aviation 2005).

- On 10 December 2005, Sosoliso Airlines Flight 1145 crashed near the runway at Port Harcourt, Nigeria, claiming 108 lives. The accident investigation determined as probable cause the crew's decision to continue the approach beyond the decision altitude without having the runway in sight (Ministry of Aviation 2006, p. 23).

- Kenya Airways Flight KQ 507, a Boeing 737–800, crashed on 5 May 2007 shortly after take-off on a flight from Douala, Cameroon, to Nairobi, Kenya. All 114 occupants on board were killed and the airplane was completely destroyed. The accident report (Cameroon Civil Aviation Authority 2010), which was prepared with assistance of the US National Transportation Safety Board, determined as probable cause the loss of control by the crew as a result of spatial disorientation after a long slow roll, during which no instrument scanning was done, and in the absence of external visual references in a dark night. In addition, inadequate operational control and lack of crew coordination, coupled with nonadherence to flight monitoring procedures and confusion in the use of the autopilot, also contributed to the accident. The report urged rigorous implementation of the accident prevention system for air carriers. It also identified as an ongoing challenge the maintenance of continuous oversight over aviation operators, who are often better equipped thanks to international commercial partnerships, by the civil aviation administration.

All of the above findings on major accidents involving African carriers reveal pilot error as the prime cause. In addition, in two cases (Kenya Airways in 2000 and Air Algérie in 2003) mechanical failure contributed to the crash, but if the crew had applied the recommended procedures the accident could have been avoided. In the Sosoliso 2005 case, poorly designed airport infrastructure contributed to accident. In the Kenya Airways 2000 case, the absence of adequate search and rescue equipment was a major factor.

The third group of carriers consists of various African carriers that operate older Western- or Eastern-built aircraft. During February 1998 through October 2007, at least 29 accidents involving such aircraft were recorded (table 3.2). The aircraft operated by this group of carriers are mostly uneconomical to operate in the West because of strict safety and environmental regulations. Many accidents among this group are never reported and the authorities of the state of occurrence investigate only a few of the accidents. The reasons for the accidents are therefore mostly unknown. However, the various small carriers that acquire one or several old aircraft on the nontransparent aircraft supply market often operate without any supervision by their national civil aviation authority. Their pilots must work long hours and regularly operate in a dangerous environment, which results in crashes with many causes. One of the most notorious countries with respect to poor safety oversight is the Democratic Republic of Congo. This large country the size of Western Europe has only 300 miles of paved roads and depends primarily on air transportation, but the presence of many small, unregulated operators and the virtual absence of regulatory oversight have resulted in various accidents (Langewiesche 2007).

Another concern in relation to air transport safety is the large number of accidents involving flights conducted by the air force, which in many African countries transports passengers and cargo for profit. The ministry

Table 3.2 Accidents of African Carriers Operating Western- or Eastern-Built Older Aircraft, February 1998–October 2007

Date	Type of aircraft	Operator (includes air force flights)	Number of deaths	Crash location
12 February 1998	Antonov 26	Sudan Air Force	26	Nasir, Sudan
12 May 1998	Yunshuji Y-7	Mauritanian Air Force	39	Nema, Mauritania
14 December 1998	Antonov 12	Khors Air	10	Kuito, Angola
26 December 1998	Lockheed L-100	Transafrik	14	Vila Nova, Angola
2 February 1999	Antonov 12	Savanair	30	Luanda, Angola
3 June 1999	Antonov 32	Sudan Air Force	50	Khartoum, Sudan
19 April 2000	Antonov 8	Rwanda Air Force	24	Pepa, Democratic Republic of Congo
12 August 2000	Antonov 26	Staer Airlines	27	Tshikapa, Democratic Republic of Congo
31 October 2000	Antonov 26	ACA Ancargo Air	49	Monaquimbundo, Angola
15 November 2000	Antonov 24	ASA Pesada	57	Luanda, Angola
4 April 2001	Antonov 26	Sudan Air Force	14	Adar Yel, Sudan
4 May 2002	BAC One-Eleven	EAS Airlines	149	Kano, Nigeria
30 June 2003	Lockheed C-130	Algerian Air Force	15	Blida, Algeria
17 November 2003	Antonov 12	Sarit Airlines	13	Wau, Sudan
29 November 2003	Antonov 26	Congolese Air Force	33	Boende, Democratic Republic of Congo
8 June 2004	HS-748	Gabon Express	19	Libreville, Gabon
5 May 2005	Antonov 26	Aeroworld	10	Kisangani, Democratic Republic of Congo
18 May 2005	Yunshuji Y-12	Zambian Air Force	13	Mongu, Zambia

(continued)

Table 3.2 Accidents of African Carriers Operating Western- or Eastern-Built Older Aircraft, February 1998–October 2007 *(continued)*

Date	Type of aircraft	Operator (includes air force flights)	Number of deaths	Crash location
25 May 2005	Antonov 12	Victoria Air	27	Biega, Democratic Republic of Congo
16 July 2005	Antonov 24	Equatorial Express	60	Baney, Equatorial Guinea
5 September 2005	Antonov 26	Aerocom	11	Isiro-Matari, Democratic Republic of Congo
9 September 2005	Antonov 26	Air Kasai	13	Brazzaville, Republic of Congo
11 February 2006	Antonov 26	Sudan Air Force	20	Aweil, Sudan
10 April 2006	Yunshuji Y-12	Kenyan Air Force	14	Marasbit, Kenya
3 August 2006	Antonov 28	Tracep	17	Bukavu, Democratic Republic of Congo
17 September 2006	Dornier DO-228	Nigerian Air Force	13	Vande Ikya, Nigeria
23 March 2007	Ilyushin 76	Transaviaexport	11	Mogadishu, Somalia
26 August 2007	Antonov 26	GLBC	14	Kongolo, Democratic Republic of Congo
4 October 2007	Antonov 26	Malila Airlift	49	Kinshasa, Democratic Republic of Congo

Source: Flight Safety Foundation 2007.

of defense generally regulates and supervises these flights, which therefore do not need to comply with the same regulations as civilian flights.

Finally, there is a general misconception that Eastern-built aircraft tend to be of poor technological quality and that accounts for the high accident rate in Africa (Usim 2007). Africa indeed has an alarmingly high rate of accidents with Eastern-built aircraft. The hull loss rate per million departures of Eastern-built aircraft reached 54.35 in 2006 in Africa, 10 times the world average (5.61) and more than 40 times the rate in the Commonwealth of Independent States (1.32), which includes most states of the former Soviet Union (IATA 2006, p. 20).

The Interstate Aviation Committee, created in 1991 by the intergovernmental Agreement on Civil Aviation and Air Space Use among various states of the former Soviet Union, compared the safety record of aircraft designed and manufactured in the former Soviet Union with the safety level of comparable aircraft over a 30-year period. The study concludes that the level of flight safety of most Soviet-made types of aircraft is not worse, and in some cases is even better, than that of their Western analogues (Interstate Aviation Committee 2006). This clearly demonstrates that high accident rates are primarily a result of poor safety standards and not a consequence of operating Eastern-built and/or older aircraft.

The obligation of ICAO contracting states to adopt and apply the regulatory framework of the SARP must translate into a strong regime of surveillance and oversight of the aviation sector of any country. ICAO's safety audits have found an interesting correlation between poor implementation of SARP and lack of oversight, resulting in high accident rates. According to audit findings of 179 contracting states (audit findings are items of noncompliance with SARP, for example, no appropriate security regulations; the higher the findings, the worse the situation in the country audited), all regions of the world experience the same correlation (ICAO 2003a, p. A5). In Africa, the two most critical problems are the lack of continued surveillance and the poor resolution of safety audits (ICAO 2003a, p. A5). In other words, when addressing high accident rates in Africa, the most important factors for improvement are compliance with SARP and establishment of an adequate regulatory oversight regime.

For an overall assessment of the current safety and security situation in Africa, the following have been evaluated on a country by country basis (see appendix C):

- ICAO audit reports: audit findings, recent improvements, and ICAO recommendations in comparison with the world average result in

4 states rated "good," 21 states rated "marginal," and 26 states rated "poor."
- FAA International Aviation Safety Assessment Program: 5 states are certified as category 1 (compliant with ICAO SARP) and 5 states are certified as category 2 (noncompliant).
- EU list of banned carriers: 9 states have one or more banned carriers.
- IATA Operational Safety Audit: 7 states have carriers certified by the IATA.
- Fatal accidents: known accidents of air transport category aircraft and reported fatalities in air transport category aircraft registered in a given state since 1943.

The application of these five elements on the current aviation safety situation of African countries permits an overall rating of these states as good (1), marginal (2), or poor (3) in terms of safety. The conclusion of this research leads to 6 states being rated "good," 16 states being considered "marginal," and 31 states being rated "poor." In other words, well over half of all African countries currently have poor aviation safety standards.

To assess progress on a regional basis (within RECs), one can review the implementation of operational regulation and the development of regional oversight capacity. However, the analysis reveals that most RECs have taken only minor steps toward regional oversight and states rated as poor can be found in most regions except North Africa (table 3.3).

Thus, the current situation with respect to safety oversight in Africa must be considered the single most important obstacle to implementation of the Yamoussoukro Decision. This is significant, especially because international air services in general, and the Yamoussoukro Decision in particular, foresee the restriction or suspension of air services in the case of poor safety standards. In addition, the costs of financing and insuring aircraft become expensive if the aircraft concerned are registered in a state with poor aviation safety standards (Chérif 2006).

Implementation: Condition Precedent or Subsequent?

Numerous meetings, conferences, and workshops have been held since the Yamoussoukro Decision was initially signed in November 1999. All these meetings included discussions about various elements of the decision that needed to be implemented. For example, the most recent high-level meeting of the African Union, namely, the Third Conference of Ministers Responsible for Air Transport, concluded with the following

Table 3.3 Quality and Progress of Safety Oversight by RECs as of 2009

REC	Safety oversight by individual REC countries (number and percentage of REC countries)			Operational regulation	Regional (REC) safety oversight
	Good	Marginal	Poor		
Arab Maghreb Union	2 (40%)	2 (40%)	1 (20%)	None	None
Banjul Accord Group	1 (14%)	3 (43%)	3 (43%)	Pending; being prepared by the Cooperative Development of Operational Safety and Continued Airworthiness Program	Ongoing; Cooperative Development of Operational Safety and Continued Airworthiness Program should lead to a new safety agency
Economic and Monetary Community of Central Africa (CEMAC)	0 (0%)	1 (17%)	5 (83%)	Joint aviation code enacted; regulations pending.	Pending; Cooperative Development of Operational Safety and Continued Airworthiness Program should lead to a new safety agency
COMESA	2 (10%)	6 (30%)	12 (60%)	None	None
EAC	0 (0%)	2 (40%)	3 (60%)	Prepared by the EAC Civil Aviation Safety and Security Oversight Agency and needs to be adopted by each member state	Regional safety agency, EAC Civil Aviation Safety and Security Oversight Agency, established in 2007
ECOWAS	2 (12%)	5 (31%)	9 (57%)	None	None
SADC	1 (7%)	8 (53%)	6 (40%)	None	None
West Africa Economic and Monetary Union	0 (0%)	6 (25%)	6 (75%)	10 safety and security regulations enacted	Ongoing; Cooperative Development of Operational Safety and Continued Airworthiness Program should lead to a new safety agency

Source: Author compilation and research.

statement: "The Ministers reaffirmed the necessity to set up the Executing Agency responsible for the economic oversight of the liberalized air transport industry in Africa with a view to speeding up the implementation of the Yamoussoukro Decision" (African Union 2007c, p. 5).

This statement gives the impression that certain steps need to be taken before the Yamoussoukro Decision can be considered implemented. However, the key question is whether the Yamoussoukro Decision can be applied before these elements are implemented or whether the aforementioned elements (for example, competition rules) or certain conditions (such as safety compliance) have to be in place before the Yamoussoukro Decision can be applied. Applying common law principles of contract law, this section seeks to examine whether, on the one hand, the Yamoussoukro Decision states that several conditions precedent (that is, a fact, act, or event that must exist or occur before a contract or obligation becomes binding), or, on the other hand, whether the decision entails certain conditions subsequent (that is, facts that would extinguish an obligation that initially became binding after the breach had occurred, for example, the conclusion that a certain measure, such as an adequate safety oversight regime at a certain date, was not implemented as planned, while a liberalized air service agreement based on the Yamoussoukro Decision was already in place and flights were operating).

The first element of implementation to consider is the establishment of competition rules. The provision on competition rules in Article 7 of the Yamoussoukro Decision obliges state parties to "ensure fair opportunity on non-discriminatory basis for the designated African airline, to effectively compete in providing air transport services within their respective territories." Strictly analyzed, and assuming that "within their respective territories" would be interpreted as a state party's own national territory, the provision would only be applicable on flights within that territory. In other words, the provision on competition rules would only concern domestic air services among carriers of a given state. However, this would contradict "designated African airline," which is a definition for carriers operating under the Yamoussoukro Decision.[14] It would also not be an adequate provision to be included in the Yamoussoukro Decision, which, by definition, regulates the liberalization of intra-African (international) air services.

If one assumes that Article 7 concerns air services between the territories of two or, in the case of fifth freedom flights, three state parties, the Yamoussoukro Decision calls upon the concerned state parties to assure fair competition among, and nondiscrimination against, the designated airlines operating between those states. This conclusion would steer away from the condition precedent of establishing general competition rules that are applicable to air transport services and put the burden of regulating competition on the bilateral relationship between state parties. If this interpretation were correct, application of the Yamoussoukro Decision would be possible as long as the concerned state parties of a given segment under the decision assure fair competition. If one applies modern principles of competition regulation, this would mainly imply that anticompetitive agreements between the different designated carriers would be sanctioned.

However, the question remains: does the absence of any guidelines or regulations on competition hinder application of the Yamoussoukro Decision? The answer lies in the fact that air transport in Africa has been, and mainly still is, regulated on a bilateral basis. While certain RECs have recently adopted competition regulations that apply to air transport, most new bilaterals that were negotiated on the basis of the principles of the Yamoussoukro Decision did not benefit from any competition regulation. The case of Ethiopian Airlines illustrates that the Yamoussoukro Decision can be applied on a bilateral basis even in the absence of competition regulation or an executing agency that could intervene and arbitrate in case of a dispute. The establishment of competition rules can therefore be considered a condition subsequent that does not hinder application of the Yamoussoukro Decision.

The dispute settlement mechanism, defined in Article 8 as the submission to arbitration after a failed settlement by negotiation, is another important element of the liberalization of air services. While the arbitration procedures remain pending, the executing agency was established by designating AFCAC to perform its duties and responsibilities. It is now the duty of the executing agency to develop the arbitration procedures in order to be in a position to arbitrate and settle disputes between Yamoussoukro Decision party states. However, as stated earlier, the absence of an arbitration procedure has not hindered several African states from agreeing to liberalized bilateral air service agreements that are fully in line with the principles of the Yamoussoukro Decision. To date, any disputes between states have been settled by negotiation. With the assignment of the responsibilities and duties of the executing agency to AFCAC, the agency can be considered established. No further conditions, other than the aforementioned establishment of competition rules, are therefore pending.

The monitoring body, which is responsible for the overall supervision, follow-up, and implementation of the Yamoussoukro Decision, was established in Article 9 of the decision. While it has met only a few times since its creation, the monitoring body can be considered to be functional.[15] The question remains whether the performance of the monitoring body can be considered to be satisfactory enough to comply with the dictates of Article 9.3, which refers to those duties and responsibilities set forth in annex 3 (actually annex 2). Given the several complex tasks of the monitoring body on the one hand, and the slow overall implementation of the Yamoussoukro Decision on the other hand, the monitoring body's performance is clearly substandard (box 3.1).

Box 3.1

Duties and Responsibilities of the Monitoring Body

The following duties and responsibilities of the monitoring body are defined in annex 2 of the Yamoussoukro Decision (quoted from UNECA 2004):

1. Prepare, for adoption by the subcommittee on Air Transport, the relevant annexes to the Decision;
2. Formulate proposals on studies, seminars, workshops and other measures aimed at enhancing and updating air transport services in Africa;
3. Use, if necessary, experts to undertake studies related to the implementation of the Decision;
4. Provide, on request, to interested organization and Member States, technical advises for the implementation of the Decision;
5. Receive declarations made in accordance with the Decision, notification of withdrawals of any declaration of complaints and requests and shall inform the Depository accordingly;
6. State its views on any disputes resulting from the application and/or interpretation of the Decision and recommend solution to the dispute;
7. State, on request of States party, its views on predatory and unfair competition practices;
8. Request the competent national and international bodies for the support required to carry out studies, seminars, work programs and other measures aimed at enhancing and updating air transport services in Africa;
9. Assist the OAU to organize the meeting of the subcommittee on Air Transport of the Committee on Transport, Communications and Tourism;
10. Analyze and plan for the periodic review of the Decision; and
11. Develop and formulate a coordinated implementation programme of the Yamoussoukro Decision between and within sub-regions.

Nevertheless, it would be too farfetched to consider this as a condition precedent for the application of the Yamoussoukro Decision, as this would include better performance of the monitoring body.

Finally, probably the most significant element of concern is the prevalent poor safety and security record in most African countries. High accident rates and poor safety and security ratings by many authorities or agencies paint an overall discouraging picture that might seriously hinder full application of the Yamoussoukro Decision. However, the decision does not directly establish the condition that all party states must fully comply with all ICAO SARP and that accident rates, for example, must remain at acceptable levels. The decision addresses safety and security by setting down several conditions that, if not met, mostly entail sanctions of a bilateral nature. For instance, in Article 5.1, a state party may unilaterally limit the volume of traffic for safety considerations; in Article 6.9, the eligibility criteria for a designated airline to operate under the decision include compliance with ICAO SARP; and, finally, in Article 6.10, a state party may revoke, suspend, or limit the operating authorization of a designated airline of the other state party if the airline fails to meet the criteria of eligibility, which include the maintenance of standards set by ICAO. Therefore, attaining and maintaining high safety standards under the Yamoussoukro Decision can clearly be seen as a condition subsequent. Traffic rights granted pursuant to the decision could be suspended or revoked if it was subsequently concluded that safety standards were not met.

Nevertheless, it remains of great concern that more than half of all African states continue to have poor safety standards. This is especially true because when strictly applying the principles of the Chicago Convention as outlined earlier, the consequence would be that more than half of African countries could not even engage in traditional international scheduled air traffic operated by aircraft registered in those states. Finally, on a more positive note, the African Union confirmed and reaffirmed its commitment to aviation security at the Third Conference of Ministers Responsible for Air Transport and plans to enhance cooperation among all member states with respect to this matter (African Union 2007c).

Notes

1. "Implementation." Wikipedia. http://en.wikipedia.org/wiki/Implementation. Accessed 11 April 2007.
2. The main reason for Mauritius' withdrawal (which was never done formally in accordance with Article 12.3 of the Yamoussoukro Decision) was apparently

that Air Mauritius feared that sixth freedom traffic from Europe over the hubs of Johannesburg or Nairobi would be operated as third and fourth freedom traffic under the Yamoussoukro Decision.

3. Heads of state and government founded the Intergovernmental Agency on Development on 21 March 1996, at the Second Extraordinary Summit in Nairobi. The objectives of this intergovernmental agency are conflict prevention, management, and resolution; humanitarian affairs; infrastructure development (transport and communications); food security; and environmental protection.

4. The 46 members states of AFCAC are Algeria, Angola, Benin, Botswana, Burkina Faso, Burundi, Cameroon, the Central African Republic, Chad, the Democratic Republic of Congo, the Republic of Congo, Côte d'Ivoire, the Arab Republic of Egypt, Eritrea, Ethiopia, Gabon, The Gambia, Ghana, Guinea, Guinea Bissau, Kenya, Lesotho, Libya, Madagascar, Malawi, Mali, Mauritania, Mauritius, Morocco, Mozambique, Liberia, Namibia, Niger, Nigeria, Rwanda, Senegal, Sierra Leone, Somalia, South Africa, Sudan, Swaziland, Tanzania, Togo, Tunisia, Uganda, and Zambia.

5. A small operator, Zambian Airways, has successfully established a regional network and is operating three Boeing 737 aircraft. However, the government of Zambia does not consider this operator to be a replacement for a national airline and continues to insist that a new national carrier must be established (interview held with Peter Tembo, permanent secretary of the Ministry of Communications and Transport, 26 March 2007, Lusaka).

6. An open skies policy is the liberal granting of at least third, fourth, and fifth freedom rights without any restrictions of frequency, capacity, or type of equipment used. An open skies policy is always translated into a bilateral air service agreement with the aforementioned liberal traffic rights. However, the Yamoussoukro Decision notification process eliminates the need for a formal Yamoussoukro Decision compliant bilateral air service agreement, but to date no case of formal Yamoussoukro Decision procedure for notification and granting of traffic rights has occurred.

7. One of these states is Somaliland, a self-declared independent republic located in the Horn of Africa within the internationally recognized borders of Somalia that is not recognized by any other country or by any international organization.

8. Kenya temporarily refused Ethiopian Airlines the right to conduct fifth freedom operations between Nairobi and Kigali, Rwanda, in breach of the Yamoussoukro Decision compliant bilateral between Ethiopia and Kenya. However, the issue was dealt with by seeking a diplomatic solution, that is, direct negotiations between the parties, rather than, for example, calling on the African Union for support. Ethiopian management considers an amicable solution paramount for any legal procedure that the Yamoussoukro Decision

framework would provide in the future (interview with Girma Wake, chief executive officer of Ethiopian Airlines, 25 April 2007, Addis Ababa).

9. The 35th Session of the ICAO General Assembly considered the council's proposal for the continuation and expansion of the Universal Safety Oversight Audit Programme as of 2005 and resolved that the program be expanded to cover all safety-related annexes (1, 2, 3, 4, 5, 6, 7, 8, 10, 11, 12, 13, 14, 15, 16, and 18) and also to transit to a comprehensive systems approach for the conduct of safety oversight audits. All states are now being progressively audited under the expanded program.

10. The list bans both individual air carriers that are considered unsafe as well as some states that do not demonstrate that they exert the necessary regulatory oversight. The latter are blacklisted by banning all carriers registered in such a state. However, this creates a false picture for travelers, because they do not know if all carriers of a given state have been checked or only the one that is banned. Industry experts therefore criticize the list and suggest a mechanism that does not mix the evaluation and banning of individual carriers with the banning of a state (interview with Günther Matschnigg, IATA senior vice president for safety, operations, and infrastructure, Montreal, 25 September 2007).

11. List of airlines banned within the EU. European Commission, Mobility and Transport. http://ec.europa.eu/transport/air-ban/list_en.htm.

12. These carriers include Air France, British Airways, Alitalia, KLM, IBERIA, TAP Portugal, Swiss International Airlines, SN Brussels, Austrian, Virgin Atlantic, Delta, North American, Etihad, and China Southern Airlines (*Official Airline Guide* 2007).

13. These aircraft include all the Boeing 700 series, as well as Airbus, McDonnell Douglas, British Aerospace, Dornier, Fairchild Swearingen Metroliner, Beech, and the DHC-6 Twin Otter aircraft.

14. Article 6.1 provides that each state party has the right to designate at least one airline to operate the intra-African air transport service in accordance with the Yamoussoukro Decision. According to Article 6.2, the designated carrier could also be from another state party.

15. The monitoring body held a total of four documented meetings until 2005 (African Union 2005a). The meetings of experts at the second and third sessions of the Conference of African Ministers Responsible for Air Transport in 2006 and 2007 represent the monitoring body even if their reports are not titled accordingly (African Union 2006c, 2007c). However, according to annex 2 of the Yamoussoukro Decision, the monitoring body shall meet, on a rotational basis, twice a year for the first year and thereafter as required.

CHAPTER 4

Regional Implementation of the Yamoussoukro Decision

It was recognized early on that implementation of the Yamoussoukro Decision depended mainly on regional initiatives that were to be carried out by regional economic groupings. The African states outlined this at the "Worldwide Air Transport Conference: Challenges and Opportunities of Liberalization," which was held in Montreal in March 2004. They stated that with reference to competition regulation, implementation of the Yamoussoukro Decision should be made through regional economic groupings. They listed the following five possible groupings (ICAO 2003b, para. 2.2):

- the Arab Maghreb Union (AMU),
- ECOWAS,
- the Central African Economic and Monetary Community (Communauté Économique et Monétaire de l'Afrique Centrale or CEMAC),
- SADC,
- COMESA.

This report examines progress made in regional implementation of the Yamoussoukro Decision by using this proposed grouping of regional economic organizations. However, in some instances other regional organizations that play a certain role in the liberalization of air transport in Africa, such as the League of Arab Nations, the West African Economic and Monetary Union (WAEMU), and the EAC, will also be examined.

North Africa

In the past, two regional organizations have played a part in trying to regulate or liberalize air transport in North Africa: the AMU and the League of Arab States.

The Arab Maghreb Union

The AMU was created on 17 February 1989, by a treaty that was signed in Marrakesh, Morocco, by the leaders of Algeria, Libya, Mauritania, Morocco, and Tunisia (Treaty Creating the Arab Union of the Maghreb 1992). The treaty was, in essence, modeled, after the European Community, now the EU. Its main objectives include integrating the member states and their peoples with the goals of achieving progress and prosperity; preserving peace; developing a common policy in certain domains; and gradually achieving free movement of people and transfer of services, goods, and capital. At the international level, the treaty (Article 3) aims to "achieve concord among the Member States and to establish between them a close diplomatic cooperation based on dialogue." The AMU's economic objectives include the achievement of industrial, agricultural, commercial, and social development of member states, with an emphasis on setting up joint ventures and common programs.

AMU members have met fairly regularly since 1990 and the five member countries have signed more than 30 multilateral agreements in several economic, social, and cultural areas; however, only five agreements have been ratified by all AMU members. The agreements that were ultimately adopted concerned trade in and tariffs on industrial products, trade in agricultural products, investment guarantees, elimination of double taxation, and common phytosanitary standards (Institute for Security Studies 2007b). Despite these agreements, the AMU has largely been paralyzed because of the dispute about the status of the Western Sahara. Morocco annexed the territories of this former Spanish colony in 1975, but ever since, the liberation movement known as the Popular Front for the Liberation of Saguia el-Hamra and Río de Oro has proclaimed its independence with Algerian backing (Aghrout and Sutton 1990, p. 119).

AMU members recognized early on that the transport sector was important for achieving the stated objective of industrial, agricultural, commercial, and social development. In 1969, members created a shipping company, the Maghreb Coast Line, which operated on a limited scale until it was dissolved 1976 because of financial problems. In 1970, the AMU's Air Transport Committee approved the concept of a jointly owned airline to be known as Air Maghreb. In the railway sector, members proposed a regional project that included the Trans-Maghreb Express, which would link Casablanca, Algiers, and Tunis (Aghrout and Sutton 1990, p. 117). Even though these three initiatives never resulted in sustainable ventures, a meeting of Maghreb transport ministers held in Tripoli in May 1989 resurrected the idea of joint air, land, and rail transport companies (Aghrout and Sutton 1990, p. 136). However, no significant progress was achieved and the idea of creating a joint airline appears to have been abandoned after the bankruptcy of Air Afrique in 2001.

The AMU did not consider the liberalization of air transport among member states even though all of them except Morocco were signatory states of the Yamoussoukro Decision. The initiative to liberalize air transport came from neighboring European countries that wanted to harmonize and gradually liberalize transport systems in the Mediterranean region. In a conference in Paris in 1995, the ministers of six western Mediterranean countries (Algeria, France, Italy, Morocco, Spain, and Tunisia) agreed to pursue a joint policy aimed at harmonizing and extending the European transport system with the Maghreb transport system. Concerning air transport, the conference set the objectives at harmonizing air traffic control systems between Europe and the Maghreb and fostering partnerships between the six countries "in the interest of gradual and controlled liberalization of the international air transport sector" (European Conference of Ministers of Transport 1995, pp. 3, 5).

The consultations between the Maghreb countries and their European counterparts were eventually elevated to the level of the EU, which began to negotiate air service agreements on behalf of its member states.[1] In May 2005, the European Commission began negotiations with Morocco on an open skies agreement. This initiative was widely seen as the test case for the new European aviation policy (European Commission 2005b). After five rounds of negotiations in Rabat, Morocco, an agreement was initialed in Marrakech on 14 December 2005. The open skies agreement has two phases. The first phase grants unrestricted third and fourth freedom rights between any point in Morocco and any point in a country in the EU for both Moroccan and EU carriers. The second phase, which will be instituted once Morocco has implemented the relevant European aviation legislation and regulation, will additionally grant consecutive fifth freedom rights to Moroccan carriers in Europe and to EU carriers "to countries involved in the Neighbourhood Policy" (European Commission 2005b, p.2). The European Neighbourhood Policy in transport, as referred to in the agreement, consists of "setting-up an integrated multimodal Euro-Mediterranean transport network, which will contribute to the strengthening of exchanges between the EU and the Mediterranean Partners, and among the Mediterranean Partners themselves" (Euromed Transport Project 2005, p. 1). The background to this policy is the EU's objective to develop the wider European common aviation area by 2010, which will include all 27 member states.

The open skies agreement between the EU and Morocco potentially has a significant impact on the liberalization of air transport in the Maghreb region. According to the agreement, any European carrier will eventually be allowed to serve any destination between two countries that are both part of the European Neighbourhood Policy.[2] Another country that is currently evaluating its bilateral relationship with the EU is Tunisia. A recent World Bank study (Kaminski 2007) concluded that Tunisia would greatly benefit from a similar bilateral air service agreement with the EU. However, while Morocco's open skies agreement with the EU marks the climax of its 10-year initiative to liberalize international air travel, Tunisia has not yet embarked on talks with the EU on liberalizing its air services (Kaminski 2007, p. 2). The initial impact of the liberalization has been that several European discount operators, such as easyJet, Ryanair, and Aigle Azur, have initiated flights between European cities (Madrid, London, Barcelona, and Paris) to several points in Morocco (Casablanca, Marrakesh, Fez, Agadir, and Oujda). At the same time, Royal Air Marco was strengthened after a successful restructuring and has expanded its network of European destinations (Kaminski 2007, p. 12). Thus given the promising initial results of the liberalization of air services between Morocco and the EU, other North African countries will certainly follow this path in the foreseeable future.

In addition to Morocco, the North African countries of the European Neighbourhood Policy include Algeria, the Arab Republic of Egypt, Libya, and Tunisia, all of which could agree to a similar air transport agreement. This may eventually lead to a situation where all Maghreb countries except Mauritania are bound to the same air service liberalization terms, which in phase two would allow fifth freedom flights of European carriers to these AMU states. Should Maghreb member states not liberalize air services among themselves, the odd situation may persist whereby European fifth freedom flights may openly compete with regional AMU traffic that is still bound to traditional bilateral air service agreements.

AMU ministers seem to have recognized the need for liberalizing air services in their region when they met in Skhirat, Morocco, in April 2007. During this meeting, they set up a committee to examine Morocco's proposal for an open skies agreement. At the conclusion of the meeting, Morocco's Transport Minister Karim Ghellab said: "For certain Maghreb countries, the liberalization of air transport will require a period of reflection, but I think the 2008 date is reasonable" (Sabooni 2007). This statement was supported by Driss Benhima, the director-general of Royal Air Maroc, who stressed the urgency of liberalizing the air transport sector, stating: "As Europe creates an open air space in which Morocco is a part, it seems more and more anachronistic that there is not a similar Maghreb open skies deal" (Middle East Online 2007). However, while the AMU has finally recognized the need to liberalize air services within the union, no considerations of the Yamoussoukro Decision and the liberalization of air traffic to Sub-Saharan Africa are currently apparent. Nevertheless, Royal Air Maroc has continuously expanded its operations in Sub-Saharan Africa, and in summer 2007 flew to 15 such destinations. In addition, Royal Air Maroc has acquired a 51 percent stake in Air Senegal International, a 51 percent stake in Air Gabon International, and a 51 percent stake in Air Mauritanie, which gives the carrier a unique advantage to expand into Sub-Saharan Africa even though Morocco did not join the Yamoussoukro Decision (Schmeling 2007).

We can conclude that the Maghreb region is confronted with the growing reality of needing to move decisively toward liberalizing air services by both the consequences of an opening of and participation in the European market and the important market potential in Sub-Sahara Africa. Because most AMU countries are bound to the Yamoussoukro Decision, which eventually will exert pressure for implementation on the region, the AMU is well advised to continue the path of liberalizing air services among its member states first. This would also provide additional leverage, for example, when negotiating with a supranational body such as the African Union about the terms of implementation of the Yamoussoukro Decision in the region.

The League of Arab States

The League of Arab States, or the Arab League, was founded in Cairo on 22 March 1945, by a treaty that was signed by the heads of state of seven Arab nations: Egypt, Iraq, Jordan, Lebanon, Saudi Arabia, the Syrian Arab Republic, and the Republic of Yemen (League of Arab States 1992, p. 148). The purpose, as defined in Article 2 of the treaty, is to strengthen relations between the member states, coordinate their policies, safeguard their independence and sovereignty, and deal with issues of general concern that are in the interests of the Arab countries. Subsequently, the Arab League extended its membership base continuously over the years to include a total of 22 members and two observing nations.[3]

In its early years the Arab League concentrated primarily on economic, cultural, and social programs. In 1959, it held the first petroleum congress, and in 1964 it established the Arab League Educational, Cultural, and Scientific Organization. However, over the years disputes about several political issues have weakened the league. Early problems arose in relation to recognition of the Palestine Liberation Organization despite Jordan's objections and Egypt's separate peace treaty with Israel on 26 March 1979, which led to the suspension of Egypt's membership and the transfer of the league's headquarters from Cairo to Tunis. However, Egypt was readmitted nine years later and the league's headquarters returned to Cairo in 1990. More recent tensions within the Arab League arose over the Kuwait crisis in 1990 and because of the invitation extended by Saudi Arabia to the United States that allowed a buildup of foreign military in the country. This issue created a fairly deep divide among the member countries that paralyzed the Arab League during the eruption of the Gulf crisis in 1990 (Geddes 1991). Subsequently, the future of the Arab League as a regional organization became highly uncertain, but this situation seems to have changed significantly during the war between Israel and Lebanon in the summer of 2006, when the Arab League displayed renewed unity and regained respect in the Arab world.

The Civil Aviation Council of the Arab States, created in 1967, dealt with the air transport sector. The original aim of this council was to study the "principles, techniques, and economics relating to air transport" (Peaslee and Xydis 1976, p. 265), and the council was to study international standards, practices, and agreements and to recommend adoption of such agreements that were in the interests of Arab states. The council also anticipated the preparation and adoption of a uniform advanced air law for Arab states; the preparation of an English-French-Arabic lexicon of civil aviation terminology; and the conclusion of various agreements on air transport, transit rights, and search and rescue (Peaslee and Xydis 1976, p. 265) Article 10 of the agreement even established a dispute settlement mechanism that was set up by the Civil Aviation Council (Peaslee and Xydis 1976, p. 265).

Despite the strong initial momentum of the Arab states' wanting to unify and harmonize their air transport sectors, and eventually creating a common Arab aviation market, there is little evidence that the Civil Aviation Council achieved major progress toward that objective. About 30 years after the creation of the council, the Arab League states launched a new initiative in 1995 when they created a new entity called the Arab Organization for Civil Aviation. The main objective of the new organization was to provide the civil aviation authorities of the Arab League member states with a joint framework for the development of air transport services between the Arab countries and to ensure the safety of the sector. Its specific aim was to promote and develop cooperation and coordination between the Arab states (Radhi 1996, p. 285). The organization, which has its own General Assembly, Executive Board, and independent budget, enjoyed a certain independence in pursuing the promotion of cooperation and integration of the air transport activities of the member countries. For example, the Arab Organization for Civil Aviation may promote integration between Arab airline companies and consolidate arrangements between member countries wherever they contribute to implementing the regional plans issued by ICAO relating to aerial navigation supplies and services (Radhi 1996, p. 286). However, the organization remained bound to the rules approved by three councils, the Economic and Social Council, the Arab League Council, and the Arab Transportation Ministers Council, with respect to Pan-Arab action organizations. Its mandate also includes implementing resolutions and programs of these councils and it must coordinate with the General Secretariat of the Arab League (Radhi 1996, p. 292). These restrictions clearly indicate that the Arab League is deciding on policy issues of the air transport sector at the highest level. However, the objectives and mandate of the Arab Organization for Civil Aviation are similar to those of the Civil Aviation Council of the Arab States, which over the course of 30 years made little progress.

Arab League Open Skies Agreement. The Arab Civil Aviation Commission, a specialized organization of the Arab League that is based in Rabat and emerged out of the Arab Organization for Civil Aviation, has continuously pushed for cooperation and for liberalization of the civil aviation sector in the Arab world. The commission's objectives are similar to those of the former council. Its creation was based on an agreement of the Council of Arab Transport Ministers, reached in 1999, to liberalize intra-Arab air services over a period of five years by gradually reducing restrictions for carriers of member states of the commission. This resulted in the signing of 17 open skies agreements among commission states that included Bahrain, Jordan, Lebanon, Morocco, Oman, Qatar, Syria, and the United Arab Emirates

(Kotaite 2006). In addition, on 19 December 2004, under the leadership of the commission, several Arab League members namely, Bahrain, Egypt, Iraq, Jordan, Lebanon, Oman, Palestine (West Bank and Gaza), Somalia, Sudan, Syria, Tunisia, and the Republic of Yemen, signed a multilateral agreement on the liberalization of air transport between the Arab states henceforth referred to as the Arab League Open Skies Agreement (Arab Civil Aviation Commission 2004a).

The agreement, which aims at liberalizing regional air services, is based on the Agreement on Facilitating and Developing Trade between the Arab Countries (known as the Agreement of Arab Free Trade), which the Economic and Social Council adopted on 27 February 1981 (Arab League 1981). Article 18 of this agreement provides for cooperation by the state parties of the Arab League to facilitate all means of transport and communication between them on a preferential basis. The preamble of the Arab League Open Skies Agreement specifically seeks to achieve greater liberalization of air transport services between the Arab countries by "coordinating Arab air transport policies in order to eliminate any obstacles to the development of Arab air transport." The preamble encourages "the gradual liberalization of air transport within a regional and multilateral framework." In Article 4, the agreement provides concrete traffic rights for any air transport company that was designated in accordance with the agreement the right to

- transit through any of the territories of the other state parties;
- land in any in any of the territories of the other state parties for non-commercial purposes;
- embark and disembark passengers, cargo, and mail, whether separately or combined, to and from any of the territories of the state parties.

The first two traffic rights represent the first two freedoms of the air as described in the International Air Services Transit Agreement of 1944, hereinafter referred to as the Transit Agreement, which was signed by 125 countries (ICAO 1944). Most of the Arab League states have already signed the Transit Agreement and are bound to grant these first two freedoms. However, for eight Arab League members (the Comoros, Djibouti, Libya, Palestine [West Bank and Gaza, not a contracting state of ICAO] Qatar, Saudi Arabia, Sudan, and the Republic of Yemen), this will become a new obligation provided they sign and ratify the agreement. The third right to be granted based on the agreement is much broader. While the

Yamoussoukro Decision clearly defines the granted rights in its Article 3 as first, second, third, fourth, and fifth freedoms, the Arab League Open Skies Agreement is less clear on what freedoms beyond the first two are granted. "To and from" a point of a state party does clearly include third and fourth freedoms, which are based on air traffic between two parties. However, the agreement seems to go beyond these freedoms, as it includes traffic "to and from any of the territories of the State parties." Clearly, fifth freedom rights are included, because any destination within state parties beyond the initial destination is included. The agreement even seems to grant seventh freedom rights, as it does not specify that traffic needs to route back over the departure point in the initial state party. The only freedom that is clearly excluded is cabotage, the eighth freedom.

The Arab League Open Skies Agreement has other provisions that are similar to the Yamoussoukro Decision. Article 5 entitles each state party to designate one or more air transport companies to benefit from the provisions of the agreement. To qualify, companies must have substantial ownership or effective control by one or more state parties or their citizens and their main place of business must be in one of the state parties. Similar to the Yamoussoukro Decision, Article 7 provides the freedom of capacity by stating that each designated air transport company is entitled to operate the capacity and number of flights it considers adequate, and that no state party may unilaterally restrict capacity, number of flights, types of aircraft, or air transport rights except on a nondiscriminatory basis for certain environmental or technical reasons when air safety or security are affected, which is similar to Article 5 of the Yamoussoukro Decision.

In terms of tariffs, the Arab League Open Skies Agreement provides a more complete framework than the Yamoussoukro Decision. According to Article 8 of the agreement, the tariffs for air transport of passengers, cargo, and mail must be determined in accordance with annex 1 of the agreement. This annex, "Criteria and Procedures for Fixing Tariffs," states that the designated air transport company should determine its tariffs for air transportation on the basis of commercial considerations. As criteria, it states that tariffs must be fixed at reasonable levels taking into account "all the relevant factors and, in particular, operating costs and types of services, a reasonable profit and the competition in the market." Civil aviation authorities do not need to approve the tariffs, but they must be filed 30 days prior to the date they come into force. However, the civil aviation authority of any state party may intervene to prevent discriminatory practices and to protect consumers, particularly as regards the provisions pertaining to guarantees and competition. Discriminatory practices are further defined as the case where tariffs are to be considered prejudicial to the air transport company of a state party, in which case the civil aviation authority of that country might object. The consumer protection provisions aim at ensuring fair competition and are defined in annex 2.

The fair competition provisions focus on air carriers belonging to a given state party, which should not benefit from special agreements between the concerned state parties when they were concluded to adversely affect competition. The consumer protection provisions of annex 1 also provide certain guarantees that should eliminate unfair practices to promote a minimum of market participation. They are listed in annex 3 and include practices such as imposing excessively low tariffs, engaging in price dumping, or providing excess capacity on the market, all of which are intended to drive other participants out of the market.

Finally, annex 1 refers to the dispute resolution mechanism of Article 30 of the agreement, which shall be invoked if an objection to a tariff for scheduled air transport was raised and the matter could not be solved by consultations between the two state parties. The dispute settlement mechanism shall be applied in the case of any disagreement between two or more state parties concerning the interpretation or application of the provisions of the agreement and its annexes. If the parties involved cannot resolve the matter through negotiation, the issue shall be submitted to the director-general of the Arab Civil Aviation Commission. If the director-general's efforts to intermediate fail, an arbitration tribunal consisting of three arbitrators shall be established. The decisions of this tribunal are final and cannot be appealed. The states parties are bound by the decision, and measures may be invoked to ensure compliance by the carrier.

Overall, the Arab League Open Skies Agreement provides the same or, in the case of seventh freedom rights, even greater liberalization of air services than the Yamoussoukro Decision. It defines the competition rules and the conflict resolution procedure well. While the agreement goes much farther in many domains that the Yamoussoukro Decision omits, the provisions of the Arab League Open Skies Agreement generally do not conflict with the Yamoussoukro Decision. However, to date, the agreement has been ratified only by Syria (24 May 2005), Jordan (30 June 2005), Palestine (West Bank and Gaza) (23 October 2005), the Republic of Yemen (24 October 2005), the United Arab Emirates (28 November 2006), and Lebanon (14 June 2006) (El Alj 2007). Nevertheless, the agreement has been in force since 18 February 2007, when according to Article 38, the necessary quorum of five countries was reached by deposition of their ratification instruments. In addition, Bahrain, Egypt, Oman, and Qatar have announced that their ratification processes are under way (El Alj 2007).

Conclusion about the Arab States and the Yamoussoukro Decision. Of the six Arab states of the African continent—Algeria, Egypt, Libya, Mauritania, Morocco, and Tunisia—four are Yamoussoukro Decision party states and are bound to the decision. Only Morocco, which never signed the Yamoussoukro Decision, and Mauritania, which deposited its ratification instruments too late, are not parties to the Yamoussoukro Decision. However, Morocco has pursued an open skies policy by agreeing to an open skies agreement with the EU and has called for liberalization within the AMU. At the same time, all the African Arab states have state-owned carriers, and except for Morocco seem to have engaged in some form of protectionism in the past that resulted in a position generally opposed to liberalization. This may also explain why none of the African Arab states have so far ratified the Arab League Open Skies Agreement even though it would eventually provide them with access to a huge market in the Middle East.

Nevertheless, the new dynamic of the Arab League toward the liberalization of air services and the Arab League Open Skies Agreement are strong pillars on which the liberalization of air services among the African Arab states can grow. Being potentially bound by two liberalization agreements, the Arab League Open Skies Agreement and the Yamoussoukro Decision, the African Arab states should recognize the market potential rather than being concerned about the threat of competition to their own carriers. Three of the Maghreb states—Egypt, Morocco, and Tunisia—operate modern and competitive carriers and have a good safety rating (see appendix B), and these are the states that should jointly act as the driving force toward liberalization. This is particularly pertinent, as the Maghreb market may soon see European carriers operating between two or more North African European Neighbourhood Policy states. In addition, the Arab League will certainly continue to develop a stronger momentum for ratification of its Open Skies Agreement. This will result in many African Arab states facing a push toward gradual liberalization of their air services. For these states to take control of the steps toward liberalization by actively cooperating with the Arab League and the Arab Civil Aviation Commission would therefore be advantageous.

Finally, the Arab League could also consider approaching the African Union, as well as neighboring subregional groupings, such as WAEMU or COMESA, to negotiate and implement an agreement with the organizations that would further liberalize air services. (Note that the Arab League states have signed an agreement for collective negotiations with regional and subregional groups [Arab Civil Aviation Commission 2004b].) This step would amount to final implementation of the Yamoussoukro Decision in the African Arab region.

West Africa

The West African states can be grouped into several economic and/or political organizations. The largest in terms of the number of member states is ECOWAS, which encompasses all 16 West African states. However, in relation to air transport policy and implementation of the Yamoussoukro Decision, the West African states split into two distinct groups early on. WAEMU comprises eight French-speaking West African states and the Banjul Accord Group (BAG) comprises seven predominantly English-speaking countries. Nevertheless, all three organizations play a role in the implementation of the Yamoussoukro Decision.

Economic Community of West African States

ECOWAS is a regional group founded in 1975 by the Treaty of Lagos that initially consisted of 15 countries: Benin, Burkina Faso, Côte d'Ivoire, The Gambia, Ghana, Guinea, Guinea-Bissau, Liberia, Mali, Mauritania, Niger, Nigeria, Senegal, Sierra Leone, and Togo. Cape Verde joined in 1976. The creation of this new economic community was initially seen as a major achievement (Adedeji 2004, p. 32). After three years of negotiations, the heads of state of the respective countries agreed to establish an organization that would not only put extremely small states on an equal footing with the large nation of Nigeria, but would also unite all West African states irrespective of the language spoken. The main languages are English and French. In addition, Portuguese is spoken in Guinea-Bissau and Arabic in Mauritania. Even though Mauritania is often referred to as a North African and not a West African country, it was a founding member of ECOWAS, but it left the organization in 2002.

From the beginning the mission of ECOWAS was to promote economic cooperation and integration by means of trade liberalization, and including the establishment of a customs union, and even a fund for economic compensation between the member states (Adedeji 2004, p. 34).

ECOWAS swiftly established its secretariat in Lagos and called for a first meeting of its Council of Ministers, which was held in Accra in July 1976. During this meeting the member states ran into some unexpected controversy when discussing the assessment of revenue losses by certain member states as a result of trade liberalization. The controversy was never fully resolved, and the initial expectations and enthusiasm about ECOWAS started to fade (Adedeji 2004, p. 33). ECOWAS then began to focus on peace-keeping operations, for which it gained some international recognition.[4] Nevertheless, in 1990 ECOWAS introduced its trade liberalization scheme, which consisted of the abolition of customs duties levied on imports and exports among member states; the adoption of a common external tariff and trade policy; and the removal of obstacles between member states to allow free movement of people, goods, services, and capital and to secure rights of residence and establishment (freedom of establishment is the right of both natural and legal persons, including companies and associations of any sort, to self-employment and to set up and manage undertakings) (Obuah 1997, p. 14).

After years of lack of political will, which resulted in member states' failure to ratify many ECOWAS protocols, ECOWAS eventually began to gain the necessary acceptance (Obuah 1997, p. 18). This resulted in the establishment of a committee in May 1990 that was charged with reviewing the Treaty of Lagos and proposing a revised version. In July 1993, at the Cotonou Summit of ECOWAS in Benin, the participants discussed and agreed on a revised version. All 16 member states, represented by their heads of state, signed the revised treaty (ECOWAS 1993). The revised treaty reaffirms the original objectives of promoting economic cooperation and integration (Article 3, para. 1). In addition, it also calls for the "harmonization and co-ordination of national policies and the promotion of integration programs, projects and activities particularly in food, ... transport and communications" (Article 3, para. 2[a]). The most significant modification in the revised treaty is the principle that decisions made by the Authority of Heads of States of ECOWAS and regulations issued by the ECOWAS Council of Ministers are binding "on the Member States and on the institutions of the Community" (Article 9, para. 4; Article 12, para. 3). The revised treaty also specifically addresses air transport by referring to the harmonious integration of the physical infrastructure of member states and to the promotion and facilitation of the movement of people, goods, and services within the community (Article 32, para. 1). It specifically mandates member states to "encourage co-operation in flight-scheduling, leasing of aircraft and granting and joint use of fifth freedom rights to airlines of the region, [and to] promote the development of regional air transport services and endeavour to promote their efficiency and profitability" (Article 32, para. 1, [f] and [g]).

According to member states, the stated objectives of airline cooperation and the promotion of regional development of air services, including the objective of granting fifth freedom rights to the region's carriers, are the principles of the Yamoussoukro Declaration of 1988. Given the new powers of ECOWAS, and given its declared policy objectives in relation to air transportation, one might have expected this regional organization to play a major role in the preparation of the Yamoussoukro Decision, which was enacted six years after the signature of the revised treaty. However, ECOWAS was soon faced with the reality that its member states began to deal with air transport matters by way of two separate regional groupings. The French-speaking countries established WAEMU in 1994, while the English-speaking states organized themselves in BAG, which was created in 1997. Both subregional organizations began implementing a range of regulations and subsequently liberalized their air service markets either through a common policy or by means of a multilateral agreement among member states.

Nevertheless, because the Yamoussoukro Decision encouraged subregional and regional organizations to "pursue and to intensify their efforts in the implementation of the Decision," the West and Central African states mandated ECOWAS and CEMAC to implement their air transport policy as defined in the Memorandum of Understanding signed in Yamoussoukro on 14 November 1999 (ECOWAS 2007, p. 1; UNECA 2004, Article 12.2). In March 2001, the ministers responsible for civil aviation in the 23 West and Central African countries met in Bamako, Mali, to discuss the steps toward implementation. At that meeting they developed the so-called Bamako Action Plan that aimed to (a) strengthen the capacity of civil aviation authorities to undertake the economic and technical regulation of civil aviation effectively, (b) harmonize the legal and institutional framework for air transport, and (c) explore options for mechanisms to ensure that oversight of the industry is carried out on a cost-effective and sustainable basis at both the state and regional levels (ECOWAS and CEMAC Project Secretariats 2004, p. 4). Based on the action plan, project secretariats were established at ECOWAS and CEMAC and several studies were initiated (World Bank 2000, 2002).

In February 2003, the Council of Ministers for the Implementation of the Yamoussoukro Decision met in Lomé, Togo, for their second meeting.

However, despite strong declarations in support of the Yamoussoukro Decision, including requesting the ministers of foreign affairs of member states to take urgent practical measures to fast-track the exchange of diplomatic notes within the framework of the designation of airlines, no significant progress was made in taking concrete steps toward implementation, for example, by adopting new regulations for the liberalization of air services (Council of Ministers for the Implementation of the Yamoussoukro Decision on Air Transport Liberalization in West and Central Africa 2003). Nevertheless, the Council of Ministers did establish the Air Transport Economic Regulation Harmonization Committee to steer the process of developing common air transport economic regulations for the two regions of West and Central Africa and to periodically monitor implementation of the Yamoussoukro Decision at the state level. In addition, to address the safety issues recognized at the Bamako meeting in 2001, the Council of Ministers also created three subregional state groups to implement the Cooperative Development of Operational Safety and Continued Airworthiness Program (COSCAP) (WAEMU 2002a, p. 9).[5] Finally, the Air Transport Project Secretariat of ECOWAS undertook regional assessments of the implementation of the Yamoussoukro Decision, which it saw as a requirement for periodic evaluation and monitoring of the implementation of the Yamoussoukro Decision (ECOWAS and CEMAC Project Secretariats 2004, p. 5). A new action plan, known as the Lomé Action Plan, was established that again focused on economic regulation and on safety and security improvements.

In November 2004, the Coordination Committee and the Council of Ministers Responsible for Civil Aviation of ECOWAS and CEMAC held their third meeting in Libreville, Gabon. At that meeting they adopted regulations on denied boarding, airport slots, and ground handling. In addition, they stressed the importance of the implementation of the Cooperative Development of Operational Safety and Continued Airworthiness Program and recommended the creation of autonomous civil aviation authorities. The Project Secretariat prepared several studies, for example, on competition rules, market access, air carrier licensing, and air carrier liability (ECOWAS 2007, p. 2; UNECA. 2004, Article 12.2).

Despite the several ministerial meetings, the various studies and reports prepared, and the financial support by international donors such as the World Bank and the African Development Bank, ECOWAS has not adopted any legally binding legislation or regulations that could be seen as steps toward implementation of the Yamoussoukro Decision. (A formal decision by the Authority of Heads of State of Government of ECOWAS is necessary for any regulation or decision of ECOWAS to be binding on its member states [ECOWAS 1993, Article 9, para. 4, Article 12, para. 3]). Member states of the other two subregional entities, WAEMU and BAG, appear to have been more successful in implementing some of the required regulatory framework.

West African Economic and Monetary Union

WAEMU, known in French as the Union Economique et Monétaire Ouest-Africaine, is a customs and monetary union of some ECOWAS members. It has its roots in the treaty signed on 12 May 1962, that established the West African Monetary Union (WAMU) (Peaslee, 1974, p. 1371). The treaty entered into force on 2 November 1962. It established the basis for issuing and managing the common currency, the Communauté Financiére Africaine (CFA) franc (Peaslee 1974, p. 1368). France had introduced his currency in 1948 in all French colonies and it remained pegged to the French franc more or less unchanged for nearly 50 years.[6] The new Central Bank of West African States was created for the WAMU region that acted in the interests of the economies of the monetary union. WAMU initially consisted of seven West African states—Côte d'Ivoire, Dahomey (now Benin), Mauritania, Niger, Senegal, Togo, and Upper Volta (now Burkina Faso)—though Mauritania withdrew from the treaty in 1973 and Mali joined in 1984. Initially, WAMU was generally seen as a success, and for many years it was defined and driven by the strong economy of Côte d'Ivoire, which accounted for about 40 percent of the region's economic output (Rother 1999). However, in the mid-1980s, WAMU started to disintegrate as a result of serious economic pressure from a structural decline in commodity prices and nominal appreciation of the French franc against the U.S. dollar. Both resulted in a serious deterioration of the WAMU economies, and in 1994 the CFA franc was devaluated by a factor of 50 percent (Van den Boogaerde and Tsangarides 2005, p. 4).

In response to the financial crisis and the devaluation of the CFA franc, WAMU members dissolved the union and on 10 January 1994, founded WAEMU. The treaty establishing WAEMU was signed in Dakar, Senegal, by the heads of state and government of Benin, Burkina Faso, Côte d'Ivoire, Mali, Niger, Senegal, and Togo. It quickly came into force on 1 August 1994, after ratification by all seven member countries (WAEMU 1994). Finally, on 2 May 1997, Guinea-Bissau became WAEMU's eighth member state. The treaty was slightly modified in 2003 to include some minor administrative and procedural changes (WAEMU 2003b).

WAEMU's overall objectives are stated in Article 4 of the treaty. They are similar to the objectives of the EU and aim at establishing a common market (EU 2002, Articles 2 and 3). The main objectives include the following:

- achieving greater economic competitiveness through open and competitive markets along with rationalization and harmonization of the legal environment;
- converging member countries' macroeconomic policies by means of a multilateral surveillance procedure;
- creating a common market among the member states on the basis of free movement of goods, services, and capital and the right to be employed or to establish a business activity with common external tariffs and a common commercial policy;
- coordinating national sectoral policies in human resources, regional planning and development, transport, telecommunications, environment, agriculture, energy, industry, and mining;
- harmonizing fiscal policies to the extent necessary to ensure the efficiency of the common market.

Notably Article 5 of the WAEMU treaty states a principle of subsidiary that is similar to that of the EU while not specifically using the term subsidiary (EU 2002, Article 5). The principle of the WAEMU provides that the union shall prepare minimal directives and core regulations that must be finalized based on the specific requirements and constitutional rules of each member state. The significant advantage of WAEMU in terms of implementing any union internal decision or an external treaty is that the legal instruments are guided by two basic and strong principles, namely:

- The principle of immediate and direct applicability, which renders community legislation incorporated into domestic legislation valid as soon as it is published. This requires no additional domestic legislative action and any individual can directly invoke community law (Charrier and Coulibaly 2007, p. 4).
- The principle of primacy of community law over domestic law, which is stated in Article 6.

These two principles constitute a favorable legal framework that facilitates the timely implementation of decisions taken at different levels of

WAEMU. They also prevent abuse by countries that might agree to new laws or regulations at the union level only to stall them later at the national level. As noted in chapter 3, the African Union does not have such powers, and consequently, all its major decisions, directives, and agreements are subject to ratification by its member states.

The Air Transport Common Program in the WAEMU States

WAEMU's involvement in air transport matters stems from Article 4 of the treaty, which sets as an objective of the union the "coordination of national sectoral policies in . . . transport and telecommunications,." To achieve this objective, on 27 June 2002, WAEMU's Council of Ministers adopted a common air transport program, which can be regarded as a sector strategy with an implementation action plan applicable to all its member states (WAEMU 2002b).

The first objective of the common air transport program is to open WAEMU territory to the outside world. To achieve this, WAEMU must establish a safe, orderly, and efficient air transport system that promotes efficient civil aviation management and the competitiveness of air transport enterprises (WAEMU 2002b). The internal objectives of the program are defined as providing cheap and accessible air transportation to the population of the WAEMU states, increasing commercial exchanges and tourist flows so as to stimulate economic growth, and supporting the integration of the member states. However, the program recognizes that member states are becoming marginalized in Africa's air transport market and many are "incapable of ensuring an orderly development of their civil aviation activities" (WAEMU 2002b). To address the objectives and challenges stated, the program focuses on four main items: (a) ensuring that infrastructure and equipment are in compliance with ICAO SARP, (b) harmonizing air transport regulations, (c) enhancing air transport systems, and (d) liberalizing air transport services (WAEMU 2002b, p. 12).

The first item refers to air navigation and aviation meteorology infrastructure and facilities. It includes implementation of the ICAO's Regional Air Navigation Plan, which requires full coverage of WAEMU airspace with communications, surveillance, and air traffic management systems. In relation to safety and security enhancement, the program aims at implementing the recommendations of ICAO and the FAA and COSCAP, which is seen as a transition toward a common agency for aviation safety oversight. In addition, several additional improvements in related areas such as search and rescue, bird hazard control, facilitation, aviation medicine, and environmental protection are planned to be addressed (WAEMU 2002b, p. 14).

The second item, harmonization of air transport regulations, aims at the union's adopting a common legal framework that regulates access to air transport markets, aircraft operations, competition rules, consumer protection, and all safety and security issues. In addition, it specifically addresses compliance with ICAO SARP by "signing and ratification of international air law instruments by Member States on the Commission's recommendation" (WAEMU 2002b, p. 15).

The third item, enhancement of air transport systems, is to be achieved by several measures. These include common regulations for civil aviation authorities' statues, which are aimed at providing legal and financial autonomy. Furthermore, aviation cooperation needed to be strengthened with several international or regional organizations, such as ICAO, IATA, ECOWAS, and CEMAC, as well as with donors, such as the EU and the governments of France and the United States. Other actions, such as creating an air transport databank, promoting investment in the union's air transport sector, establishing an air transport development fund, and undertaking measures to develop aviation human resources, are also planned (WAEMU 2002b, p. 16).

The most relevant measure in relation to implementation of the Yamoussoukro Decision is the fourth item, liberalization of air transport services. The two main elements of liberalization of air services in WAEMU are (a) the disengagement of member states in the "industrial and commercial air transport sector," which is defined as airlines, airports, ground handling, and catering; and (b) the full liberalization of access by allowing, in the long-term, cabotage, or eighth freedom flights for WAEMU carriers. Additional actions are planned to implement these two important steps, such as the development of common competition regulation, the enhancement of facilitation by eliminating restrictions to the free movement of people and goods, and the adoption of consumer protection regulations (WAEMU 2002b, p. 17).

For implementation of the common air transport program, the plan was to prepare and adopt a common air transport legal framework in three phases (WAEMU 2002b, p. 21). The first phase had to be adopted before March 2002 and included (a) regulations on market access; (b) regulations on air carriers' certification; (c) regulations on passengers, freight, and mail; and (d) regulations on accident and incident investigations. The second phase, to be implemented before December 2002, included (a) competition regulation, and (b) consumer protection regulation. The third and final phase consisted of (a) the regulation of the creation of regional and national facilitation committees, and (b) the union's Aviation Code. In addition, the program also set clear deliverables for the Cooperative Development of Operational Safety and Continued Airworthiness Program in order to address the safety and security challenges that a common air transport market must regulate and supervise (WAEMU 2002b, p. 23). These included legislation or regulations covering (a) aviation safety, (b) air transport and the organization of civil aviation, (c) personnel licensing and training, (d) aircraft operations and airworthiness, (d) transport of dangerous goods by air, (e) bird hazard control, and (f) aviation safety oversight by means of a regional agency in the future.

In the five years since adoption of the common air transport program, WAEMU has made progress by adopting several regulations. Appendix D provides an overview of all aviation-related laws and regulations adopted and enacted. In summary, WAEMU has adopted most of the regulations necessary to implement its union-wide air transport liberalization program, which at the same time comply with or exceed the provisions and requirements of the Yamoussoukro Decision.

The most significant regulations are as follows:

- *Traffic rights (Yamoussoukro Decision, Article 3)*: Regulation No. 24/2002 on conditions for market access of air carriers within WAEMU grants all freedoms, including cabotage, after entitlement by the member states. This regulation clearly exceeds the requirements of the Yamoussoukro Decision, which includes third, fourth, and fifth freedom traffic rights.

- *Tariffs (Yamoussoukro Decision, Article 4)*: Regulation No. 07/2002 on tariffs on air service for passengers, freight, and mail within WAEMU allows carriers to freely fix tariffs, which need to be filed only 24 hours in advance. The Yamoussoukro Decision requires filing at least 30 days in advance.

- *Competition regulation (Yamoussoukro Decision, Article 7)*: Regulation No. 24/2002 on conditions for market access by air carriers makes the exercise of traffic rights subject to competition legislation. Enforcement action may be taken by the WAEMU Commission. Regulation No. 2/2002 outlines the union's competition regulation applicable to the air transport sector. Article 6 of the Yamoussoukro Decision notes that state parties shall ensure competition, which implementation of this WAEMU regulation accomplishes.[7]

- *Safety and security (Yamoussoukro Decision, Article 6.12)*: WAEMU has adopted a total of 10 safety and security regulations to address the region's safety and security challenges (appendix D). However, while the necessary regulations are in place, the overall safety and security situation remains unsatisfactory. According to the assessment in appendix C, the safety situation is rated as poor in six WAEMU member states and fair in two. The WAEMU Commission has signed and launched an implementation program with ICAO that should build the necessary human technical capacity and eventually lead to the establishment of a regional safety oversight agency (WAEMU 2003a).

In addition to dealing with the main provisions of the Yamoussoukro Decision, WAEMU has also addressed some consumer protection and carrier liability issues. Regulation No. 03/2003 provides for specific compensation for denial of embarkation, flight cancellation, or major flight delays (appendix D). The regulations, as well as the predefined amounts, are similar to the EU regulation on compensation for and assistance to passengers in the event of denied boarding and of cancellation or long flight delays.[8]

WAEMU took a similar approach when it issued Regulation No. 02/2003 on air carriers' liability in case of an accident. This regulation is tailored after the Montreal Convention of 1999 (ICAO 1999) and includes strict liability per the convention's Article 21 up to SDR 100,000 and its presumed liability above this limit if the carrier cannot demonstrate that the damage was not caused by its negligence or lack of oversight. The regulation is significant because only Benin has signed and ratified the Montreal Convention. The other seven countries of WAEMU have either not ratified (Burkina Faso, Côte d'Ivoire, Niger, Senegal, and Togo) or not signed the convention (Guinea-Bissau and Mali). The simple adoption of WAEMU Regulation No. 02/2003 by the Council of Ministers has effectively bound all WAEMU member states to the main principles of the Montreal Convention. Another provision that was also incorporated in Regulation No. 02/2003 is the requirement for advance payment by the carrier of SDR 15,000 in the case of the death of a traveler, which has its roots in a similar earlier EU regulation (Article 5 of European Commission Regulation No. 2027/97 of 9 October 1997, on Air Carrier Liability in the Event of Accidents).

Thus, WAEMU has established most of the necessary regulatory framework that implements the main provisions of the Yamoussoukro Decision within its territory, and even goes beyond the Yamoussoukro Decision in relation to market access. However, integration of WAEMU's air service market into the continental African region, which is covered by the Yamoussoukro Decision, is not effectively dealt with. Even though each regulation related to air transport includes a reference to the Yamoussoukro Decision in its preamble, it also limits the scope of the air transport policy on WAEMU territory.[9] Reference to air traffic of non-member states is only dealt with by Article 5 of Regulation No. 24/2002, which empowers WAEMU member states to grant access to outside carriers to intracommunity links. This provision includes fifth freedom rights by nonmember states to destinations within the WAEMU. As it is based on "international agreements in force," it can be applied to any member state of the Yamoussoukro Decision. However, while Article 3 of the Yamoussoukro Decision states that "State parties grant to each other the free exercise of the rights of the first, second, third, fourth, and fifth freedoms of the air," WAEMU Regulation No. 24/2002 only states that non-WEMUA carriers "may be authorized by a member State to operate traffic rights . . . on intercommunity links." This indicates that WAEMU maintains reservations about full, continent-wide implementation of the Yamoussoukro Decision.

Nevertheless, WAEMU's full liberalization of air services within its territory must be considered a successful step toward ultimate implementation of the Yamoussoukro Decision. A future regulation by the Council of Ministers, which clarifies access by carriers of non-WAEMU, but Yamoussoukro Decision, states would finalize this step.

The Banjul Accord Group
BAG was created on 29 January 2004, when seven West African states—Cape Verde, The Gambia, Ghana, Guinea, Liberia, Nigeria, and Sierra Leone—signed the BAG Agreement (BAG 2004a, p. 19). This new agreement builds on the initial Banjul Accord signed on 3 April 1997 (BAG 1997, appendix A). The initial Banjul Accord aimed primarily at ensuring and accelerating implementation of the Yamoussoukro Declaration of 1988. Accordingly, the Banjul Accord states as its prime objective the safeguarding of international air transport in the region and the promotion of cooperation among national carriers. Similar to the Yamoussoukro Declaration, the integration of airlines into larger entities, even joint multinational carriers, became the declared objective of the Banjul Accord (UNECA 1988, p. 2). The preamble to the Banjul Accord foresaw cooperation among airlines at three levels: (a) the provision and management of air traffic services, (b) the establishment and exercise of safety oversight procedures, and (c) the establishment of a coordinated multinational

approach for the negotiation of agreements with respect to the granting of air traffic rights. However, the initial Banjul Accord, like the Yamoussoukro Declaration, did not liberalize traffic rights, but primarily maintained the view that African air carriers would cooperate, eventually leading to the elimination of the need to grant traffic rights (UNECA 1988, p. 2). The Banjul Accord became an integral part of a memorandum of understanding that was signed on 26 November 1997, between the civil aviation authorities of four West African states and nine airlines (Cape Verde, The Gambia, Ghana, Nigeria, Air Dabia, Cape Verde Airlines, Ghana Airways, MUK Air, Far Airways, Bellview Airlines, Gambia International Airlines, Mahfooz Aviation Ltd., and Nigeria Airways). Even though this memorandum of understanding did not include all member states of the Banjul Accord, it was one of the few attempts to establish cooperation among air carriers, the declared objective of the Yamoussoukro Declaration. However, there is no evidence that the memorandum of understanding or the Banjul Accord ever resulted in any operational cooperation between carriers of the Western African region.

Article 3.1 of the BAG Agreement of 2004 explicitly states implementation of the Yamoussoukro Declaration and the Yamoussoukro Decision as an objective. In addition, member states agree to enter into joint ventures and or cooperative arrangements to foster the development of international civil aviation among both member states and nonmember states and organizations (Articles 3.2 and 3.3). However, while the intent of the Yamoussoukro Decision is to liberalize access to air transport markets in Africa, the BAG Agreement seems to emphasize airline cooperation rather than to focus primarily on liberalization and free competition as stipulated in the Yamoussoukro Decision. By agreeing on implementation of both the Yamoussoukro Declaration and the Yamoussoukro Decision, the BAG Agreement creates a certain contradiction, or at least confusion, about its real focus with respect to the development of air services. The crux of the issue is that the policy focus clearly shifted from cooperation to liberalized competition in the 11 years between the signing of the Yamoussoukro Declaration and the enactment of the Yamoussoukro Decision. Nevertheless, the BAG Plenary produced two documents in addition to the BAG Agreement. The first is the Multilateral Air Services Agreement (MASA) (BAG 2004c) and the second is the memorandum of understanding for the implementation of a technical cooperation project (COSCAP) for BAG (BAG (Article 3.1).

The MASA was signed on 29 January 2004, by all seven West African states that signed the BAG Agreement. The MASA is, in essence, an identical application of the Yamoussoukro Decision for the BAG member states. For example, the MASA includes the following:

- *Traffic rights (Yamoussoukro Decision, Article 3)*: First and second freedom rights are granted without conditions or restrictions. Third, fourth, and fifth freedom rights are granted for any scheduled and nonscheduled passenger, cargo, and mail flights that are conducted in the territory of the contracting states (MASA, Article II, para. 1). The MASA also stimulates that each contracting state will enjoy fifth freedom traffic rights with respect to other African states in accordance with the Yamoussoukro Decision (MASA, Article II, para. 2). As all BAG member states are full Yamoussoukro Decision member states, this can be interpreted as an acknowledgement and reaffirmation of the Yamoussoukro Decision by BAG.

- *Designation of carrier (Yamoussoukro Decision, Article 6)*: Each contracting state may designate one or more airlines to operate on the specified routes in accordance with the MASA. The carriers can be of another contracting state, and the designation may be refused only if the chosen airline does not conform to the eligibility criteria as defined in Article 6.9 of the Yamoussoukro Decision (MASA, Article 3).

- *Tariffs (Yamoussoukro Decision, Article 4)*: Tariffs are to be freely established based on commercial considerations and are not subject to approval (MASA, Article XII, para. 1). Nevertheless, if tariffs are discriminatory (unreasonably high, restrictive, or artificially low), the contracting parties may intervene. Upon request by the other contracting states, their aeronautical authorities may have to be notified about the tariffs no more than 30 days before the proposed date of effectiveness. If a contracting state considers an announced tariff inconsistent with the above-mentioned principles, consultations between the contracting states should settle the matter. If no mutual agreement can be reached between the parties, the existing tariff shall continue in effect (MASA, Article XII, para. 4). However, the MASA does not provide for a situation in which no prior tariff existed.

- *Capacity and frequency (Yamoussoukro Decision, Article 5)*: Except for considerations concerning safety, security, and environmental requirements, no restrictions shall be imposed on the frequency, capacity, and/or types of aircraft used on air services under the agreement (MASA, Article II, para. 4).

In addition to granting traffic rights in conformity with the Yamoussoukro Decision, the MASA also emphasizes safety and security beyond the principles of the Yamoussoukro Decision. For example, while the state parties of the Yamoussoukro Decision only reaffirm their obligation to comply with the civil aviation safety standards and practices recommended by ICAO (UNECA 2004, Article 6.12, para. c), MASA contracting states may request consultations on the safety standards of any other contracting states relating to aeronautical facilities and services, air crews, aircraft, and operations of designated airlines (MASA, Article VII, para. 1). In addition, each contracting party may withhold, revoke, or limit the operating authorization or technical permission of an airline designated by the other contracting party in the event that the other contracting party does not take appropriate corrective action (MASA, Article VII, para. 2). This unusually strong rule gives any BAG state the right to revoke the operating permit of a foreign BAG airline and effectively ground its operations. The BAG member states recognized that the level of regulatory safety oversight did not meet required international standards, and to address the shortcomings, BAG signed a memorandum of understanding to implement a technical cooperation project that was subsequently launched under the management of ICAO's Technical Cooperation Bureau (BAG 2004b). The program focuses primarily on preparing the required technical regulation and on building capacity for regulatory supervision. Its cost is borne by international donors such as the African Development Bank, the French government, and the EU.

The MASA also goes far beyond the provisions of the Yamoussoukro Decision in relation to security. While the Yamoussoukro Decision stipulates in Article 6.12 that state parties must reaffirm their obligations to protect the security of civil aviation in accordance with annex 17 of the Chicago Convention, the MASA specifically reminds contracting parties that they must act in conformity with the provisions of the Convention on Offences and Certain other Acts Committed on Board Aircraft, signed in Tokyo on 14 September 1963; the Convention for the Suppression of Unlawful Seizure of Aircraft, signed in The Hague on 16 November 1970; and the Convention for the Suppression of Unlawful Acts against the Safety of Civil Aviation, signed in Montreal on 23 September 1971, which all BAG members have signed and ratified. In addition, the MASA obligates the contracting parties to provide assistance to prevent or to take action in the case of unlawful acts prejudicing the safety of aircraft, passengers, crew, airports, and air navigation facilities (MASA, Article VIII). The signing of the Yamoussoukro Decision before the events of 11 September 2001, which triggered a renewed and strong focus on aviation security, and the signing of the MASA two years later explains the latter's relatively strong focus on security in comparison with the Yamoussoukro Decision.

Finally, the settlement of disputes that may arise between two or more contracting parties relating to the interpretation or application of the MASA is to be settled primarily by negotiation (MASA, Article XVI). If the parties fail to reach a settlement by negotiation, they may refer to an arbitration mechanism as set forth in Article XVII of the MASA or to any arbitration mechanism available within the African Union (MASA, Article XVI, para. 2). The MASA outlines the arbitration procedure well, including the appointment of arbitrators and the establishment of its procedural rules. The clear definition of an arbitration procedure, as well as the option of referring to the African Union, is a consequence of the fact that BAG is not an international body, which means that it does not have the necessary infrastructure, human resources, and regulations, like, for example, WAEMU does. Nevertheless, dispute settlement by negotiation or by arbitration may in many cases be a more effective way to deal with issues of air transportation, an ever-changing industry.[10]

In conclusion, by means of the MASA, BAG has established a liberalized regime that is fully compatible with the provisions and obligations of the Yamoussoukro Decision. Its clear obligations and focus on safety and security, as well as the simplified dispute settlement mechanism, should be an inspiration to implement, the Yamoussoukro Decision within the BAG region. It can also serve as a good example that liberalized air transport markets may not require costly and complicated institutional supervisory mechanisms such as the executing agency and monitoring body of the Yamoussoukro Decision.

Central Africa

Central Africa has one regional economic community, CEMAC, which is made up of the six central African states.

Economic and Monetary Community of Central Africa

CEMAC was established to promote economic integration among countries that share a common currency, the CFA franc. (Although Central African CFA francs and West African CFA francs have the same monetary value against other currencies, West African CFA coins and banknotes are not accepted in countries using Central African CFA francs, and vice versa [Van den Boogaerde and Tsangarides 2005, p. 4].) The legal basis of CEMAC is a treaty that was signed in 1994 between Cameroon, the

Central African Republic, Chad, the Republic of Congo, Equatorial Guinea, and Gabon (CEMAC 1994). The annex to this treaty includes the Convention Governing the Economic Union of Central Africa, which was created by Article 2 of this treaty. CEMAC became the successor of the former Customs and Economic Union of Central Africa, which it completely replaced in June 1999.

The main objectives of CEMAC are similar to those of WAEMU. The overall goal is the harmonized development of member states within the institutional framework of CEMAC's two main institutions, the Economic Union (Union Economique de l'Afrique Centrale) and the Monetary Union (Union Monétaire de l'Afrique Centrale). The more specific objectives are stated in Article 2 of the convention governing the Economic Union, namely:

- strengthening economic and financial competitiveness by harmonizing members' regulatory frameworks;
- converging overall macroeconomic policy by coordinating the economic and monetary policies of member states to assure an improved economic outcome;
- creating a common market on the basis of free movement of goods, services, and capital;
- coordinating national sectoral policies of member states in agriculture, livestock, fisheries, industry, trade, tourism, transport, telecommunications, energy, environment, research, and education.

As an institution, CEMAC benefits from a distinct legal personality that is based on public law. It has its own equity, budget, organs, and agents. This is specifically confirmed by the statement that CEMAC is to be recognized as a full and legally independent entity by all member states regardless of any contradictory rules or regulations (CEMAC 1994, annex, Article 35). Article 36 of the treaty also empowers CEMAC to sign agreements of cooperation with international, regional, or subregional organizations. Member states are called upon to contribute to achievement of the general objectives of the community and to "assure all internal measures to secure the implementation of their community obligations" (Articles 8 and 10 of the convention regulating the Economic Union and the Monetary Union). Finally, the institutional treaty and any annexes are considered to be the constitutional basis of the community, which also entails certain limitations to member states' autonomy, namely, in line with the same principles governing the European Community, CEMAC member states must apply community law without any further national rulemaking procedure (Kamtoh 2002).Overall, CEMAC's legal and regulatory basis is sufficiently well structured for the community to act as an entity. CEMAC's defined legal entity, and the fact that decisions taken by the Conference of Heads of States and regulations or directives set forth by the Council of Ministers are legally binding for member states, are the necessary powers for the community to decide on and implement a community-wide regulatory framework. CEMAC is also entitled to engage in international agreements with third parties. Both the necessary powers and the entitlement to engage in agreement are required tools for regional implementation of the Yamoussoukro Decision.

The Air Transport Program of the CEMAC States

Since early on, the CEMAC states have aimed at developing the region's air transport sector. They have done so in view of the specific objective, stated in Article 2 of the convention governing the Economic Union of "coordinating national sectoral policies of Member States in . . . trade, tourism, transport." The three measures that were taken before the Yamoussoukro Decision was signed or took full effect in the CEMAC region included the Agreement on Air Transport, the Civil Aviation Code, and the Joint Competition Regulation.

The Agreement on Air Transport, which the Council of Ministers adopted on 18 August 1999, is a program that aims to develop CEMAC's intracommunity air transport sector to establish greater access within the region and to promote economic and commercial relations between member states (CEMAC 1999b, Article 2). It also includes a provision for the creation of an entity for supervising flight safety and fosters technical and commercial cooperation among CEMAC air carriers. Several provisions of the program, such as the designation of participating carriers or the freedoms of the air provided in the program, are similar, or even identical to, the Yamoussoukro Decision, for example:

- *Designation of carrier (Yamoussoukro Decision Article 6)*: Each member state designates two carriers to participate in the intracommunity air service market. The carriers can be of another CEMAC member state and the designation has to be communicated to CEMAC's Executive Secretariat, which will publish the selection in the community's official bulletin (CEMAC 1999b, Article 4). The member states must grant the same treatment and access to infrastructure and equipment to all carriers and may not give their own carriers preferential fees (CEMAC 1999b, Article 5)

- *Traffic rights (Yamoussoukro Decision, Article 3)*: First and second freedom rights are granted without conditions (CEMAC 1999b, Article 11). Third and fourth freedom rights are granted for any scheduled passenger, cargo, and mail flights that are conducted within the CEMAC region (CEMAC 1999b, Article 12). Fifth freedom rights were initially restricted to 40 percent of the previous annual capacity (reserving 60 percent for third and fourth freedom operators on the same leg), but became fully liberalized for community operators after a two-year transition period that ended in August 2001 (CEMAC 1999b, Article 13). Sixth and seventh freedoms are not mentioned, but eighth freedom rights (cabotage) are possible if a member state specifically grants this right to a designated carrier of another member state (CEMAC 1999b, Article 16).

- *Tariffs (Yamoussoukro Decision, Article 4)*: Tariffs are freely determined based on commercial considerations. They must be communicated to the civil aviation authorities of respective states at least 60 days in advance. Carriers must, however, comply with the community's Competition Regulation (CEMAC 1999b, Article 18).

- *Capacity and frequency (Yamoussoukro Decision, Article 5)*: The member states must grant a maximum of frequencies, but the designated carriers must coordinate their schedules (CEMAC 1999b, Article 14). No restriction of capacity and types of aircraft shall be imposed. Nevertheless, in the case of significant disparity between capacity and type of aircraft, the carriers must enter into commercial arrangements between themselves (CEMAC 1999b, Article 15).

In addition to the foregoing basic rules of the CEMAC Agreement on Air Transport, it includes additional provisions in relation to the implementation of intracommunity liberalization of the sector. These include the establishment of an executing agency that shall be designated and supervised by the Council of Ministers in charge of civil aviation. The agency will responsible for implementing and supervising the liberalized air transport policy (CEMAC 1999b, Article 21), although sanctions against carriers, such as the revocation or suspension of granted traffic rights, are decided by the Council of Ministers after considering the recommendations of the executing agency (CEMAC 1999b, Article 23). Finally, the agreement permits nonmember states to join this framework and to participate in its air transport market (CEMAC 1999b, Article 24), but existing bilaterals with member states or participating nonmember states remain valid and may have to be modified to comply with the provisions of the agreement (CEMAC 1999b, Article 25). Member states also have the right to terminate their rights and obligations under the agreement by opting out (CEMAC 1999b, Article 25).

Given the objective of establishing a coordinated and harmonized legal framework for the air transport sector, in July 2000, the Council of Ministers adopted the CEMAC Civil Aviation Code (CEMAC 2000b). The code became legislation in all member states of the community, replacing obsolete or contradictory aviation legislation (CEMAC 2000a, Article 335). However, it also provides for member states to regulate certain domains at the national level that the code does not cover (CEMAC 2000a, Article 333). Nevertheless, the new Civil Aviation Code incorporated most of the provisions that had been decided just one year earlier in the CEMAC Agreement on Air Transport. The code is structured into the following 10 main sections:

- general provisions defining the scope and applicability of the code;
- supervision of the civil aviation sector and the requirement for autonomous civil aviation authorities;
- regulation on aircraft, including requirements for registration, nationality and ownership, airworthiness, operations, and liability insurance;
- regulation of air navigation;
- regulation of airports, airport operations, and facilitation of air services;
- public air transport and on-demand operators, including requirements for certification, ownership requirements, and access to markets;
- personnel licensing;
- aviation security;
- environmental protection;
- criminal and civil enforcement.

In terms of the Yamoussoukro Decision, all major provisions that have been developed for the CEMAC member states in the Agreement on Air Transport have been included in the code. In particular, these include regulations governing the following:

- *Market access (Yamoussoukro Decision, Article 3)*: Liberalization of scheduled air services within the community of first to fifth freedom rights (CEMAC 2000a, Article 214) and full liberalization of cargo and on-demand traffic (Article 219).

- *Tariffs (Yamoussoukro Decision, Article 4)*: Free, but "reasonable" tariff fixing by carriers to be filed 60 days in advance (CEMAC 2000a, Article 219) and interdiction of anticompetitive practices, such as dumping, with the possibility of temporary intervention on tariffs by the civil aviation authorities (Article 215).
- *Frequency and capacity (Yamoussoukro Decision, Article 5)*: No restrictions on frequency and capacity (CEMAC 2000a, Article 219), but commercial activities must be coordinated among operators and their programs must be approved by the civil aviation authorities (Article 209).
- *Designation and establishment (Yamoussoukro Decision, Article 6)*: Single or multidesignation of operator by each member state (CEMAC 2000a, Article 205), with requirements for community nationality in relation to ownership and minimum standards for technical, financial, and managerial qualification (Article 204).
- *Competition regulation (Yamoussoukro Decision, Article 7)*: Code of conduct for carriers that aims at developing a sound competitive environment by prohibiting all forms of price and capacity dumping (CEMAC 2000a, Article 215), as well as discrimination against a given designated carrier by another member state (Article 216).

The third element of liberalization of air services among the CEMAC member states is the Joint Competition Regulation, which the Council of Ministers adopted on 25 June 1999 (CEMAC 1999a). The competition regulations are general in nature and cover all domains or industries of the CEMAC common market. Their primary objective is to prevent any form of interference with free and efficient competition (CEMAC 1999a, Preamble, Article 2). The provisions that are applicable to the air transport sector include anticompetitive agreements between suppliers, market domination through mergers, and abuse of a dominant position.

The provision on anticompetitive agreements between suppliers prohibits any price fixing, limitation of production, market segmentation with competitors, or any other way of preventing efficient competition (CEMAC 1999a, Article 3). However, in cases where such an agreement could lead to more efficient market development, this interdiction might exempt certain agreements or coordinating measures between market participants.[11] The prohibition of market domination through mergers concerns any merger or acquisition of independent enterprises that leads to the elimination of a competitive environment (CEMAC 1999a, Article 5). The prohibition is applicable in cases of market concentration within the community, which are defined as involving two entities each having an annual turnover of CFAF 1 billion or both entities controlling more than 30 percent of a given market (CEMAC 1999a, Article 6). The abuse of a dominant market refers to maintaining abusive pricing practices or severely limiting production in order to stimulate demand (CEMAC 1999a, Article 16). A dominant market position is again defined as controlling more than 30 percent of a given market (CEMAC 1999a, Article 15).

A specialized CEMAC monitoring body is established by the Joint Competition Regulation and is responsible for controlling and supervising the market and its participants with respect to the Completion Regulation (CEMAC 1999a, Article 17). The monitoring body is composed of an executive secretariat that investigates anticompetitive practices and reports to the Regional Council that considers cases and renders judgments (CEMAC 1999a, Article 19). To appeal a decision rendered by the Regional Council, an arbitration court is to be set up that includes three arbitrators each appointed by a different party or entity (CEMAC 1999a, Article 24). The sanctions against an entity found guilty of infringement of the Joint Competition Regulation include fines of up to 5 percent of turnover achieved in the common market during the past year or of 75 percent of the profits gained from the prohibited practice (CEMAC 1999a, Article 37). In addition, the Regional Council can decide that a merger of an anticompetitive nature must be dissolved (CEMAC 1999a, Article 39).

Thus, like WAEMU, CEMAC has implemented most of the necessary framework that constitutes the main provisions of the Yamoussoukro Decision.

Southern and East Africa

Southern and East Africa have three RECs that address the air transport sector. The largest in terms of member states and territory covered is COMESA, which currently includes 20 countries from Egypt in the north to Zimbabwe in the south. The next largest REC is SADC, which comprises 15 member states in southern Africa. The smallest REC is the EAC, which comprises the five East African states. Some of the member states of these communities are also members of neighboring and overlapping organizations. For example, in East Africa, Burundi, Kenya, Rwanda, and Uganda are members of COMESA and the EAC, and in southern Africa, Angola, the Democratic Republic of Congo, Madagascar, Malawi, Mauritius, the Seychelles, Swaziland, Tanzania, Zambia, and Zimbabwe are members of COMESA and the SADC. Nevertheless, each of the three RECs has taken on the issue of liberalization of air services.

The Common Market for Eastern and Southern Africa

COMESA has its origins in the Preferential Trade Area (PTA) for Eastern and Southern Africa, which was established in 1981. Its principle objectives included increasing economic and commercial cooperation between member states, harmonizing tariffs, and reducing trade barriers with the eventual outcome of creating a common market (the PTA was created based on the framework of the Lagos Plan of Action of the Organization of African Unity [OAU 1980]). The PTA's headquarters were in Lusaka, Zambia. UNECA had supported an arrangement whereby the PTA would have comprised all 18 southern and East African states, including the African Indian Ocean islands. However, because of several local disputes, for example, the border dispute between Kenya and Tanzania following the termination of the EAC in 1977, six countries never signed the treaty (Matthews 1984, p. 174). On 8 December 1994, the COMESA treaty formally succeeded the PTA upon ratification of the treaty by 11 signatory states. The establishment of COMESA was a direct fulfillment of the requirements of Article 29 of the treaty establishing the PTA, which provided for the transformation of the PTA into a common market 10 years after the entry into force of the PTA Treaty (COMESA Secretariat 2007, p. 1).

COMESA is Africa's largest REC. It currently includes 20 member states, of which 15 were signatory states of the former PTA. The member states are (effective 21 December 1981, unless another date is shown) Angola, Burundi, the Comoros, Democratic Republic of Congo, Djibouti, Egypt (6 January 1999), Eritrea (1994), Ethiopia, Kenya, Libya (3 June 2005), Madagascar, Malawi, Mauritius, Rwanda, the Seychelles (2001), Sudan, Swaziland, Uganda, Zambia, and Zimbabwe. The main aims and objectives of COMESA are stated in Article 3 of the COMESA Treaty (COMESA Secretariat 1994), and include (a) promoting sustainable growth and development of the member states; (b) jointly adopting supporting macroeconomic policies and programs; (c) creating an enabling environment for foreign, cross–border, and domestic investment; (d) promoting peace, security, and stability among member states; (e) strengthening relationships between the common market and the rest of the world; and (f) contributing toward the establishment and realization of the objectives of the EAC.

To achieve these objectives, Article 4 of the COMESA Treaty laid out a set of specific undertakings. These undertaking are (a) establishing a customs union; (b) adopting a bond guarantee scheme; (c) trading documents and procedures; (d) establishing regulations governing the re-exportation of goods from third countries within the common market; (e) establishing rules of origin for products originating in member states; and (f) granting a temporary exemption for Lesotho, Namibia, and Swaziland from the full application of specific provisions of the treaty. Article 4 goes on to list specific undertakings in several specialized fields such as transport, communications, industry, and energy. In the field of transport, the undertaking focuses on regulations for facilitating transit trade within the common market (COMESA Secretariat 1994, Article 4, para. 2 [b]).

COMESA has launched and implemented several programs since its creation. In 2000 it established the COMESA Free Trade Area, a declared prerequisite for the pending customs union (COMESA Secretariat 2007, p. 3). To support trade liberalization, various technical harmonization projects were implemented, such as harmonized road transit charges, a common carrier's license, joint customs bond guarantee schemes, and telecommunications interconnectivity. Liberalization of air transport services is also addressed under the main objective of trade facilitation among member states (COMESA Secretariat 2007, p. 8).

The COMESA Air Transport Liberalization Program

COMESA's policy on air transport was already well established in the COMESA Treaty. Article 84 of the treaty notes that member states should undertake to develop coordinated and complementary transport and communications policies. To facilitate the movement of interstate traffic and promote greater movement of people, goods, and services within the Common Market, member states "shall take all necessary steps" to maintain, upgrade, and rehabilitate the roads, railways, and harbors in their territories (COMESA Secretariat 1994, Article 84, para. a).

The essence of the air transport policy is outlined in Article 87, which seems to be drafted in line with the Yamoussoukro Declaration of 1988. The main focus of Article 87 is cooperation between Common Market operators, namely: "The establishment of joint ventures for co-operation in the use of equipment, in the pooling of aircraft maintenance and training facilities, in the acquisition and use of fuel and spare parts, in insurance schemes, in the coordination of flight schedules and the improvement of managerial techniques and skills" (COMESA Secretariat 1994, Article 87, para. 1). However, it goes on to say that member states "shall in particular" liberalize the granting of air traffic rights for passenger and cargo operations, to harmonize civil aviation rules and regulations by implementing the provisions of the Chicago Convention, to establish common measures for the facilitation of passenger and cargo air services, to develop and maintain a common navigation and communications infrastructure for air space management, and to harmonize rates for and rules and regulations on scheduled air transport services (COMESA Secretariat 1994, Article 87, para. 3).

In 1999, practically in parallel with the AEC-initiated agreement of the Yamoussoukro Decision, COMESA's Council of Ministers issued the Regulation for the Implementation of the Liberalised Air Transport Industry (COMESA Secretariat 1999). The regulation was issued as a directive entitled Legal Notice No.2, which became binding on the member states and on all subordinate organs of the Common Market (COMESA Secretariat 1994, Article 9, paras. 2[c], 3). Legal Notice No. 2 aims at liberalizing air transport services as a step toward creating a free trade area guaranteeing the free movement of goods and services produced within COMESA and removing all tariff and nontariff barriers (COMESA Secretariat 1999, Preamble). However, even though Legal Notice No. 2 goes beyond the scope of liberalization of the Yamoussoukro Decision, it does not mention the Yamoussoukro Decision as a basis of or inspiration for COMESA's air transport policy.

According to Legal Notice No. 2, air transportation within COMESA was to be liberalized in two phases. Phase I, which was initiated in October 1999, (a) introduced free movement of air cargo and nonscheduled passenger services within COMESA, (b) introduced free movement of intra-COMESA scheduled passenger services with a frequency limit of up to two daily flights between any city pair within COMESA, and (c) adopted multiple designations and the elimination of capacity restrictions (COMESA Secretariat 1999, Preamble). Fifth freedom rights, which many liberalization policies such as the Yamoussoukro Decision viewed as essential, were already granted in phase I of COMESA's liberalization, whereby fifth freedom rights were limited to 30 percent of a carrier's capacity on routes where third and fourth freedom traffic were provided, but no restrictions were put on fifth freedom traffic on routes where no third and fourth traffic by another operator existed (COMESA Secretariat 1999, Article 5 [a]).

The main liberalization of air transportation within COMESA was reached one year after the commencement of phase I, when in October 2000 phase II became the new policy. This, in essence, introduced free movement of air transport services within COMESA (COMESA Secretariat 1999, Article 5 [b]). Phase II of Legal Notice No. 2 liberalized air services far beyond the scope of the Yamoussoukro Decision by implementing the following:

- *Market access (Yamoussoukro Decision, Article 6)*: Any air carrier is eligible provided it is substantially owned and effectively controlled by a COMESA member state or its nationals. It must demonstrate financial, managerial, and technical ability to perform the services, which is also a condition for receiving an air operator's certificate (COMESA Secretariat 1999, Article 3). However, in contrast with the Yamoussoukro Decision where traffic rights are notified on a bilateral basis between two or, in cases of fifth freedom flights three, countries, COMESA carriers are able to operate between any destination within COMESA. Carriers can also use aircraft registered in and owned by any COMESA state or its nationals (Article 4).

- *Traffic rights (Yamoussoukro Decision, Article 3)*: Legal Notice No. 2 set forth the principle of free movement of air transport services within COMESA (COMESA Secretariat 1999, Article 2 [b]). This explicitly includes cabotage rights, which were only excluded during phase I.

- *Tariffs (Yamoussoukro Decision, Article 4)*: No specific regulations are set forth with regard to air services, but the preamble to Legal Notice No. 2 states that all COMESA member states have agreed on the removal of all tariff and nontariff barriers to facilitate the establishment of a free trade area, implying that air services would also be free from any tariff regulation.

- *Capacity and frequency (Yamoussoukro Decision, Article 5)*: Legal Notice No. 2 notes that no restriction of capacity shall be imposed during phase II. This is explicitly mentioned in the case of fifth freedom rights even though traffic in COMESA is free, including cabotage. (COMESA Secretariat 1999, Article 5, para. 2 [c]) As concerns equipment, another explicit rule states that no restrictions on types and capacity of aircraft shall be made (Article 7). Nevertheless, similar to Article 11.4 of the Yamoussoukro Decision, COMESA carriers are encouraged to establish intra-COMESA airline alliances and commercial arrangements as long as these arrangements do not undermine COMESA's competition rules and regulations (Article 6).

Despite the clear and concise liberalization program contained in Legal Notice No. 2, its adoption was stalled in 2001 when COMESA's Council of Ministers decided to "defer the implementation of Phase 2 awaiting the preparation of competition regulations" (COMESA Secretariat 2005, p. 3). Subsequently, the implementation of liberalized air services within COMESA, as specified in phase II, remained pending for several years. By 2004, only 12 member states had implemented phase I and only Djibouti had opened its airspace to COMESA carriers in line with Legal Notice No. 2 (COMESA Secretariat 2004, p. 22). Indeed, Legal Notice No. 2 did not mention issues of fair competition and the procedure for dealing with disputes resulting from liberalization of international air traffic in the region. In addition to the missing competition regulations, several other elements were subsequently identified that were required to "successfully complete this regional air transport liberalization agenda" (COMESA Secretariat 2003b, p. 7). These elements included the following:

- the adoption of a COMESA air transport policy,
- the implementation of provisions for air transport competition rules,
- the creation of a joint institutional and monitoring mechanism for the liberalization and competition rules,
- the drafting of a memorandum for the Court of Justice and Tribunal on the jurisdiction and enforcement of decisions under the competition rules,
- the drafting of a standardized mechanism for entry into the market and for enjoying the rights enshrined in Legal Notice No. 2 and in the Yamoussoukro Decision,
- the sensitization of airlines and other key stakeholders on the implementation of Legal Notice No. 2 and the Yamoussoukro Decision,
- the drafting of a comprehensive regulation on consumer protection in the air transport sector,
- the harmonization of the regulatory framework, and
- the incorporation of all Council of Ministers' regulations into individual state's legal and administrative procedures.

The key issue is whether implementation of this agenda for the liberalization of regional air transport can be seen as a condition precedent for the application of liberalization as set out in Legal Notice No. 2. Given that the Yamoussoukro Decision does not deal with detailed competition regulation or the various aforementioned regulations, the application of a liberalized air transport policy may be beneficial in general, or may benefit the air transport sector or industry, but does not need to exist *a priori*. As outlined in chapter 3, air transport and its liberalization in Africa is still mainly regulated on a bilateral basis between member states of the

Yamoussoukro Decision. There is no reason why the principles of Legal Notice No. 2 could not be applied by agreeing to new bilaterals that conform to both Legal Notice No. 2 and the Yamoussoukro Decision. Legal Notice No. 2 does not refer to bilateral relationships between states. In Article 2 (b) it primarily aims at establishing free movement of air transport services within COMESA. At the same time, Article 2 of the Yamoussoukro Decision, Scope of Application, provides that the Yamoussoukro Decision has precedence over any multilateral or bilateral agreements on air services between state parties that are incompatible with the decision. However, provisions that are included in such agreements and that are not incompatible with the decision remain valid and are supplementary to the decision. Article 10.5 states that state parties shall not be precluded from maintaining or developing on a bilateral basis or among themselves arrangements that are more flexible than those contained herein. A bilateral solution among COMESA member states could therefore at least provide a temporary solution, which would allow the application of the principles of liberalization as agreed upon in both Legal Notice No. 2 and the Yamoussoukro Decision.

Nevertheless, COMESA began to prepare specialized competition regulations for the air transport sector even though its secretariat had already drafted general competition regulations that it could have adapted or extended to include the sector (COMESA Secretariat 2003a). COMESA issued a first draft of its air transport competition regulations, but soon after recognized the need to develop common regulations for the entire southern and East Africa region, where member states belonged to a number of RECs. Subsequently, COMESA's draft competition regulations and those prepared by SADC were considered together and a common draft was adopted by a joint ministerial meeting of COMESA, EAC, and SADC ministers responsible for civil aviation in September 2002 (COMESA 2005, p. 3).

The draft regulations for competition in air transport services within COMESA, the EAC, and the SADC include three main provisions (Council of Ministers of COMESA and EAC Responsible for Civil Aviation and the Committee of Ministers of Transport and Communications of SADC 2004). Article 4 prohibits any anticompetitive agreements and practices, such as fixing prices, limiting or controlling markets, providing excessive capacity or frequency of services, dividing markets or sources of supply, or entering into agreements that place trading partners into a competitive disadvantage by applying dissimilar conditions to similar transactions. Article 5 aims at preventing the abuse of a dominant position, which may occur when a carrier introduces unfair trading conditions to the prejudice of competitors, such as excessively low or high prices; limits capacity or markets to the prejudice of consumers, including excessive pricing or oversupply and undersupply on certain routes to drive out another competitor; or applies dissimilar conditions to similar transactions with other trading parties, effectively placing them in a disadvantaged competitive situation. Article 6 reminds member states not to discriminate in national legislation or administrative measures against carriers or associations of carriers of other member states. Article 9, para. 1, entrusts the application and enforcement of the joint competition regulation to the RECs, which are responsible for investigating violations of the rules and for granting, refusing, or revoking exemptions. However, Article 9, para. 2, states that the Council of Ministers responsible for civil aviation of COMESA, EAC, and SADC will establish a joint body responsible for monitoring implementation of the Yamoussoukro Decision and the joint competition regulations.

According to an interview with Amos Marawa, COMESA's director of infrastructure development (28 March 2007, in Lusaka, Zambia), the adoption of both the COMESA and SADC draft competition regulations by the joint ministerial meeting of COMESA, EAC, and SADC in September 2002 and the adoption of the resulting common draft regulations by SADC and the COMESA Council of Ministers in 2004 was primarily seen as a policy decision. All those involved understood that the application or implementation of the principles of Legal Notice No. 2 of 1999 depended on the finalization of the pending competition regulations and their "implementation." In November 2006, COMESA, SADC, and EAC ministers responsible for civil aviation jointly adopted the Guidelines, Provisions, and Procedures for the Implementation of the Regulations for Competition in Air Transport Services within COMESA, EAC, and SADC (SADC 2007, p. 1). According to these guidelines, implementation of the competition regulation includes the establishment of a joint competition authority that would be responsible for monitoring implementation of the Yamoussoukro Decision and competition regulations in air transport services within the RECs (SADC 2007, p. 1). Even though the Twelfth Summit of the COMESA Authority of Heads of States formally agreed to the speedy establishment of a joint competition authority in May 2007, implementation of the joint competition regulations remains pending in all three RECs, COMESA, SADC, and the EAC.

Thus, more than eight years after COMESA liberalized air services within its territory by instituting phase II of Legal Notice No. 2 of 1999, application of this liberalization remains pending. Currently, the understanding of all COMESA member states is that the establishment of a joint competition authority remains the missing link before liberalization of air services can be applied.

The Southern African Development Community

SADC's roots were created in the 1960s and 1970s, when the leaders of countries with black majorities and national liberation movements coordinated their efforts on a political and military level to bring an end to colonial and white minority rule in southern Africa. The initial grouping was the so-called Front Line States, an informal organization founded in the mid-1970s with the goal of achieving black majority rule in South Africa. Its members consisted of Angola, Botswana, Lesotho, Mozambique, Tanzania, Zambia, and Zimbabwe (Rowlands 1998, p. 926). On 1 April 1980, these seven states plus Malawi and Swaziland, all black majority-ruled southern African countries, issued the so-called Lusaka Declaration, which paved the way for the establishment of the Southern African Development Coordination Conference on 17 August 1981, in Maseru, Botswana (Tsie 1996, p. 84). This organization was not a formal authority based on a treaty, but primarily the outcome of a conference of independent southern African states whose primary objective was to reduce their dependency on South Africa by coordinating interstate projects in a decentralized manner. Soon the Southern African Development Coordination Conference experienced its own limitations, because the decentralized set-up did not include clear lines of reporting or accountability, both of which are necessary when implementing regional projects (Mandaza and Tostensen 1994, p. 109).

On 17 August 1992, SADC was formally founded by treaty (SADC 1992, p. 17). The SADC Treaty, which basically transformed the Southern African Development Coordination Conference into SADC, was later called the Windhoek Declaration and was adopted by the founding members of the Southern Africa Development Community and newly independent Namibia. The main objectives of SADC include development and economic growth, poverty reduction, and enhancement of the standard of living and quality of life of the peoples of southern Africa while supporting the socially disadvantaged through regional integration (SADC 1992, Article 5, para. 1). The objectives also include developing common political values, systems, and institutions and promoting and defending peace and security. To achieve the objectives, SADC is to harmonize the political and socioeconomic policies and plans of member states. This could be achieved by encouraging the peoples of the region and their institutions to take initiatives to develop economic, social, and cultural ties across the region, and to participate fully in implementing SADC's programs and projects (SADC 1992, Article 5, para. 2).

While these objectives were generally less specific in terms of concrete measures than those of other African RECs, they at least included the development of policies aimed at progressive elimination of obstacles to free movement of capital and labor, goods and services, and people of the region among member states (SADC 1992, Article 5, para. 2). On 14 August 2001, the SADC Treaty was slightly amended by overhauling some of the community's structures, policies, and procedures. One of the major changes was the institutionalization of political and security cooperation in the Organ on Politics, Defense, and Security. Currently, SADC comprises 15 member states (date of joining is 17 August 1992, unless shown otherwise): Angola, Botswana, the Democratic Republic of Congo (8 September 1997), Lesotho, Madagascar (18 August 2005), Malawi, Mauritius (28 August 1995), Mozambique, Namibia (31 March 1990), the Seychelles (15 August 2007), South Africa (30 August 1994), Swaziland, Tanzania, Zambia, and Zimbabwe. The SADC maintains its headquarters in Gaborone, Botswana.

In relation to decision making and its applicability to member states, Article 4 of the SADC Treaty declares that member states are expected to demonstrate their commitment to act in accordance with a set of principles. These include sovereignty and equality of member states, solidarity, peace and security of human rights, democracy, rule of law, and peaceful settlement of disputes. However, only decisions made by the Summit are legally binding on member states unless otherwise noted in the treaty. To enforce decisions made by the Council or to make member states fulfill other obligations under the treaty, including implementing policies or settling arrears of contributions to SADC, the SADC Treaty provides for sanctions that may be imposed against member states (SADC 1992, Article 33). However, these sanctions have to be determined by the Council.

To foster the development and implementation of the main objectives of the SADC Treaty, it defines certain main areas of cooperation in which member states are expected to coordinate, rationalize, and harmonize their overall macroeconomic and sectoral policies and strategies (SADC 1992, Article 21, paras. 1, 2). These areas include infrastructure and services, industry, trade, investments and finance, international relations, and peace and security (SADC 1992, Article 21, para. 3). To better define the policies for these areas of cooperation, member states are encouraged to conclude specific protocols to spell out the objectives and scope of cooperation and integration of a given sector (SADC 1992, Article 22, paras. 1, 2). These protocols shall be approved by the Summit on the recommendation of the Council and become an integral part of the SADC Treaty. However, other than the decisions of the Summit that are generally applicable to member states without any further ratification, each protocol must be signed and ratified by each member state that becomes party thereto (SADC 1992, Article 22, paras. 1, 2). Since 1992, in addition to the initial treaty, the SADC member states have signed more than 37 protocols in a variety of sectors, for example, protocols on energy (1996); trade (1996); the Regional Tourism Organization of Southern Africa (1997); health (1999); wildlife conservation and law enforcement (1999); politics, defense, and security cooperation (2001); corruption (2001); and fundamental social rights (2003) (SADC 2005, p. 35). Of the 37 protocols, 26 have attained the necessary quorum and entered into force.

The objectives and development priorities of the transport sector of SADC were defined in a relatively early protocol, known as the Protocol on Transport, Communications, and Meteorology, which was signed on 24 August 1996, and came into force on 6 July 1998 (SADC 2005, p. 34). This protocol deals with a variety of transport sectors, including integrated transport (logistics), road transport, railways, maritime and inland waterway transport, and civil aviation. In addition, it defines similar objectives and implementation programs for the telecommunications sector, for postal services, and for meteorology (SADC 2005, p. 3). Civil aviation is defined in chapter 9 of the protocol, which starts by setting the objectives for the sector. These include providing safe, reliable, and efficient air transportation within member states (SADC 2005, Article 9.1). The protocol further recognizes that member states must enhance co-operation within the regional air transport market "in order to overcome the constraints of small national markets, market restrictions and the small size of some SADC airlines" (SADC 2005, Article 9.1). Liberalization of air services is only mentioned once, in Article 9.2, which is titled Civil Aviation Policy and notes that member states will develop a harmonized regional aviation policy that includes the "gradual liberalization of intra-regional air transport markets for the SADC airlines" (SADC 2005, Article 9.2). Civil aviation policy also focuses on developing regionally owned airlines by restructuring existent SADC airlines, airports, and air navigation service providers and on promoting fair competition between these service providers. In addition, it aims at expanding and strengthening governments' capacity to provide adequate policy frameworks and to establish an appropriate regional institutional mechanism (SADC 2005, Article 9.2, paras. b, c, d).

The SADC Protocol on Transport, Communications, and Meteorology, which was agreed upon three years before the signing of the Yamoussoukro Decision, clearly reflects the objectives of the former Yamoussoukro Declaration, whose primary aim was to integrate African air carriers (UNECA 1988, p. 2). While most of the other RECs have agreed upon or issued legislation aimed at implementing the Yamoussoukro Decision, SADC did not further define liberalization in relation to implementation of the Yamoussoukro Decision. Nevertheless, even though SADC never formally agreed on intraregional liberalization of its air services, it worked continuously to implement the Yamoussoukro Decision, to which all SADC member states except Madagascar, South Africa, and Swaziland are bound (see appendix B). The only regional aspect of implementation of the Yamoussoukro Decision is the joint COMESA, SADC, and EAC approach toward preparing regulations for competition in air transport services. However, even though the three RECs laid out a concrete road map for implementation on several occasion, the adoption of the joint competition regulations and the establishment of a joint competition authority remain pending (SADC 2006, p. 9).

Thus, SADC has not taken any steps toward implementing the Yamoussoukro Decision that can be considered binding for its member states. However, it has at least acknowledged the Yamoussoukro Decision and its objective of liberalizing air transportation across the continent. The SADC Summit has the necessary power to decide by consensus to adopt the Yamoussoukro Decision in the region, which would be a binding decision on all member states, but the matter has never been presented for decision by the Council. The SADC member states therefore cannot be considered to have liberalized air transport in the spirit of the Yamoussoukro Decision.

The East African Community

The history of the EAC goes back as far as 1917, when Kenya and Uganda formed one of the first cooperative entities in Africa by establishing a customs union. Tanganyika, now Tanzania, joined the union in 1927 after being freed from German colonial rule (Kayizzi-Mugerwa 1999, p. 178). The main role of the customs union was to provide for a common customs administration. In 1948, it was replaced by the more formal East African High Commission, which was enacted under British colonial oversight. However, the populations of the countries involved saw the East African High Commission as a regime imposed on the three British territories of East Africa, Kenya, Tanganyika, and Uganda. (The British Settlement Acts of 1887 and 1945 and the British Foreign Jurisdiction Act of 1890 in essence allowed the British Crown to make laws for British possessions without recourse to the British Parliament [Akintan 1977, p. 124].) Nevertheless, in 1961, when Tanganyika entered into formal negotiations for independence with the British government, it was recognized that the "common services at present provided by the East African High Commission should continue to be provided on an East African basis" (Akintan 1977, p. 125). Subsequently, on 12 December 1961, 11 days after Tanganyika's independence, representatives from Kenya, Tanganyika, Uganda, the East African High Commission, and the British government established a new institution known as the East African Common Services Organisation.

In 1967, Kenya, Tanzania, and Uganda formed the EAC as an economic cooperative. One of the objectives of the treaty establishing the EAC was to maintain the cooperative regional trade framework that had initially been mandated by the British Crown. An earlier attempt to create a cooperative, the East African Federation, had failed in 1964 because of strong nationalistic attitudes and the divergence of the three countries' economic and political priorities.

The declared long-term objective of the EAC was to set up an East African common market to promote, strengthen, and regulate common industrial and commercial development (Mead 1969, p. 277). However, soon after its creation, it became apparent that the EAC Treaty had failed to address several important issues, which resulted in many instances of stalled application of the principles of the common market, for instance, the external tariffs of the three countries, a crucial element of a common market, could not be harmonized because of flaws in the community's institutional arrangements (Mead 1969, p. 277).

The main challenge facing the new organization was the increasing divergence in the three member governments' ideological and political views. The ideological split was caused by the dictatorship under Idi Amin in Uganda, socialism in Tanzania, and capitalism in Kenya. In addition, Kenya demanded more seats than Tanzania and Uganda in decision-making organs (Petersen 2005). Indeed, Mugomba (1978, p. 262) summarizes the situation as "a three-dimensional verbal 'guerrilla' war ... waged by Kenya, Tanzania, and Uganda against one another; ... sometimes it has come very close to physical combat." The result was the collapse of the

EAC in 1977, only 10 years after its creation. The triggering event was the bankruptcy and liquidation of the joint airline, East African Airways, with Kenya immediately creating its own national carrier in response (Mugomba 1978, p. 264). The EAC collapsed quite swiftly despite its initial recognition by the international community as a promising example of regional cooperation.

Soon after the EAC's dissolution in 1977, the member states negotiated a mediation agreement for the division of assets and liabilities, which they signed in 1984. One of the provisions of the agreement was that the three states would explore areas of future cooperation and prepare concrete arrangements for such cooperation. This eventually led to the signing on 30 November 1993, of the Agreement for the Establishment of the Permanent Tripartite Commission for East African Co-operation by the heads of state of Kenya, Tanzania, and Uganda. Formal cooperation started in March 1996 with the launch of the Secretariat of the Permanent Tripartite Commission, headquartered in Arusha, Tanzania.

The leaders of the three governments quickly recognized that the regional cooperation between the three states needed to be consolidated. At their second summit in Arusha on 29 April 1997, the East African heads of state directed the Permanent Tripartite Commission to initiate the process of transforming the Agreement for the Establishment of the Permanent Tripartite Commission for East African Co-operation into a treaty reestablishing the EAC (Kayizzi-Mugerwa 1999, p. 179). Three years later, on 30 November 1999, the three so-called partner states signed the treaty in Arusha. Following ratification and deposit of the instruments of ratification with the secretary general by all three member states, the treaty entered into force on 7 July 2000. Initially comprising three partner states, the EAC was enlarged in 2007 when Burundi and Rwanda joined (Ford 2007).

The objectives of the EAC are outlined in Article 5 of the EAC Treaty of 1999 (EAC 1999). The EAC's prime objective is to "develop policies and programs aimed at widening and deepening cooperation among the Partner States in political, economic, security and legal and judicial affairs, for their mutual benefit" (EAC 1999, Article 5, para. 1). To achieve these objectives, the EAC shall establish a customs union, a common market, and subsequently a monetary union ultimately leading to a political federation (EAC 1999, Article 5, para. 2). The EAC Treaty lays out a set of fundamental and operational principles that must govern the achievement of the set objectives (EAC 1999, Articles 6, 7). The most significant fundamental principles include "mutual trust, political will and sovereign equality," as well as peaceful coexistence and peaceful settlement of disputes (EAC 1999, Article 6). The community's key operational principles are "the establishment of an export oriented economy for the Partner States in which there shall be free movement of goods, persons, labor, services, capital, information and technology" and the principle of subsidiary of the EAC, which secures multilevel participation and the involvement of a wide range of stakeholders during the integration process (EAC 1999, Article 7).

Overall, the institutional framework of the newly established EAC is well defined and consists of all the necessary elements for effective implementation of its goals, economic cooperation, and integration among its partner states. The decision making is, in general, consensus based, which does not seem to pose a major problem given the small number of partner states and their long history of economic cooperation.

The East African Community's Air Transport Program

Chapter 15 of the EAC Treaty (EAC 1999) outlines the modalities of cooperation in infrastructure and services by partner states. The sectors for which policies and concrete programs are outlined are

- transport and communications (Article 89),
- roads and road transport (Article 90),
- railways and rail transport (Article 91),
- civil aviation and civil air transport (Article 92),
- maritime transport and ports (Article 93),
- inland waterways transport (Article 94),
- multimodal transport (Article 95),
- freight booking centers (Article 96),
- freight forwarders, customs clearing, and shipping agents (Article 97);
- postal services (Article 98),
- telecommunications (Article 99),
- meteorological services (Article 100), and
- energy (Article 101).

The objectives of the civil aviation program are to harmonize civil aviation policies among partner states and to facilitate the establishment of joint air services (EAC 1999, Article 92, paras. 1, 2). In particular, the treaty provides a list of concrete steps to reach these goals (EAC 1999, Article 92, para. 3). The main steps are

- adopting common policies to develop civil air transport in collaboration with other relevant organizations (for example, airline associations or ICAO);
- liberalizing the granting of air traffic rights for passenger and cargo operations;
- harmonizing civil aviation rules and regulations;
- establishing an upper area control system, that is, a system of air traffic control for the upper flight levels;
- coordinating the flight schedules of designated carriers;
- applying ICAO guidelines to determine user charges for scheduled air services; and
- adopting common aircraft standards and technical standards.

Some of these steps match elements of the Yamoussoukro Decision, which was signed the same year as the Treaty of the EAC, but the latter is basically limited to liberalizing the granting of air traffic rights for passengers and cargo operations and does not further specify the extent of liberalization. The other steps are, at most, secondary measures of the Yamoussoukro Decision. Furthermore, the concrete objectives of establishing joint air services and facilitating the efficient use of aircraft are elements of the Yamoussoukro Declaration of 1988 (UNECA 1988, p. 2). At the same time, Article 11.3 of the Yamoussoukro Decision does provide for a mild form of cooperative arrangements among designated carriers.

Even though the EAC Treaty did not incorporate all the principles of the Yamoussoukro Decision, the EAC's Sectoral Council on Transport, Communications, and Meteorology worked continuously on several key measures of the Yamoussoukro Decision. The most important was the application of a liberalized air transport policy for scheduled air services. While other RECs developed specific regulations that liberalized air services within their REC, for example, WAEMU, the EAC choose to focus on amending the bilaterals between the partner states. The 11th Meeting of the Council of Ministers of the EAC formally approved several projects pertinent to air transport and issued the necessary directives, namely (EAC Secretariat 2006, p. 61):

- The amendments to the bilaterals between the EAC states toward full implementation of the Yamoussoukro Decision on air transport liberalization are approved and must be incorporated into the respective bilaterals (EAC Secretariat 2006, Decision 44, p. 61).

- The amendments include full liberalization of air services between any points within the territory of the EAC. Following the principles of the Yamoussoukro Decision, no restriction shall be posted on frequency, capacity, or types of aircraft operated by designated EAC carriers.
- The EAC Secretariat is to inform the Economic Commission for Africa, with copies to COMESA and SADC, that the EAC is fully compliant with the Yamoussoukro Decision. The latter two organizations are urged to "expedite the move towards continental implementation of the Yamoussoukro Decision" (EAC Secretariat 2006, Directive 13, p. 62).
- The EAC Air Transport Subcommittee for implementation of the Yamoussoukro Decision will be staffed with an official responsible for administering the bilaterals and with officials from the civil aviation authorities, airport authorities, and the attorneys general chambers of each partner state (EAC Secretariat 2006, Decision 45, p. 62).
- The heads of civil aviation and airport authorities of each partner state are authorized and instructed to renegotiate the funding for civil aviation safety and airport projects with their respective ministers of finance and to seek other resources for such projects (EAC Secretariat 2006, Decision 46, p. 62).
- The revised civil aviation regulations for the EAC are to be promulgated to facilitate establishment of the East African Civil Aviation Safety and Security Agency (EAC Secretariat 2006, Decision 47, p. 62). The implementation of priority airport projects is approved (EAC Secretariat 2006, Decision 48, p. 62).
- The EAC Secretariat must develop a comprehensive funding arrangement for the priority airport projects for consideration by the Sectoral Council on Transport, Communications, and Meteorology.

The EAC took the first step toward implementing these decisions and directives on 18 April 2007, when the Extra Ordinary Council of Ministers Meeting in Arusha approved the establishment of the EAC's Civil Aviation Safety and Security Oversight Agency (EAC Secretariat 2007). The main objective of this agency is to promote safe, secure, and efficient use and development of civil aviation by having the partner states meet their obligations and responsibilities under the Chicago Convention (EAC Secretariat 2007, Article 4). In this respect, the revisions and harmonization of the civil aviation regulations in the EAC cover the domains of personnel licensing, flight operations, and airworthiness in accordance with annexes 1 and 6 of the Chicago Convention. The main functions of the agency are to strengthen the institutional framework within the partner states in aviation security, to coordinate civil aviation security oversight activities among partner states, and to evaluate and monitor compliance of partner states with ICAO SARP (EAC Secretariat 2007, Article 5).

Even before the establishment of the Civil Aviation Safety and Security Oversight Agency in 2007, the EAC's civil Aviation Authorities were working on the development and adoption of harmonized civil aviation safety and security regulations for the region. These regulations contain specific rules for most operational aspects of air transportation. Uganda has established regulations that were formally adopted in 2006 on

- personnel licensing (Government of Uganda 2006, p. 571);
- approved training organizations (Government of Uganda 2006, p. 853);
- aircraft registration and marking (Government of Uganda 2006, p. 929);
- airworthiness (Government of Uganda 2006, p. 955);
- approved maintenance organizations (Government of Uganda 2006, p. 1019);
- instruments and equipment (Government of Uganda 2006, p. 1099);
- operation of aircraft (Government of Uganda 2006, p. 1207);
- air operator certification and administration (Government of Uganda 2006, p. 1471);
- commercial air transport operations by foreign air operators in and out of Uganda (Government of Uganda 2006, p. 1615);
- aerial work, that is, operations of aircraft used for specialized services, for example, agriculture, surveying, or search and rescue (Government of Uganda 2006, p. 1639);
- rules of the air and air traffic control (Government of Uganda 2006, p. 1707); and
- parachute operations (Government of Uganda 2006, p. 1815).

However, as of April 2008, only Tanzania and Uganda had formally adopted the harmonized civil aviation regulations into national law. Kenya reported that its civil aviation regulations had been submitted to the Attorney General's Chambers for promulgation, while the two new members of the EAC, Burundi and Rwanda, requested assistance to harmonize their civil aviation regulations with those of the EAC (EAC Secretariat, 2008, p. 3).

Thus, the EAC has displayed great interest in and motivation toward liberalizing and developing air services within its territory. As a relatively small REC, the EAC relies mainly on mutual consent with respect to major decisions and program implementation. The notion of cooperation among partner states has a long history in the region and must be regarded as the best way forward. Therefore the approach of agreeing to bilaterals that conform to the principles of the Yamoussoukro Decision is the most appropriate manner of implementation. However, this key element of the EAC's approach toward implementing the Yamoussoukro Decision, that is, amending the bilaterals between EAC states, is still pending. Currently, the existing bilaterals regime among the EAC partner states is more restrictive than that established by the Yamoussoukro Decision framework. For example, Tanzania's current bilaterals with Kenya and Uganda generally have no limitations on capacity or types of aircraft, but they limit frequencies, and in the case of Kenya, the destinations to be served in both countries, and there are also no provisions for fifth freedom traffic (Munyagi 2006). Finally, the creation of the regional Civil Aviation Safety and Security Oversight Agency is an important step, not only for implementation of the Yamoussoukro Decision, but for the development of international air services by any EAC state. However, it is only an important support tool and revision of the bilaterals remains the more important step.

Conclusion

The Yamoussoukro Decision explicitly encourages subregional and regional organizations to pursue and intensify their efforts to implement the Yamoussoukro Decision (UNECA 2004, Article 12.2). It does so because Africa is a fragmented continent with heterogeneous economic and political organizations. Expecting full and harmonious application of the mechanism of the Yamoussoukro Decision and liberalization of air services in all Yamoussoukro Decision party states two years after the decision came into force was probably excessively optimistic. A better strategy is to encourage the various subregional and regional organizations that are involved in air transportation to begin implementing the steps of the Yamoussoukro Decision, while at the same time pan-African efforts are driven by the African Union. The underlying idea clearly seems to be to reach a situation where many RECs have applied the Yamoussoukro Decision and then start to agree on liberalizing air traffic between them. This last step would eventually complete full continent-wide implementation.

When one reviews the different regions, a fairly heterogeneous picture appears. The Arab states of North Africa have not begun liberalizing air services among themselves, even though certain instruments, such as the Arab League Open-Skies Agreement, exist. Morocco, the only North African country that is not a Yamoussoukro Decision party state, is the most active nation with respect to liberalizing and expanding its air services, as it has signed an open skies agreement with the EU and has acquired controlling stakes in two African air carriers.

In West Africa, the overarching organization, ECOWAS, has been unable to take any significant steps toward liberalizing air services. However, the smaller REC, WAEMU, went even beyond the principles of the Yamoussoukro Decision when it agreed to an EU model that includes cabotage rights. Finally, BAG has agreed to a multilateral air service agreement that establishes a liberalized regime that is fully compatible with the Yamoussoukro Decision.

In Central Africa, CEMAC has implemented all the necessary legislative and regulatory elements to comply with the provisions of the Yamoussoukro Decision.

In southern and East Africa, COMESA has achieved the most progress by issuing a legal instrument that would effectively have liberalized air services in 2001. However, after delays, application of the legal notice was suspended until other elements, such as competition regulations, were prepared. The EAC, which has the longest history of cooperation of any of the RECs, especially in the field of aviation, has chosen an effective strategy of revising bilaterals to conform to the Yamoussoukro Decision. However, while implementation remains pending, progress in other relevant matters, such as the establishment of a joint air safety and security agency, are significant steps forward. Finally, SADC has achieved the least progress. Apparently, the dominant position of South Africa and the fear that its national carrier, South African Airways, would quickly wipe out competition in a liberalized southern African market, remain the main obstacles toward more progress in implementing the Yamoussoukro Decision.

Of the 10 African states that cannot be considered Yamoussoukro Decision party states, two, Equatorial Guinea and Gabon, have implemented the Yamoussoukro Decision by means of their REC (CEMAC). This means that eight African states—Djibouti, Eritrea, Madagascar, Mauritania, Morocco, Somalia, South Africa, and Swaziland (see appendix B)—remain uncommitted to any obligations to liberalize air transportation according to the Yamoussoukro Decision on either a continental or a regional level.

Notes

1. In November 2002, the EU's Court of Justice ruled that several member states (Austria, Belgium, Denmark, Finland, Germany, Luxembourg, and Sweden) had failed to fulfill their obligations under the European Community Treaty when they had agreed to individual open skies agreements with the United States in 1994, 1995, and 1996 (European Court of Justice 2002, pp. 2–8). This marked the beginning of new EU external aviation policy that aims to (a) bring existing bilateral agreements in line with community law, and (b) gradually adopt ambitious agreements between the community and third countries (European Commission 2005a).
2. These economies are Algeria, Armenia, Azerbaijan, Belarus, the Arab Republic of Egypt, Georgia, Israel, Jordan, Lebanon, Libya, Moldova, Morocco, the West Bank and Gaza, the Syrian Arab Republic, Tunisia, and Ukraine (European Commission 2007a).
3. Current members are Egypt (1945), Iraq (1945), Jordan (1945), Lebanon (1945), Saudi Arabia (1945), Syria (1945), Yemen (1945), Libya (1953), Sudan (1956), Morocco (1958), Tunisia (1958), Kuwait (1961), Algeria (1962), Bahrain (1971), Oman (1971), Qatar (1971), United Arab Emirates (1971), Mauritania (1973), Somalia (1974), Palestine (West Bank and Gaza) `(1976), Djibouti (1977), and the Comoros (1993). The observer states are Eritrea (2003) and India (2007) (League of Arab States 2007).
4. ECOWAS was the first regional organization to intervene militarily to resolve a conflict in the post-Cold War period. It set up the Economic Community Monitoring Group in 1990 to resolve the Liberian civil war. It began its peace-keeping operations in December 1989 when Libyan-backed rebels invaded Liberia from Côte d'Ivoire. The war ended in 1996, but President Charles Taylor's autocratic and dysfunctional government led to a new rebellion in 1999. Estimates suggest that more than 200,000 people were killed in the civil wars since 1998. In 2006, former President Charles Taylor was arrested and extradited to the International Criminal Court at The Hague to face 17 counts of alleged war crimes (Blackwell Synergy 2007).
5. The Cooperative Development of Operational Safety and Continued Airworthiness Program is a regional initiative of ICAO aimed at improving aviation oversight using a regional approach. Several such programs have been initiated in Africa, Asia, and Latin America. Most are financed by ICAO contracting states or by development partners such as the African Development Bank or the EU (ICAO 2006).

6. Between 1945 and 1958, CFA stood for Colonies françaises d'Afrique (French colonies of Africa). Thereafter, it stood for Communauté française d'Afrique (French Community of Africa), which existed from 1958 (establishment of the French Fifth Republic) to the colonies' independence at the beginning of the 1960s. The use of the term CFA in connection with the franc continues to this day. Two regional currencies are denominated CFA: the Central African franc and the West African franc.

7. In May 2002, WAEMU's Council of Ministers adopted in the Community Competition Law, which consists of five parts: (a) control of anticompetitive behavior within WAEMU; (b) rules and procedures related to the control of cartels and abuse of a dominant position within WAEMU; (c) control of state support within WAEMU that could distort competition, for example, subsidies or no landing taxes for a particular corporation or airline; (d) transparency of the financial relationship between member states and public enterprises and between public enterprises and international or foreign organizations; and (e) cooperation between the WAEMU Commission and national authorities in law enforcement. According to a ruling by the WAEMU Court of Justice (opinion 003/2000/CJ/WAEMU), the WAEMU Commission has exclusive authority to implement these provisions as they relate to competition. National competition authorities still do enforce national competition laws where they exist, but WAEMU competition law takes precedence when in case of a conflict with national law (WAEMU 2002c).

8. For example, the EU sets the compensation for passenger delays at €250 for flights of less than 1,500 kilometers (km), €400 for flights of between 1,500 and 3,500 km, and €600 for flights of more than 3,500 km. WAEMU fixes the compensation at CFA100,000 (€150) in economy or CFA200,000 (€300) in business class for flights of less than 2,500 km and CFA400,000 (€600) in economy or CFA800,000 (€1,200) in business class for flights of 2,500 km or further (European Parliament and the European Council 2004).

9. Regulation No. 07/2002/CM/UEMOA, "Passengers, Freight and Cargo, and Mail Tariffs Applicable to Air Services within, from and to WAEMO Member States," states in its preamble: "Considering the Decision dated 14 November 1999 relating to the implementation of the Yamoussoukro Decision on the liberalization of air transport markets access in Africa signed on 12 July 2000 by the current Chairperson of OAU." But it limits the scope in the same preamble to the territory of WAEMU: "Anxious to promote the development of a safe, orderly and efficient air transport within the Union."

10. Girma Wake, chief executive officer of Ethiopian Airlines, confirmed some issues were pending concerning the denial of fifth freedom traffic rights by Kenya. However, rather than trying to settle the matter via the auspices of the African Union, he considered direct negotiations with the Kenyan authorities

to be a much more effective way to reach a solution (interview held with Girma Wake, 25 April 2007, Addis Ababa).

11. Both Article 5 of the Yamoussoukro Decision and Article 14 of CEMAC's Civil Aviation Code state that designated carriers must coordinate their schedules. In the spirit of CEMAC's Competition Regulation, the requirement for coordination is justified as long as it leads to more efficient market development.

CHAPTER 5

Impact of Liberalization

The liberalization of air services, or as it is referred to in the United States, airline deregulation, the process of removing entry and price restrictions on airlines affecting, in particular, the carriers permitted to serve specific routes, has had a severe impact on the growth of air transport markets in the developed world. The African continent, however, started to liberalize its markets about 20 years later, with different progress in various regions. Nevertheless, there are some clear indicators that liberalization has already had an impact on African air transport services.

Data Sources and Methodology

Several methods are available for analyzing air service markets in any given region of the world. For air carriers, one of the most important indicators is the revenue passenger-kilometer, which represents one fare-paying passenger transported 1 km. The revenue passenger-kilometers of a given flight can be divided by available seat-kilometers, which are the total number of seats available for the transportation of paying passengers multiplied by the number of kilometers flown. This provides the load factor, which for most airlines is one of the leading performance indicators of how well a given route performs within the network. While these data would generally provide a comprehensive picture of an air service market, the revenue passenger-kilometers and available seat-kilometers of an air carrier are mostly disclosed on a fleet-wide basis only so as not to indicate specific route profitability to competitors.[1] This is especially true in fragmented international markets, where often only a few carriers dominate certain routes.

The standard source for air traffic data collected by airlines and airports is ICAO, which has developed statistics and forecasting programs that are based on data it collects from its contracting states that it then compiles into multiple data series. ICAO's database is known as the integral statistical database (ICAO 2007). The data include information on commercial air carriers (traffic, on-flight origin and destination, traffic by flight stage, fleet personnel and financial data), on airports (airport traffic by passengers and aircraft movements from international airports, and financial data), on air navigation service providers (financial and traffic data), and from civil aircraft registries.[2] However, the data are based on reporting by states and are often incomplete, inaccurate, and/or unreliable, especially when provided by developing countries whose statistical capacity is limited often because of a lack of training and of funding for adequate staff. Indeed, during several missions to Africa from 2002 to 2008 the author observed, for example, that actual passenger counts were often maintained on paper ledgers with no computerization. In many cases these data were never submitted to ICAO, leaving exceptionally large data holes in any time series. In addition, many contracting states believe that they need to report data only about international traffic to ICAO given that ICAO's mandate focuses primarily on international air services.

As an alternative, official airline schedules, which are in the public domain, are the best source of data for air traffic analysis for developing countries. The limitation of such data published by airlines is that schedules capture the capacity offered only in terms of seats between two points, not the number of actual passengers carried. Nevertheless, given the assumption that no airline would, over time, operate an aircraft that is not filled sufficiently to render the flight economically feasible, one could hypothesize that at any given point in time, 50 to 70 percent of the seat capacity offered on a route would approximate the actual number of passengers carried. One could also hypothesize that even with certain changes in load factors, the overall trend in seat capacity would approximate actual traffic trends over time. Finally, given that airline schedules are readily available and provide additional information such as type of aircraft, frequency of the routes, and scheduled times of the flight, the analysis of the air service market presented in this chapter will depend primarily on such data.

The traditional source for airline data is the Official Airline Guide, a company with a more than 150-year history of publishing travel schedules. The company provides global flight information and data for the passenger aviation, air cargo logistics, and business travel markets. The firm was founded in the United Kingdom in 1853. In 1993, it merged with a company founded in the United States in 1929 that provided similar information. For many years the Official Airline Guide was the only provider of such data until the creation of the Airline Data Group of the Seabury Group in 2000. Founded in 1995, the U.S.-based Seabury Group provides investment banking, financial advisory, restructuring, and consulting services primarily for transportation companies and companies in related industries around the world. Both sources depend on airlines reporting their routes, and both have captured 99 percent of scheduled airline data, with about 900 to 1,000 airlines participating. While the Official Airline Guide is the more established data collector, both companies enjoy an excellent industry reputation and are endorsed by the IATA.

For the research of air service markets in Africa in this study, a defined set of data was procured from the Airline Data Group and compiled in electronic form (Abbey 2008). To cover the period of implementation of the Yamoussoukro Decision, 12 extractions in time were assembled, four each for 2001, 2004, and 2007. These extractions cover all scheduled flights within, to, and from Africa. To assure the capture of seasonal trends, the four samples for each year consist of data for one week in the months of February, May, August, and November. To annualize these figures, the total sum of the four observations for a given year was multiplied by 13. As these are weekly data, the multiplier 13 ($4 \times 13 = 52$ weeks) is more precise than 12 ($4 \times 12 = 48$).

The data consist of one record of each flight occurring during the sampled week, with relevant entries on the origin and destination airports, the changeover airport in the case of flights with one intermittent stop, the number of miles of the flight, the duration of the flight, the number of seats available on the flight, the number of times the flight occurred during the week, the days the flight was scheduled, the aircraft type used, the carrier, and the actual operator. Using the relational database management system Microsoft Access, the data were normalized and linked to other relevant tables to develop a relational database for extensive summarization and querying. In addition, flights from one airport to another final destination with an intermediate scheduled stop had their capacity allocated by assigning even proportions to each leg. This implies that a flight from airport A to airport C via airport B would have only half the capacity going from airport A to C while the other half would deplane at airport B. This allocation was made for each leg, that is, if a flight had four legs, each of the destination airports would only have a quarter of the overall capacity allocated. Even though the even distribution among the legs is just an assumption, this methodology prevents double counting of capacity for flights with more than one leg. The overall impact of these calculations resulted in about a 10 percent adjustment of capacities.

To provide safeguards and "sanity checks" (basic tests to quickly evaluate the validity of statements or calculations), some of the airport aggregates were compared with actual data from ICAO and other sources, where available. The ratio of scheduled seats to reported passenger traffic found hinted at a load factor of about 65 to 69 percent for most of the routes tested. This result is a solid and reliable figure that supports the credibility of the data used. Other more general and rougher summaries resulted in a load factor between 50 and 60 percent. However, these were large aggregates measured against each other, most likely also having significant assumptions in the index they were measured against, and therefore less accurate. Overall, when estimating traffic in terms of passengers this study assumes a load factor of 70 percent when deriving seat capacity from flight schedules.

The data used are particularly helpful for capturing trends in city and country pairs, fleet renewal (in most cases the type of aircraft is provided down to the level of detail of series number, for instance, Boeing 737–100 versus Boeing 737–800), and airline market share. However, the data analyzed reflect only scheduled and advertised services. Any data on informal carriers with no public reservation systems that issue paper tickets at the airport and provide only a chalkboard or a printed flyer setting out their schedules was not captured. For example, the Airline Data Group data include virtually no older, Eastern-built aircraft operating in Africa, yet much anecdotal evidence about such operations exists, as do accident statistics. Nevertheless, the overall proportion of such flights is generally considered to be relatively small and they are operated primarily in larger domestic markets, which would not be of significance for the Yamoussoukro Decision.

Finally, to confirm the fleet analysis derived from the Airline Data Group data, the registration information for each aircraft for each African-registered carrier for the years 1997, 2001, 2004, and 2007 was compiled in an electronic spreadsheet. The data were summarized and entered manually from the *JP Airline-Fleets International* publications for the respective years (Klee 1997, 2001, 2004, 2007).

General Traffic Analysis

The traffic analysis to measure the impact of liberalization focuses on two types of main markets for each REC, namely, international traffic in terms of seat capacity within a REC and international traffic between REC countries and countries in Africa that do not belong to the given REC. The data collected as explained earlier, were annualized and provided an estimated seat capacity for 2001, 2004, and 2007. The change in seat capacity can thus be measured for two periods: between 2001 and 2004 and between 2004 and 2007. However, as most measures to implement the Yamoussoukro Decision were only achieved in recent years, and given the worldwide drop in air traffic after 11 September 2001, the latter dataset provides more evidence of the impact of liberalization.

The RECs were rated in terms of their progress toward implementation of the Yamoussoukro Decision and the extent of liberalization achieved (table 5.1).

A first glance at the resulting changes in offered seats could lead to the erroneous conclusion that liberalization has had a negative effect on traffic (table 5.2). The REC that scored the highest in relation to liberalization had the steepest drop, or slowest growth, in traffic. Air traffic within the two most liberalized regions (CEMAC and WAEMU) dropped significantly between 2004 and 2007, while traffic between the RECs dropped only slightly between 2001 and 2004, and generally experienced good growth in the period between 2004 and 2007. However, the second most liberalized region, BAG, saw a healthy development in traffic, especially during the years when liberalization took effect (2004–07). Note also that traffic experienced a steep drop within the two fully liberalized regions, but the traffic between these regions and other regions remained stable or stagnant. Nevertheless, the drop in traffic in West and Central Africa was not a direct effect of the Yamoussoukro Decision, but can be attributed to other factors.

A similarly revealing result is achieved when analyzing city pairs served. The analysis shows that the number of city pairs served declined substantially in the most liberalized regions of West and Central Africa, but grew in BAG as well as in the less liberalized RECs in southern and East Africa. A much smaller, but still negative, trend can be observed

Table 5.1 Grading of RECs on Their Liberalization of Air Services as of 30 June 2009

Community	General status of Yamoussoukro Decision implementation	Status of air services liberalization	Overall implementation score[a]
AMU	No implementation has occurred.	No liberalization within the AMU has been initiated, but the need for liberalization is recognized.	1
BAG	The principles of the Yamoussoukro Decision have been agreed upon in the MASA.	Up to fifth freedom rights have been granted, tariffs are free, and capacity and frequency are open.	4
CEMAC	The principles of the Yamoussoukro Decision have been agreed upon in an air transport program. Some minor restrictions remain.	Up to fifth freedom rights have been granted, tariffs are free, and capacity and frequency are open. A maximum of two carriers per state may participate.	5
COMESA	Full liberalization has been agreed on (Legal Notice No. 2), but application and implementation remain pending until a joint competition authority has been established.	Liberalization is pending. Once applied, operators may be able to serve any destination (all freedoms) and tariffs, capacity, and frequency will be free.	3
EAC	The EAC Council issued a directive to amend bilaterals among EAC states to conform to the Yamoussoukro Decision.	Air services are not liberalized because the amendments to bilaterals remain pending.	3
SADC	No steps toward implementation have been taken, even though SADC's civil aviation policy includes the gradual liberalization of air services within SADC.	No liberalization has been initiated within SADC.	2
WAEMU	The Yamoussoukro Decision has been fully implemented.	All freedoms, including cabotage, have been granted. Tariffs have been liberalized.	5

Source: Author's calculations.
a. The rating scale ranges from no progress toward liberalization (1) to full liberalization (5).

Table 5.2 Estimated Number of Seats on International Flights within and between RECs, Selected Years

REC	Number of seats 2001	2004	2007	Growth 2001–07 (percent)	Growth 2004–07 (percent)
International flights within RECS					
AMU	799,719	943,345	1,294,189	8.4	11.1
BAG	549,105	425,427	568,306	0.6	10.1
CEMAC	498,708	495,158	152,984	−17.9	−32.4
COMESA	2,952,372	2,745,938	4,484,675	7.2	17.8
EAC	1,384,894	1,458,539	1,751,811	4.0	6.3
SADC	4,033,387	4,465,842	5,663,632	5.8	8.2
WAEMU	983,167	849,818	763,472	−4.1	−3.5
International flights between RECS					
AMU	617,747	879,595	1,641,705	17.7	23.1
BAG	1,911,861	1,573,379	2,130,360	1.8	10.6
CEMAC	1,206,595	1,044,355	1,266,196	0.8	6.6
COMESA	1,675,538	2,075,502	2,961,023	10.0	12.6
EAC	623,131	815,557	1,069,575	9.4	9.5
SADC	1,660,856	1,980,463	2,296,398	5.6	5.1
WAEMU	1,877,875	1,907,297	2,352,456	3.8	7.2

Source: Airline Data Group data and author's calculations.

when looking at city pairs between RECs, where the most liberalized regions experienced slow or negative growth (table 5.3).

This trend is linked to an ongoing consolidation of networks, which are focusing on the most profitable routes. It is a consequence of the collapse of the former business model that was based on cross-subsidizing local and regional routes using the income generated on strongly regulated and highly profitable intercontinental routes.

General Fleet Analysis

The fleet analysis was conducted by attributing a specific aircraft group code to each type of aircraft. The codes ranged from extremely old Western aircraft, commuter jets and commuter propeller aircraft, city jets, and wide-body jets, to several Eastern-built aircraft types. The changes in fleet composition by region are calculated as a percentage of seat miles flown. A grading was applied to the overall fleet age, with the highest score (5) being applied to the newest fleet.

The result of the analysis shows an overall improvement in fleet age and types of aircraft across all the regions with the exception of the BAG countries (table 5.4). The two most liberalized regions, CEMAC and

Table 5.3 International Flights, REC City Pairs, Selected Years

REC	Liberalization score[a]	Number of cities end of 2007	Net change in number of cities from 2001	Number of city pairs end of 2007	Net change in number of city pairs	Annual change 2001–07 (percent)	Annual change, 2004–07 (percent)	Overall change 2001–07 (percent)	Average aircraft seating capacity 2001	Average aircraft seating capacity 2007
Within RECs										
AMU	1	9	1	14	2	6.71	11.12	47.68	147	159
BAG	4	8	0	15	1	−0.16	10.13	−0.95	144	117
CEMAC	5	7	−2	9	−9	−18.48	−32.40	−70.66	128	78
COMESA	3	34	−2	71	−3	7.25	17.76	52.20	129	147
EAC	3	10	0	18	−2	3.34	6.30	21.78	113	95
SADC	2	37	4	72	5	4.75	8.24	32.12	98	88
WAEMU	5	9	0	21	−3	−5.32	−3.51	−27.99	150	102
Between RECs										
AMU	1	30	11	7	−3	8.13	15.37	59.85	146	142
BAG	4	28	−5	9	0	−0.84	5.23	−4.96	177	118
CEMAC	5	17	−4	20	3	−2.67	0.24	−14.97	192	170
COMESA	3	74	5	43	6	4.67	6.89	31.47	128	122
EAC	3	42	8	19	3	11.42	17.03	91.29	156	149
SADC	2	50	−2	44	6	3.74	5.74	24.62	135	122
WAEMU	5	30	−8	14	−4	0.96	12.94	5.88	187	198

Source: Airline Data Group data and author's calculations.
Note: In the second panel, the data do not take into account when countries belong to more than one REC.
a. See table 5.1.

Table 5.4 Changes in Fleet Composition by REC, 2001–07

REC	Fleet age grade 2001[a]	Fleet age grade 2007[a]	Difference in age grades between 2001 and 2007	Comments	Typical aircraft size 2001[b]	Typical aircraft size 2007[b]
AMU	4	5	1	Almost all old aircraft replaced	Nearly all Boeing 737-type city jets	Almost 100% city jets
BAG	2	1	−1	Very large proportional shift from old to even older aircraft	Roughly 60% city jets, about 30% wide-bodies	Almost 100% city jets
CEMAC	3	4	1	From mixed (50% old) to about 75% recent, but also an increase in very old aircraft	About 80% city jets	Large shift toward commuter turboprops
COMESA	3	4	1	Shift from 50% relatively recent to almost 75% recent	About 65% city jets, 35% wide-bodies	Shift to about 80% city jets, 20% wide bodies
EAC	3	3	0	Roughly the same proportion, 33%, of old aircraft, with the remainder being renewed	About 75% city jets, 20% wide-bodies, 10% commuter props	About 80% city jets, wide-bodies down to 5%, remainder reflects increase in commuter props
SADC	3	4	1	Increase of recent jetliners from roughly 20% to nearly 66%	About 75% city jets, 20% wide-bodies	About 85% city jets, only 5% wide-bodies
WAEMU	3	4	1	Percentage of recent airliners about as high as BAG, but the remainder still old	About 60% wide-bodies, about 10% commuter jets, 30% city jets	Large shift toward 80% city jets, 20% commuter props, no wide-bodies

Source: Airline Data Group data and author's calculations.

a. The newer the fleet, the higher the number with a maximum of 5.

b. For the analysis of the African fleet all aircraft were grouped into the following categories: (a) wide-body (for example, A340, B747), (b) large jet (for example, B757, DC8), (c) city jet (for example, A320, B737, DC9), (d) commuter jet (for example, CRJ, F100), (e) commuter prop (for example, F28, SB200), and (f) general aviation (for example, PC12, BE200, C421).

WAEMU, experienced a clear shift toward smaller and newer aircraft. In essence, CEMAC was replacing all city jets with newer turboprop aircraft and WAEMU was replacing wide-body aircraft with city jets and commuter aircraft.

A similar trend replacement is observed in BAG, where the rapid growth of air services in Nigeria resulted in a shift to primarily smaller, but older, city jet aircraft. Nonliberalized regions experienced both a renewal in terms of newer aircraft as well as a shift to smaller aircraft. Nevertheless, more wide-body aircraft seem to remain in less liberalized regions such as COMESA and SADC.

Effects of Liberalization on Traffic and Air Carriers by Region

The result of the analysis of traffic and fleet changes must be analyzed within each region by taking into account progress made toward liberalization by the individual RECs along with some external factors that may have occurred independently of the effects of the implementation of a liberalized air services framework.

For analysis of the effects of liberalization in selected countries in each REC, aircraft fleet data were compiled and summarized by country. Only aircraft with more than 30 seats were included on the assumption that despite the number of smaller aircraft, they do not significantly change the conclusions drawn, as they participate only marginally in country-to-country air services. The samples also exclude all aircraft that are not involved in public air transportation, such as aircraft belonging to government air services, corporate fleets, air ambulance operators, and aerial surveyors.

In addition to the fleet analysis the study analyzes changes in traffic flows with a focus on service providers. For example, in 2001, a few large carriers dominated West Africa and Central Africa, but disappeared during the early years of liberalization. After 1994, the traffic served by these air carriers, which were often fifth, or even seventh, freedom flights, started to be replaced by carriers that were not registered in either the departure country or the destination country. Such changes are clearly signs of the impact of liberalization, because new carriers are serving fifth freedom flights, which is one of the basic elements of the Yamoussoukro Decision.

Development across Africa

As table 5.5 shows, the number of carriers increased steadily between 1997 and 2004. The collapse of some of the African legacy carriers such

Table 5.5 Fleet Analysis, Africa, Selected Years

Item	1997	2001	2004	2007
Number of carriers	104	125	166	168
Number of aircraft	585	706	895	978
Seat capacity	76,615	95,828	118,803	123,896

Source: Klee 1997, 2001, 2004, 2007.

as Air Afrique and Ghana Airways during that period has been more than compensated for by the entry of several new carriers into the market. Between 2004 and 2007, the number of carriers stabilized across the continent, but several carriers that existed in 2004 had been replaced by new operators by 2007. The general increase in carriers is due primarily to the reform of domestic policies to allow new carriers to compete with or replace the former national carrier. There is little evidence to indicate that the observed fleet development is only the result of the intra-African liberalization driven by the Yamoussoukro Decision.

The number of aircraft has increased along with the number of carriers, and both grew faster (9 percent) between 2004 and 2007 than between 1997 and 2004. During 1997–2007, the fleet of aircraft with more than 30 seats increased by 67 percent, which represents an annual growth rate of 5.3 percent. The total seat capacity initially grew more rapidly than the number of aircraft, but slowed after 2004. The average fleet size (aggregated number of aircraft in fleets divided by the number of carriers) remained steady at 5.6 during 1997–2001 period and decreased slightly thereafter because of the entry into the market of smaller operators and the growth of existing small carriers, which have added some aircraft with a capacity of more than 30 seats to their fleets. However, average fleet size grew again as of 2004, which reflects a certain trend of consolidation of the industry, with stronger growth by the major carriers.

Between 1997 and 2001, average aircraft capacity increased from 131 to 136 seats per aircraft, but since that time a clear trend toward smaller aircraft resulted in an average seat capacity of 127 seats by 2007. This trend reflects the introduction of smaller aircraft by some major operators to develop new routes; the phasing out of older, sometimes underutilized, aircraft such as the B-727 series; and the removal of several wide-body "flag of convenience" aircraft from the registries of some certain states. (This study considers flag of convenience registrations to be all carriers whose head offices are located outside the country of registration and that do not operate listed air services to and from their country of registration.)

The Yamoussoukro Decision has helped new airlines to enter markets that were abandoned by failing carriers. In many regions, new carriers made up for some of the lost capacities (table 5.6). In many cases, carriers from outside a given REC were allowed to take over unserved capacity, often by adding fifth freedom operations. In this way, Ethiopian Airlines and Kenyan Airways, both East African carriers, gained market share predominantly in West and Central Africa. In other words, as the markets shrank in capacity and older carriers either abandoned those markets or went under, every one of the remaining 6 country pair markets of an original 12 country pairs is being served by a new market entrant. At times, this was undertaken by operators such as Ethiopian Airlines and Libya's Afriqiyah Airways. The latter now provides the only intraregional service connecting the Central African Republic. What seems to be a clear application of the Yamoussoukro Decision can be seen in most of the services reflected in table 5.6. However, caution should be applied when interpreting these findings because many of the airlines that served these routes and are no longer active have also often been foreign to both countries in a pair as far back as 2001.

Most of the RECs saw a reduction in fifth freedom traffic by carriers of their own REC between 2001 and 2004 (table 5.7). This was primarily because large carriers such as Air Afrique and Air Gabon had left the market, but by 2007, fifth freedom flights in most regions had increased. Especially in West and Central Africa, fifth freedom flights accounted for about a third of all traffic.

Table 5.6 Changes in the Number of Seats by REC

REC	International travel within RECs			International travel between RECs		
	Seats available in 2007	Seats from airlines that had left the market by 2007	Seats from airlines that were new to the market in 2007	Seats available in 2007	Seats from airlines that had left the market by 2007	Seats from airlines that were new to the market in 2007
AMU	1,294,189	90,998	45,396	1,641,705	186,977	554,030
BAG	586,306	457,422	432,907	2,130,360	1,265,446	980,850
CEMAC	152,984	663,116	152,984	1,266,196	1,103,435	777,976
COMESA	4,484,675	1,170,550	990,390	2,961,023	674,559	707,209
EAC	1,751,811	806,977	472,030	1,069,575	223,160	217,291
SADC	5,663,632	1,396,004	1,891,595	2,296,398	972,450	722,042
WAEMU	763,472	932,675	408,288	2,352,456	1,550,345	1,395,286

Source: Airline Data Group data and author's calculations.

Table 5.7 Fifth Freedom Flights by Carriers of Each REC, Selected Years
(percentage of flights in a REC that are fifth freedom)

Year	AMU	BAG	CEMAC	COMESA	EAC	SADC	WAEMU
2001	7.63	45.26	38.00	25.35	33.01	18.68	47.66
2004	8.27	36.27	11.76	9.86	12.21	2.25	43.70
2007	4.13	43.25	28.48	14.10	16.38	5.68	43.75

Source: Airline Data Group data and author's calculations.

Most interesting, however, is the development of African carriers that operate within an REC other than the one where they are based, thus providing fifth freedom traffic (table 5.8). West and Central Africa in particular experienced a significant increase in non-REC fifth freedom flights after 2004. There are strong indications that East African (Ethiopian Airlines and Kenya Airways) and North African (Afriqiyah Airways and Royal Air Maroc) carriers had taken over traffic within BAG, CEMAC, and WAEMU.

Non-African carriers had a remarkable share of fifth freedom flights in Sub-Saharan Africa, accounting for 6 to 29 percent in 2001 (table 5.9). However, this traffic declined steeply when African carriers began to take over such fifth freedom operations. This can be seen as a successful response to concerns expressed at the Summit of the OAU in 1979, which feared that European carriers would replace African airlines. Clearly the Yamoussoukro Decision did facilitate the expansion of African carriers in domestic markets.

Development in North Africa

North Africa has made little progress toward liberalizing its air services and no liberalization of international air services took place within the AMU. Nevertheless, some countries have achieved some domestic liberalization by allowing more than one carrier, and some of these carriers have begun to serve international destinations.

In Algeria, the national carrier, Air Algérie, benefited for several decades from a monopoly both in the domestic and international markets, but liberalization of the domestic market in 2000 resulted in the entry of a few new carriers. This resulted in a more than 70 percent increase in aircraft and seat capacity. The most significant new operator, Khalifa Airways, embarked on an ambitious and aggressive growth policy, but subsequently collapsed. In addition, the liberalization of domestic market entry was not accompanied by adequate new regulatory instruments (World Bank 2005, p. 34). By 2004, only two carriers remained in the domestic

Table 5.8 Fifth Freedom Flights by African Carriers of Other RECs, Selected Years
(percentage of fifth freedom flights by carriers of other RECs within the given REC)

Year	AMU	BAG	CEMAC	COMESA	EAC	SADC	WAEMU
2001	0.00	39.11	35.23	20.79	32.63	17.95	25.73
2004	0.00	24.43	3.19	3.63	11.50	1.48	29.34
2007	0.00	27.99	28.48	7.22	14.56	3.97	28.74

Source: Airline Data Group data and author's calculations.
Note: During the selected years, there were no African Carriers from other RECs operating fifth freedom flights in AMU.

Table 5.9 Fifth Freedom Flights by Non-African Carriers, Selected Years
(percentage of fifth freedom flights)

Year	AMU	BAG	CEMAC	COMESA	EAC	SADC	WAEMU
2001	5.62	28.64	11.02	19.39	26.48	13.35	16.52
2004	8.27	19.71	2.02	2.59	6.77	0.63	0.00
2007	4.13	15.19	0.00	3.86	0.77	2.55	0.37

Source: Airline Data Group data and author's calculations.

market, and by 2007, Algeria's air transport industry had reverted to a de facto monopoly (table 5.10).

Libya experienced steady progress toward liberalization that resulted in the number of carriers increasing from one in 1997 to nine in 2007, while seat capacity doubled. This development is a result of the opening of the country following the end of the international embargo. In addition, Libya seems to have focused on a policy of developing an air transport sector that is competing with sixth freedom flights between West Africa and Europe. In addition, Libya seems to support primarily its new carrier Afriqiyah Airways by designating it for all the new routes that were opened to the detriment of its legacy state-owned carrier Libyan Airlines.

Morocco appears to have a more restrictive policy that seems to control liberalization by allowing the introduction of only a few new operators. The number of carriers increased from one in 1997 to four in 2007. However, the only major operator among the new entrants, Atlas Blue, is a subsidiary of the legacy carrier Royal Air Maroc.[3] It is strictly focused on low-cost operations and on supplementing the traffic of Royal Air Maroc under franchise or code-sharing agreements on low-density routes. The policy seems to have succeeded, as the fleet size more than doubled during the period, whereas unit capacity increased slightly from 149 in 1997 to 155 in 2007 (table 5.10).

Tunisia's air carrier development in terms of fleet size and seat capacity has been fluctuating. This seems to be due primarily to the changing

Table 5.10 Fleet Analysis, North Africa, Selected Years
(number)

Country	1997			2001			2004			2007		
	Carriers	Aircraft	Available seats	Carriers	Aircraft	Available seats	Carriers	Aircraft	Available seats	Carriers	Aircraft	Available seats
Algeria	1	40	5,035	5	68	8,885	2	55	6,692	1	58	7,854
Egypt, Arab Rep. of	9	56	10,289	15	71	12,445	8	63	11,418	12	72	12,229
Libya	1	27	2,346	2	21	2,673	7	58	4,969	9	51	5,369
Morocco	1	28	4,176	1	41	5,617	3	49	7,364	4	73	11,303
Tunisia	3	31	4,533	3	49	7,317	5	59	9,552	4	49	7,692
Total	15	182	26,379	26	250	36,937	25	284	39,995	30	303	44,447

Source: Klee 1997, 2001, 2004, 2007.

relative competitiveness between Tunisian charter operators and their European counterparts on the international market with Europe. In addition, the national carrier, Tunisair, seems to have been less successful than Royal Air Maroc in capturing sixth freedom traffic between West Africa and Europe. This is probably due to its smaller size and its stronger exposure by geographic proximity to competition from Libya's Afriqiyah Airways on this particular market segment.

The Arab Republic of Egypt is not a member of the AMU, but a member of COMESA. COMESA has made some progress toward liberalization, but still falls short of fully implementing the Yamoussoukro Decision. The number of carriers in Egypt fluctuated during 1997–2007, whereas total seat capacity has remained more or less steady. The fluctuation was mainly due to changes in the industry's structure, which consisted of one dominant flag carrier, EgyptAir, and several smaller charter operators, some of which ceased operations soon after they entered the market. A variety of factors appeared to account for this, such as the volatility of the international tourist market given recurrent security problems and the domination of this segment of the industry by financial investors some of which have only short-term investment strategies.

Overall, the Yamoussoukro Decision has had little impact within the North African market. However, some North African carriers have begun to expand their operations into Sub-Saharan Africa, where most can benefit from being located in state that is party to the decision.

Development in West Africa

West Africa has done quite well in implementing the principles of the Yamoussoukro Decision. WAEMU has fully liberalized its internal market and BAG has applied most of the principles in a multilateral agreement. The regional development of West African countries can be examined by grouping certain smaller players, while reviewing dominant countries separately.

The first group of small countries comprises Benin, Burkina Faso, Guinea, Guinea-Bissau, Mali, Mauritania, Niger, and Togo, most of which are members of WAEMU. The development of the air transport industry of these countries was unstable, consisting of the entrance of only a few carriers with low capacities (table 5.11). In some of countries, for instance, Mali and Togo, the air transport industry completely disappeared after some unsuccessful attempts to develop new operators. Niger has only one operator that apparently has no aircraft. Burkina Faso has been able to maintain its flag carrier, which continues to operate at a reduced scale,

Table 5.11 Fleet Analysis, West Africa, Selected Years
(number)

	1997			2001			2004			2007		
Country	Carriers	Aircraft	Available seats	Carriers	Aircraft	Available seats	Carriers	Aircraft	Available seats	Carriers	Aircraft	Available seats
Benin	0	0	0	1	1	118	1	1	108	1	3	324
Burkina Faso	1	1	85	1	1	85	1	4	369	1	1	189
Cape Verde	1	5	367	2	5	353	1	5	508	1	6	554
Gambia, The	2	12	1,370	3	7	1,040	5	9	1,433	2	7	789
Ghana	1	5	748	1	6	1,312	3	12	1,600	4	8	670
Guinea	3	5	318	2	4	274	3	3	220	2	2	172
Guinea Bissau	1	1	44	0	0	0	0	0	0	1	1	48
Côte d'Ivoire	2	16	2,613	1	11	2,395	1	4	385	3	7	546
Liberia	1	1	40	3	4	409	2	2	100	1	2	96
Mali	1	2	168	1	1	65	1	2	180	0	0	0
Mauritania	1	4	254	1	2	158	1	5	566	1	5	545
Niger	0	0	0	1	0	0	0	0	0	1	0	0
Nigeria	12	83	10,431	15	64	7,316	20	78	10,285	20	98	11,789
Senegal	1	1	37	1	1	50	2	5	452	2	5	452
Sierra Leone	0	0	0	0	0	0	8	24	5,596	4	13	3,731
Togo	1	3	225	1	1	281	1	1	46	0	0	0
Total	28	139	16,700	34	108	13,856	50	155	21,848	44	158	19,905

Source: Klee 1997, 2001, 2004, 2007.

whereas Mauritania created a new carrier after its national carrier, Air Mauritanie, went out of business.

The second group comprises Cape Verde and Senegal, where the flag carriers have been able to develop their markets and have performed reasonably well. Cape Verde's national carrier, Transportes Aéreos de Cabo Verde, has reduced its focus on the regional market in West Africa to concentrate on long-haul routes to Europe and the United States (Sterling Merchant Finance, Ltd. 2007, p. 82). Air Sénégal International, a re-emergence of the former national carrier with participation by Royal Air Maroc, has successfully carried out a strategy of developing its business on the routes to and from Dakar, which had been abandoned by the defunct Air Afrique (Sterling Merchant Finance, Ltd. 2007, p. 86). Air Sénégal's success on regional fifth freedom sectors, such as Bamak–Abidjan and Bamako–Niamey, may have contributed to driving Mali's, Niger's, and Togo's carriers out of business. This is a direct consequence of the effects of liberalization induced by the Yamoussoukro Decision.

The third group of countries is composed of The Gambia, Liberia, and Sierra Leone. The flag of convenience phenomenon has become particularly important in these countries. In The Gambia, fleet size and seat capacity remained at a high level well in excess of the country's market potential from 1997 to 2004. However, it had dropped significantly by 2007, apparently because of the authorities' efforts to remove flag of convenience registrations from the country's registry. In Sierra Leone, the trend was opposite to what was observed in The Gambia. While no carrier operating aircraft with more than 30 seats was listed in 1997 and 2001, by 2004 the country had 8 carriers and 24 aircraft with almost 5,600 seats, obviously reflecting flag of convenience registrations. The figures had dropped by 2007, reflecting the authorities' efforts to remove flag of convenience registrations. Finally, Liberia's fleet figures are similar to those of the first group of countries with small air transport industries. However, large numbers of freighter aircraft not shown in table 5.11 appear on its registry, most operated by carriers based outside the country.

Three countries, Côte d'Ivoire, Ghana, and Nigeria, are countries where specific circumstances have influenced market and fleet development. Nigeria accounts for nearly half the region's air carriers and well over half the region's air fleet and seat capacity. The country experienced in-depth reform of the air transport sector, resulting in the full liberalization of domestic air services, in the late 1990s. Its flag carrier,

Nigeria Airways, then faced tough competition on its domestic market and subsequently collapsed in 2003. The new private carriers initially operated a massive fleet of old aircraft, such as 30-year-old Romanian-built BAC-111s, most of which were phased out between 2004 and 2007 and replaced by newer aircraft, predominately of the Boeing 737 series. The average seat capacity slowly increased from about 116 in 2001 to about 120 in 2007, but remained relatively low because carriers competed for high-frequency services on major domestic routes. In 2005 a new flag carrier, Virgin Nigeria, was established as a public-private partnership to operate Nigeria's international traffic rights. In 2007, the government of Nigeria indicated its intent to designate Arik, a carrier created in 2006 by Nigerian private investors, to operate most long-haul routes previously assigned to Virgin Nigeria. Arik subsequently placed a large order for Boeing 777 and 787 aircraft to be delivered in the next few years (Atiba 2007, p. 26).

The fleet size of Côte d'Ivoire and its capacities dropped dramatically from 2,395 seats in 2001 to 385 seats in 2004. This was due to the collapse of Air Afrique, whose fleet was registered in Côte d'Ivoire. A new national carrier, Air Ivoire, was established on a modest scale and has been building up its capacities to serve regional destinations and a few routes to Europe.

Ghana's fleet size and seat capacity increased steadily from 1997 (5 aircraft and 748 seats) to 2004 (12 aircraft and 1,600 seats). Since then, and despite a large increase of carriers to four in 2007, fleet size and seat capacity fell significantly to only 8 aircraft and 670 seats in 2007. This was followed by the collapse of the legacy carrier Ghana Airways, which suffered a freeze in traffic rights with the United States because of safety concerns and subsequent downgrading to FAA International Aviation Safety Assessment Program category 2. In addition, Ghana's aircraft registry lists a significant number of freighter aircraft, including seven B-747-200s, that are operated by carriers based in the United Kingdom and the United Arab Emirates that are supposedly using Ghana as a flag of convenience.

Overall, the region underwent a fundamental change from a few major national air carriers to various smaller operators. There is no evidence that liberalization contributed to the disappearance of unsustainable flag carriers. However, the Yamoussoukro Decision provided both the political and the regulatory basis for a few carriers, such as Air Sénégal International, to expand into abandoned markets. In addition, several carriers both from within the West African RECs as well as from other RECs have expanded their services with fifth freedom operations.

Development in Central Africa

The Central African region consists of two distinct main groups with quite different characteristics. On the one hand are the CEMAC countries and on the other are the Democratic Republic of Congo and the small island state of São Tomé and Principe.

The Democratic Republic of Congo is the largest and most populated country of the region. It accounts for about half the region's fleet and seat capacity, although the numbers fluctuate somewhat erratically. This may attributed to successive periods of relative peace and internal fighting, but may also be a result of a lack of appropriate reporting. The country experienced a sharp drop in the number of operators, aircraft, and seats from 1997 to 2001 (table 5.12), which probably reflects the crisis experienced following the fall and death of its long-time leader President Sese Seko Mobutu. However, a strong upturn followed from 2 carriers in 2001 to 12 carriers in 2004 with 25 aircraft and 2,871 seats. The situation then stabilized, with some consolidation of the industry resulting in a reduction to nine carriers. However, most of the country's fleet consists of old aircraft models. In addition to its passenger fleet, the Democratic Republic of Congo also has a large number of freight carriers. One of the major carriers, Hewa Bora Airways, seemed to be becoming an international carrier of some standing serving routes to Johannesburg and Brussels, but blacklisting by the EU and a recent accident suspended its plans (European Commission 2007b).

São Tomé and Principe has two airlines operating aircraft with fewer than 30 seats. Its registry also includes several flag of convenience listings, including a large fleet of B-727 and L-100 freighters (not shown in table 5.12) that are owned by a carrier based in Angola. Of the CEMAC countries, both Cameroon and Gabon are special cases. The two countries withdrew from Air Afrique in the early 1970s to set up their own flag carriers in the belief that their traffic potential would be able to sustain their operations (Kofele-Kale 1981, p. 202). Both Cameroon Airlines and Air Gabon were initially successful operators, but experienced serious financial and operational problems in the late 1990s that led to the collapse of both carriers. (Note that the figures for Cameroon shown in table 5.12 for 2007 were collected before Cameroon Airlines finally went out of business.) The disappearance of these carriers resulted in the progressive phasing out of wide-body aircraft in the region. What remained was a few niche carriers operating local routes with smaller aircraft.

Table 5.12 Fleet Analysis, Central Africa, Selected Years
(number)

	1997			2001			2004			2007		
Country	Carriers	Aircraft	Available seats	Carriers	Aircraft	Available seats	Carriers	Aircraft	Available seats	Carriers	Aircraft	Available seats
Cameroon	2	5	551	2	7	751	2	6	1,162	2	5	730
Central African Republic	0	0	0	0	3	90	0	0	0	0	0	0
Chad	1	1	44	1	1	44	1	1	87	1	1	72
Congo, Rep. of,	3	9	455	2	7	590	4	10	669	4	13	803
Congo, Dem. Rep. of,	9	22	1,777	2	9	965	12	25	2,871	9	27	2,984
Equatorial Guinea	2	2	64	3	4	212	4	9	447	3	7	301
Gabon	2	8	944	4	11	1,113	7	20	1,692	5	17	1,022
São Tomé and Principe	1	1	118	0	0	0	2	3	315	0	0	0
Total	20	48	3,953	15	42	3,765	32	74	7,243	24	70	5,912

Source: Klee 1997, 2001, 2004, 2007.

The Republic of Congo showed steady growth in the number of aircraft and seat capacity, whereas the number of operators stabilized, indicating that consolidation was taking place. However, the aircraft fleet consists primarily of older aircraft ranging from earlier Boeing 727 to Antonov aircraft.

Chad and the Central African Republic are completely marginalized in terms of their air transport industry. Central Africa does not have any air carriers and the planned establishment of Chad's new carrier Air Toumaï did not materialize.

Equatorial Guinea, whose territory is split between a continental part, the former Rio Muni, and its islands, offers an opportunity for the development of niche domestic air transport. At the same time, the oil boom has become a major driver for international travel to the country, which is an important petroleum producer. Nevertheless, the carriers of Equatorial Guinea are weak, as demonstrated by major fluctuations in the number of aircraft and seats. In addition, flag of convenience registrations account for a large part of the capacities listed.

Even though the CEMAC countries are fully liberalized, there is little evidence that to date the Yamoussoukro Decision has facilitated the establishment of new carriers in the region. However, this might be because the two main national carriers in Cameroon and Gabon have only recently disappeared and have not yet been replaced by new operators. On the positive side, the decision has clearly facilitated the ability of carriers from other RECs to operate in Central Africa. In CEMAC, for example, most fifth freedom flights by carriers from another REC in 2001 were presumably Air Afrique flights, a carrier registered in Côte d'Ivoire. These flights disappeared in 2004 and were replaced by nearly the same percentage of fifth freedom flights from non-CEMAC carriers. As table 5.13 indicates, carriers from Benin, Ethiopia, Libya, and Nigeria, now have an important market share of fifth freedom traffic in the region.

Table 5.13 Out of Region Carriers Providing Intraregional Service in CEMAC, 2007

Country pair	Airline	Nationality	Market share (percent)
Cameroon–Gabon	Ethiopian Airlines	Ethiopia	22
	Bellview Airlines	Nigeria	11
Cameroon–Central African Republic	Afriqiyah Airways	Libya	100
Republic of Congo–Gabon	Benin Golf Air	Benin	11
Equatorial Guinea–Gabon	Benin Golf Air	Benin	11
Equatorial Guinea–Cameroon	Benin Golf Air	Benin	31

Source: Airline Data Group data and author's calculations.

The principles of the Yamoussoukro Decision are thus clearly affecting traffic flows, both on a regional as well as a continent-wide basis. The prime indicator is traffic that is now served by carriers from outside the region that are replacing flights that in the past were carried out by the former major regional carriers. Full liberalization of air services within the region has apparently had little effect yet on the replacement of lost capacity from within CEMAC. This, however, is positive, signaling that implementation of the decision on a regional basis has not shut the door to carriers from other RECs that are operating under the continent-wide principles of the decision.

Development in East Africa

East Africa's air transport sector has experienced remarkable growth, both in terms of number of carriers and markets. However, this growth is unevenly distributed, as only two countries, Kenya and Ethiopia, represent about two-thirds of the region's seat capacity (table 5.14). Both countries operate strong flag carriers, but the situation of each nation is entirely different. In terms of RECs, Kenya is within the EAC, where Burundi, Rwanda, Tanzania, and Uganda are relatively small players in the regional air transport market. COMESA, which includes most East Africa states, is dominated by Ethiopia, but also includes Egypt with its strong national carrier.

Kenya has reformed its air transport policies with the aim of liberalizing the domestic air transport sector. The number of carriers doubled from 1997 to 2007 and average fleet size and seat capacity have trebled, reaching 6,045 seats in 2007. Implementing domestic liberalization has, however, been less successful. One example concerns a privately-owned carrier that operated on the domestic market during 2002 and 2003 under a franchise agreement with British Airways, quickly becoming a strong competitor to Kenya Airways. However, this undertaking was short-lived, and British Airways abruptly terminated the franchise agreement. Kenya Airways subsequently remained as the only major operator, and all other carriers were either small charter companies or local operators on low-density routes. Note that the Kenyan government has carried out a partial privatization of Kenya Airways, with KLM (today Air France-KLM) owning a 27 percent share and providing support services in the role of a technical partner.

Ethiopia shows no sign of effective internal liberalization of the air transport market. Ethiopian Airlines still remains a de facto monopoly and enjoys strong support from the government in negotiating new air service

Table 5.14 Fleet Analysis, East Africa, Selected Years
(number)

Country	1997			2001			2004			2007		
	Carriers	Aircraft	Available seats	Carriers	Aircraft	Available seats	Carriers	Aircraft	Available seats	Carriers	Aircraft	Available seats
Djibouti	1	2	222	3	8	735	1	1	48	3	12	1,443
Eritrea	0	0	0	0	0	0	1	2	412	1	2	403
Ethiopia	1	17	1,668	1	17	1,920	1	25	3,558	2	25	3,547
Kenya	5	17	1,914	7	28	3,894	10	40	4,219	10	56	6,045
Rwanda	0	0	0	1	1	79	1	1	142	1	1	37
Somalia	0	0	0	1	1	164	0	0	0	1	1	48
Sudan	3	12	1,478	3	121	2,213	3	15	1,359	5	21	2,169
Tanzania	2	6	390	2	7	516	4	14	916	4	10	674
Uganda	1	3	249	0	0	0	1	1	103	1	1	103
Total	13	57	5,921	18	73	9,521	22	99	10,757	28	1,29	14,469

Source: Klee 1997, 2001, 2004, 2007.

agreements (see appendix A for a complete list of bilaterals negotiated by the Ethiopian government). The fleet experienced steady growth, with a 50 percent increase in the number of aircraft from 1997 to 2007, while average seat capacity doubled during the same period. This illustrates Ethiopian's strategic priorities in favor of fostering the development of long-haul routes. At the same time, Ethiopian Airlines continues to establish its intra-African network, which in the past essentially aimed at playing a feeder role for its intercontinental services. Nevertheless, increased fifth and some seventh freedom routes indicate clear intra-African market development, with Ethiopian Airlines becoming a major operator serving several RECs.

Tanzania, despite being a relatively large market for air transport compared with other countries of a similar size, is dominated by several smaller carriers flying aircraft with fewer than 30 seats that primarily serve the domestic tourism market. As concerns international carriers, two major operators stand out. The national carrier, Air Tanzania, was partly privatized in 2002 when South African Airways acquired a 49 percent stake and was becoming a major shareholder and technical partner. However, the partnership ended in 2006 when South African Airways sold back its stake.[4] The other carrier is Precision Air, which is a privately owned carrier with substantial shareholding by Kenya Airways. Precision Air has been steadily gaining ground against Air Tanzania, effectively becoming the country's most important operator in the domestic and regional market within the EAC. Other Tanzanian carriers are small operators serving selective local routes, for instance, to and from Zanzibar and Arusha. Nevertheless, Tanzania has also become one of the most competitive domestic markets compared with other African countries, where at least two carriers compete on any major domestic destination.

Sudan, the largest country in Africa, has the region's third largest fleet. Its air transport market seems to be volatile, resulting in fleet size and capacity fluctuating between the years analyzed. Most of Sudan's fleet is composed of older Western- and Eastern-built aircraft split among a few operators. None of these operators has been able to dominate the country's air transport sector by becoming a serious contender on international routes. In addition, Sudan's safety record is particularly worrying, which led to the recent suspension of the national carrier's air operator certificate (Henshaw 2008).

The other countries of the region include Burundi, Rwanda, and Uganda, which belong to the EAC; Djibouti and Eritrea, which belong to COMESA; and Somalia, which is not part of any REC. Each of these states has a marginal and relatively unstable air transport industry, with Burundi not even having a carrier operating aircraft over 30 seats. Nevertheless, Uganda is a good example in terms of policy, as it completely opened up its air transport market after its national carrier was liquidated. While its own fleet remains stagnant, traffic by other carriers, which have been allowed to operate quite freely, has risen steadily.

Another special case in the region is Djibouti. The relatively large number of aircraft and seats in 2007 is deceptive, as carriers based out of the country seem to account for most of them. Apparently Djibouti, which was flagged with respect to safety oversight after the 2008 ICAO universal safety oversight audit, has recently become a provider of flag of convenience registrations (ICAO 2008).

East Africa experienced a strong development of its air transport services since 2001. Liberalization has helped two main carriers, Ethiopian Airlines and Kenya Airways, to expand their regional operations. As a consequence, however, fifth freedom operations from carriers that are not based in either the EAC or COMESA have lost importance in the region, suggesting a lesser influence of the continent-wide Yamoussoukro Decision. Nevertheless, strong growth of intraregional traffic, including fifth freedom operations, confirm that regional liberalization of air services is taking place in East Africa.

Development in Southern Africa

Southern Africa's air transport industry is predominately located in SADC countries, which have generally made relatively little progress in implementing the Yamoussoukro Decision on a regional basis. However, several SADC states are also members of COMESA (Angola, Malawi, Swaziland, Zambia, and Zimbabwe), which has made far more progress in liberalizing air services.

One of the prime factors underlying SADC's slow progress is South African carriers' domination of the air transport market (table 5.15). These represented 68 percent of the region's aircraft in 1997, growing to more than 80 percent in 2007. At the regional level, the number of carriers, aircraft, and seats has grown steadily, resulting in a 60 percent increase in carriers, a 112 percent increase in aircraft, and a 72 percent increase in seat capacity. These figures reflect a certain consolidation of the industry and stronger growth of regional and domestic routes. However, given the magnitude of South Africa's air transport industry, it is primarily the region's domestic market that is driving the region's fleet and seat capacity indicators.

Table 5.15 Fleet Analysis, Southern Africa, Selected Years
(number)

Country	1997			2001			2004			2007		
	Carriers	Aircraft	Available seats	Carriers	Aircraft	Available seats	Carriers	Aircraft	Available seats	Carriers	Aircraft	Available seats
Angola	4	21	2,136	4	20	2,238	4	15	1,976	8	33	2,818
Botswana	1	2	84	1	3	138	1	4	211	1	5	281
Lesotho	1	1	44	0	0	0	0	0	0	0	0	0
Malawi	1	2	177	1	2	177	1	2	177	1	3	287
Mozambique	1	4	654	1	5	613	1	5	520	3	9	886
Namibia	2	6	1,435	2	6	680	2	5	679	2	7	1,044
South Africa	8	85	13,960	16	161	21,853	20	206	27,364	19	220	28,039
Swaziland	1	2	156	2	3	660	2	8	2,275	4	4	503
Zambia	2	4	360	0	0	0	1	1	48	1	2	236
Zimbabwe	2	11	1,374	1	6	836	1	6	836	1	9	968
Total	23	138	20,380	28	206	27,195	33	252	34,086	37	292	35,062

Source: Klee 1997, 2001, 2004, 2007.

South Africa has been liberalizing its domestic market for several years, but with its flag carrier, South African Airways, still not privatized, implementation of the liberalization policy remains incomplete. The number of South African carriers increased from 8 in 1997 to 16 in 2001, and to 20 in 2004, dropping slightly to 19 in 2007. The number of passenger aircraft with more than 30 seats doubled from 1997 to 2001, reaching 220 in 2007. Seat capacity also doubled from 1997 to 2004, but had stabilized by 2007.

Other important South African carriers include the following:

- Comair and Nationwide, both of which operate domestic trunk routes and a few short- to medium-haul international destinations. Comair operates under two different brands: regular services are flown under a franchise agreement with British Airways and "low-cost" operations are flown as Kulula.com.
- South African Express and South African Airlink are both equipped with 50-seater aircraft and operate feeder services to smaller South African towns and neighboring countries (Lesotho and Swaziland) under franchise agreements with South African Airways.

In recent years, the industry has modernized its fleets by replacing aging Boeing 737-200s with newer versions (table 5.16). However, the figures shown in the table are not by themselves sufficient to provide a

Table 5.16 Fleet Evolution of Major South African Carriers, Selected Years
(number)

Carrier	Aircraft types	1997	2001	2004	2007
Comair	B-727 and 737-200	8	15	10	6
	MD-80 series	0	0	6	6
	B-737 newer versions	0	0	4	12
Nationwide	B-727 and 737-200	1	7	14	16
	B-737 newer versions	0	0	1	2
	BAC111	12	11	0	0
South African Airlink	F-28	0	0	1	0
	EMB-135	0	0	0	5
	Bae-146	0	0	0	3
South African Airways	B-727 and 737-200	1	1	11	0
	B-737 newer versions	0	11	21	21
	A-320 and 319	7	5	4	11
	A-300	7	3	3	3
South African Express	DHC-8	0	7	7	9
	CRJ	0	6	6	9

Source: Klee 1997, 2001, 2004, 2007.

clear picture of South Africa's aircraft fleet given the extent of modernization and the creation of small, new carriers.

Botswana's fleet experienced steady growth, with just one carrier operating aircraft with more than 30 seats, but with the number of aircraft and overall seat capacity growing. Namibia's fleet has fluctuated. The number of operators and aircraft remained stable, but capacities were halved before timid growth resumed. This was partly due to Air Namibia's difficulties in sustaining its long-haul operations in the face of aggressive competition from South African Airways, which was using low-fare connections based on sixth freedom rights via its Johannesburg hub to a much wider range of long-haul and medium-haul destinations than Air Namibia could achieve.

Malawi, Mozambique, Zambia, and Zimbabwe faced the same problem. In Zambia, the flag carrier, Zambia Airways, was liquidated in 1994. In Zimbabwe, Air Zimbabwe's capacity stabilized after a significant drop from 1997 to 2001. Linhas Aereas de Mozambique, the national carrier of Mozambique, experienced a continued drop in unit capacities, reflecting limited liberalization of the domestic market and the difficulties of competing on long-haul routes, as the South African Airways hub in Johannesburg is increasingly capturing its international traffic. The Mozambican authorities have tried to limit this competition by imposing a cap on frequencies and capacities on the Johannesburg–Maputo route. This attempt has been challenged by competitors wanting to enter the market based on the liberalization of third and fourth freedoms by the Yamoussoukro Decision.

Malawi's flag carrier seems to be able to maintain a niche market strategy, capturing a substantial proportion of the passengers traveling to and from the small country. The situation is similar for Lesotho, which is also a small and landlocked country with limited traffic potential, but the only flag carrier went of business, partly because of competition from South African carriers and partly because of competition from cheaper transportation services offered by bus operators on the routes to Bloemfontein (200 km) and Johannesburg (500 km). Swaziland's national airline has also not been successful in competing with South African carriers. Nevertheless, the country's registry lists several aircraft, some of which are flag-of-convenience registrations. The reduction of aircraft in the registry from 2004 to 2007 was a consequence of international pressure to reduce flag of convenience registrations.

Overall, the southern African region provides little evidence of an impact from the liberalization of air services. The SADC countries remain dominated by the South African flag carrier, and as a consequence, fifth freedom operations from both the SADC and from other RECs have declined steeply. However, some of the SADC states are also members of COMESA and there are some indications that these states have benefited in a few isolated cases from fifth freedom flights to other COMESA states that were requested on the basis of the Yamoussoukro Decision (see the case of Malawi, which requested several fifth freedom operations that were mostly refused [Bofinger 2007b, p. 15]).

Development in Indian Ocean Island Countries

The Indian Ocean island countries depend heavily on air transportation for both domestic and international destinations. Of the four countries in this group, two belong to COMESA (the Comoros and the Seychelles) and two belong to both COMESA and SADC (Madagascar and Mauritius). However, only the Comoros and the Seychelles are parties to the Yamoussoukro Decision, while Madagascar is not and the case of Mauritius remains unclear (see appendix B).

Only one carrier was listed for the Comoros in 1997 and none was listed for the subsequent years (table 5.17). Nevertheless, the country operates a national carrier with two aircraft that are not registered in the Comoros. In the Seychelles, the number of aircraft registered rose and then dropped, while capacities dropped from 2004 to 2007 following a peak accounted for by the registration of a carrier based abroad.

Mauritius represented two-thirds of seat capacity in 1997, but its relative share then declined even though its total seat capacity grew slowly during the period, but at a slower pace than total traffic, reflecting a loss of market share by Mauritius. However, the upward trend in unit capacity reflects Air Mauritius' developing of its long-haul services, as well as its difficulties in diversifying its markets at the regional level. A recent reform of air transport policy has ended Air Mauritius' monopoly by allowing the entry of the new carrier Catovair, but its operations remain limited, concentrating on services between the mainland of Mauritius and the outer island of Rodrigues (Bernard Krief Consultants 2008, p. 4).

Madagascar's aviation capacity doubled between 1997 and 2001, but then dropped. The number of medium-haul aircraft remained steady, but newer models replaced aging ones. The long-haul fleet was increased from one Boeing 747 to two Boeing 767-300ER aircraft to help meet the objective of opening new routes and increasing the frequency of services on existing ones. Similar to other African countries, reformed policies have liberalized domestic market entry, and a second carrier was

Table 5.17 Fleet Analysis, Indian Ocean Island Countries, Selected Years
(number)

	1997		2001			2004			2007		
Country	Carriers	Aircraft	Available seats	Carriers	Aircraft	Available seats	Carriers	Aircraft	Available seats	Carriers	Aircraft	Available seats
Comores	1	1	44	0	0	0	0	0	0	0	0	0
Madagascar	2	7	788	1	12	1,642	2	11	1,341	2	10	1,074
Mauritius	1	11	1,996	1	12	2,216	1	12	2,222	2	12	2,463
Seychelles	1	2	454	1	3	696	2	8	1,311	1	4	564
Total	5	21	3,282	3	27	4,554	5	31	4,874	5	26	4,101

Source: Klee 1997, 2001, 2004, 2007.

established with a limited fleet operating on domestic routes (Bernard Krief Consultants 2008, p. 4).

The analysis of the region's air transport industry would be incomplete without mention of La Réunion Island, a French territory. The local carrier, Air Austral, which flies two Boeing 737-300/500 and one ATR72-500 aircraft on regional routes, has recently added three Boeing 777-200s to its fleet to operate its new routes to France and Southeast Asia.

Conclusions

The general move toward liberalizing air services in Africa resulted from the following three different set of causes:

- worldwide trend toward liberalization that had a strong impact on African carriers' long-haul operations, especially through increased competition that resulted in lower fares, as well as their past business model, which consisted of cross-subsidizing domestic and regional services with profits made on intercontinental traffic;
- domestic liberalization policies that caused the end of domestic monopolies, and in some cases the disappearance of state ownership of flag carriers, and the arrival of new entrants on domestic markets, mostly privately owned, that began competing with legacy carriers for international routes;
- continent-wide liberalization of intra-African air services promoted by the Yamoussoukro Decision and already implemented by some RECs.

The first two causes of liberalization produced strong and conspicuous impacts during 2001–04, in particular, the collapse of some major legacy carriers, demonstrable by significant drops in seat capacities and the supply of air services. However, the impact of the Yamoussoukro Decision only became sizable during 2004–07. The most remarkable impacts of the Yamoussoukro Decision on the African air transport sector during this period were

- the relative strengthening of a limited number of stronger African carriers, such as Ethiopian Airlines and Kenya Airways, that reaped the benefits of their comparative advantages in terms of geographical location; financial, commercial and managerial strength; and access to intercontinental markets;

- the marginalization of many already weak carriers, some of which ultimately disappeared, for instance, Air Tanzania, Nigerian Airways, and Cameroon Airlines;
- the consolidation of networks through the phasing out of a number of low-density routes and growth of routes to and from the main hubs, most significant in East Africa;
- the development of fifth freedom traffic, especially in regions and country pairs that lacked strong local carriers, often offered by dominant carriers at marginal cost, effectively resulting in pressure on regional fares, which is forcing locally-based third and fourth freedom carriers to accept lower fares;
- the significant development of sixth freedom traffic, fostered by the liberalization of third and fourth freedom capacities within Africa, and in some cases with intercontinental counterpart countries.

With respect to the last point, some of the sixth freedom services are increasingly competing with point-to-point intercontinental traffic, especially on West African routes to and from Europe and over certain hubs in East Africa. These carriers, which appear to be the main beneficiaries of the ongoing liberalization, are mostly based in North and East Africa and are likely to emerge as key actors in relation to the future consolidation of Africa's air transport industry.

On a regional basis, only West and Central Africa have fully achieved the liberalization of air services in terms of policy implementation. While these regions experienced a high turnover of carriers, they also felt the largest impact in terms of fifth freedom flights. Nevertheless, while a high percentage of these fifth freedom flights are of carriers registered in the RECs of West and Central Africa (WAEMU and CEMAC), African carriers of other RECs also account for a significant number of fifth freedom flights. As no strong regional carrier has emerged in West or Central Africa, the question of whether regional liberalization or continent-wide liberalization will ultimately shape the market in West and Central Africa remains open.

Regions that have not implemented the Yamoussoukro Decision, such as North and southern Africa, would generally benefit from the decision. However, some countries, such as South Africa, are facing strong, continued resistance by neighboring states with weak carriers. Nevertheless, the examples of several North African carriers that have begun expanding their route networks into Sub-Saharan Africa are inspiring continent-wide liberalization.

The most inspiring development is the progress in East Africa, where a few operators have aggressively expanded their air services into other regions of Africa. Both Ethiopian Airlines and Kenya Airways are good examples of how to replace the capacity of failed operators, often found in smaller, unviable markets. However, the final steps to liberalize East Africa's regional market must still be taken.

Notes

1. International publicly listed airlines have become increasingly transparent by generally disclosing a set of data that includes number of passengers transported, available seat-kilometers, revenue passenger-kilometers, passenger load factor, amount of freight transported, cargo load factor, available cargo-ton-kilometers, revenue cargo-ton-kilometers, total revenue ton-kilometers, overall load factor, and number of flights flown in a given year (see, for example, Deutsche Lufthansa AG 2007, p. 46).

2. On-flight origin and destination data show, on an aggregate basis, the number of passengers and tons of freight and mail carried between all international city pairs on scheduled services. Traffic data by flight stage indicates traffic on board aircraft on flight stages of international scheduled services. The data are classified by international flight stage for each air carrier and aircraft type used and by the number of flights operated, the aircraft capacity offered, and the traffic (passengers, freight, and mail) carried. These data are provided to contracting states and are publicly available at http://icaodata.com/Trial/WhatIsICAO.aspx.

3. One of those included in the group of new entrants is privately-owned Regional Air Lines, which actually already existed in 1997 and 2001, but was not yet operating aircraft with more than 30 seats, which is why it is not listed in table 5.10 for those years.

4. On 32 March 2006, the government of Tanzania declared that it would dispose of Air Tanzania following four years of losses amounting to TZS 24.7 billion. The director-general of Tanzania's Civil Aviation Authority stated that Air Tanzania was in worse shape than before the involvement of South African Airways. Meanwhile South African Airways blamed the Tanzanian government for not releasing about US$ 30 million that were needed to implement Air Tanzania's restructuring and to stop continued losses. On 7 September 2006, the government of Tanzania bought back the 49 percent stake for US$ 1 million (*East African Business Week* 2009).

CHAPTER 6

Economic Aspects of Liberalizing Air Services in Africa

Africa is a large continent of about 30.37 million square km and a population of about 900 million (World Bank 2007, p. 42). However, while it is three times larger than Europe, its population density is low. Africa only has 33 people per square kilometer, compared with 128 in Europe and 307 in South Asia, and Africa's figure is about 30 percent below the world average of 50 people per square kilometer (World Bank 2007, p. 42). In addition, a much lower percentage of Africa's population is urban than in many other parts of the world, for example, in 2005 only 35 percent of Africa's population was urban, compared with a world average of 49 percent (World Bank 2007, p. 164). Africa also has the greatest share of people living in poverty: about 41 percent of Africa's population lives on less than US$1 a day compared with 32 percent in South Asia and almost 10 percent in China (World Bank 2007, p. 63). Economic development to reduce poverty must therefore be considered one of the key priorities for the African continent.

A review of economic indicators for Sub-Saharan Africa reveals that Africa's overall gross domestic product (GDP) has one of the highest percentages of merchandise trade and trade in services: in 2005, merchandise trade accounted for 57.8 percent of Sub-Saharan Africa's GDP, compared with a world average of 47.3 percent, and trade in services accounted for 13.1 percent of GDP, compared with a world average of 11 percent (World Bank 2007, p. 318). A large part of trade in Africa is undertaken at the local level. However, expanding economies aim at developing new markets, first at the regional level and then on a continent-wide basis. In addition, an increase in local trade depends on imports of goods, or at least of raw materials for production. For Africa, as for many other emerging regions, the transportation of goods and people is becoming an increasingly important element of economic development. This has been confirmed, especially in the case of Africa. A recent study showed that trade in Africa was highly sensitive to transportation costs: a 10 percent reduction in transport costs would increase trade by 25 percent (Gwilliam 2007, p. 39).

Africa's road infrastructure is for the most part less developed than in any other region of the world. A World Bank study (Gwilliam 2007, p. 5) shows that African countries have lower levels of paved roads per capita, per square kilometer, and per GDP per capita than any other low-income countries. Another study (Gwet and Rizet 1998, p. 80) reveals that transport costs in Africa are far higher than in other regions. For instance, for distances of up to 300 km the unit cost of road transport is 40 to 100 percent higher in Africa than in Southeast Asia. In addition, the fixed costs of trucking in Africa are low, while the variable costs are extremely high, which is different from most other regions. Given the less developed road network and bearing in mind that reduced transportation costs would stimulate trade, the pertinent question is what role air transportation plays in economic development in Africa. To address this issue we need to review the benefits generated by the liberalization of air transportation and to ask whether liberalizing air services is indeed one of the key issues for economic development in Africa.

Economic Benefits of the Air Transport Sector

Direct, Indirect, and Induced Effects

Commercial air transportation started as early as during World War I, when bomber aircraft begun transporting passengers or goods. For example, in the United States, regular passenger service across Tampa Bay started in 1914, and in the United Kingdom, regular service across the English Channel commenced in 1919 (Thomas and Smith 2003, p. 8). However, in its early days, the public viewed air transport as a risky endeavor both with respect to safety and economic stability, and because of its high cost was reserved for a very few affluent passengers. Nevertheless, several air carriers were created between World Wars I and II, some of which still exist today such as American Airlines, Lufthansa, Air France, and South African Airways. Commercial air transportation of passengers and goods experienced increased growth after World War II because of the huge inventory of transport aircraft that had been built and operated during the war. In addition, the technology gained by building large bombers during the war strongly benefited the development of more efficient passenger and cargo airplanes. For example, the first aircraft with cabin pressurization (though restricted to crew areas) was the B-29 Superfortress, a bomber developed by Boeing.

Nevertheless, for many decades air transportation remained expensive. Expense then began to decline, especially when jets became widely used during the late 1960. For example, in 1940, passenger fares in cents per mile (expressed in 1978 cents) were 25 cents on the widespread DC-3 aircraft (Thomas and Smith 2003, p. 177). The fare halved to 12.14 cents per mile in the mid-1960s, when jet aircraft were introduced. Another decline to 6.37 cents per mile was achieved in the early 1990s with the introduction of more fuel-efficient aircraft, and the new Airbus A380 allows an estimated passenger fare of about 3 cents per mile. An illustrative example is the cost of flying from Sydney to London expressed in average weekly earnings in the United Kingdom (per capita, 2005). In 1945, the fare would have been the equivalent of 130 weeks' pay. By 1965, the cost had declined to the equivalent of 22 weeks' pay, and the current fare is equivalent to about 2 weeks' pay (Thomas and Smith 2003, p. 181). This example illustrates that the cost of commercial air transportation has reached a level that is affordable for a wide range of passengers and goods.

With the decline in airfares came rapid growth of the air transport sector. The introduction of jet aircraft resulted in worldwide passenger traffic nearly tripling in the 1960s and early 1970s, doubling in the 1980s, and growing at around 50 percent per decade in recent decades (Thomas and Smith 2003, p. 222). This rapid growth developed the global air transport sector into a major industry with a significant economic impact. The air transport industry consists of an aviation sector and a civil aerospace sector. The aviation sector includes airlines (passengers, cargo, general aviation), airports and related services (civil airports, handling and catering, freight services, aircraft maintenance, fueling, retail), and providers of air navigation services. The civil aerospace sector develops and manufactures airframes, engines, and equipment and performs off-site maintenance.

The air transport industry generates about 5 million direct jobs globally (airlines employ 4.3 million people and the civil aerospace sector about 730,000) (Oxford Economic Forecasting 2005, p. 6). Its contribution to the global economy was around US$275 billion in 2004, similar to that of the pharmaceutical sector. The air transport sector has an even greater indirect and induced effect with respect to the industry's supply chain, which includes suppliers (for example, off-site suppliers of fuel, food and beverages, and construction services), manufacturing (for instance, computers and retail), and business services (such as call centers, accountants, lawyers, and financial services). The induced effect is generated by the spending of direct and indirect employees on such items as food and beverages, recreation, transport, clothing, and household goods (Oxford Economic Forecasting 2005, p. 5). Oxford Economic Forecasting (2005, p. 6) estimates that the indirect impact of the sector in 2004 represented 5.8 million jobs, with a global contribution to GDP of US$375 billion. The induced effect of the air transport sector generated another 2.7 million jobs and contributed US$175 billion to global GDP (Oxford Economic Forecasting 2005, p. 6). Overall, in 2004, the air transport sector was a global industry with about 13.5 million jobs that accounted for well over US$ 800 billion of global GDP.

Effects on Other Industries

In addition to its direct, indirect, and induced effects, air transportation also generates a significant catalytic effect that is the most important economic contribution of air transportation. This catalytic effect is the impact of air transportation on the performance and growth of a range of other industries, for example, international trade. Air cargo has become a key element of efficient, on-time delivery of many manufactured goods as well as a large range of perishables. Estimates indicate that about 40 percent of the value of all interregional trade is transported by air (Oxford Economic Forecasting 2005, p. 15). This translates on a global scale to 25 percent of the value of all goods being transported by air, which corresponded in 2004 to a value of about US$1.75 trillion. Some developing countries have specialized in manufacturing high-value goods such as electronic components for the computer industry. These countries can only participate in the global trade of these products if they have access to a reliable and cost-effective transportation network. As many high-value computer components are time sensitive because of the successive development of newer versions of such products, air transportation is the often the most cost- and time-effective mode of transportation.

A good example is the Malaysian electronics export industry, which is dominated by semiconductor manufacturing and computer component production for major computer manufacturers such as NEC and DELL. The factors influencing a manufacturer to use air cargo are the degree to which production has been internationalized, the nature of the good produced, the importance of speed in a supply and distribution chain, and the degree of liberty of decision making on the part of the manufacturer in the production network. Air transportation has become the prime mode of transportation in the case of the production of high-value electronic components with the aforementioned factors playing a dominant role (Leinbach and Bowen 2004, p. 301).

The role of trade in economic development is another important element to examine when reviewing the economic aspects of liberalizing air services in Africa. In an extensive cross-country analysis involving all African, European, and Latin American countries and many Asian countries (a total of 150 countries), Frankel and Romer (1999, p. 394) conclude that a one percentage point increase in the trade share of a given country's GDP increases per capita income by 2 percent. Several subsequent studies confirm the effect of trade on per capita income, even though more recent research estimates that a one percentage point increase in trade share increases per capita income by only 0.48 percent, which is still significant (Aradhyula, Rahman, and Seeivasan 2007, p. 25). One of the key elements of trade is transport. The development of trade, which leads to economic development, is only possible if the transport services used to ship the traded goods grow along with the growth in trade volume. Several studies conclude that high transport costs pose a barrier to trade that is at least of the same, if not a higher, magnitude than tariffs (see, for example, Feige 2007, p. 31). Low transport costs and the absence of trade barriers are commonly seen as the two most important ingredients for developing trade. As Feige (2007, p. 29) puts it, low transport costs are a "necessary but not a sufficient condition," indicating that efficient transportation is the basic element of trade, next to low tariffs.

Air transportation has become the mode of choice of many time-sensitive and high-value internationally traded goods as well as a powerful tool for the implementation of just-on-time procurement and production strategies. In addition to manufactured goods, perishables are also becoming increasingly dependent on a well-functioning air transport sector. Many developing countries have built a solid export industry trading agricultural products, including cut flowers, exotic fruits, seafood, and meat, on a global scale. One of the prime examples of a strong perishables export industry is Kenya's cut flower exports to the EU. Over the past 40 years, Kenya has become the largest cut flower producer and exporter to the European market, maintaining a solid market share of 31 percent (Bofinger 2007a, p. 10). Since the industry's inception, the global distribution of Kenya's perishable goods has depended on air transportation. Even though Kenya's national air carrier does not have any dedicated freighter aircraft the airline transports about 90 percent of the country's air cargo exports in the cargo holds of regular passenger aircraft with destinations in the Netherlands and the United Kingdom. Only a small part of overall exports is transported on dedicated cargo aircraft (Bofinger 2007a, p. 11). This underscores the importance of passenger air services for air cargo, especially for countries that do not possess a large air cargo fleet or whose volume of cargo business is too small to support dedicated cargo operations.

Another illustrative example of perishables is the export of fresh fish and other seafood products. Traditionally, countries with shorelines have developed a fishing industry, providing opportunities for export. However, such countries have often developed their fishing industry over centuries and have well-established local distribution networks. Some nations have organized and managed fisheries exports by traditional means, such as transportation by sea or processing offshore and freight forwarding by land, while others have assigned fishing rights to foreign operators. Mauritania is an example of a developing country whose fishing industry remains dominated by foreign operators that control the sector's exports: estimates indicate that Mauritanian vessels account for only 2 to 3 percent of the total maritime catch. In some cases, foreign vessels have maintained some colonial fishing rights (for example, Spain), while others operate without any formal agreement with the state (Gibbs 1984, p. 81).

Air transportation has created a new export market for some landlocked countries and for countries with access to large freshwater reservoirs. The production of freshwater fish, such as West Nile perch or tilapia, has become a lucrative export sector for a few developing countries. A good example is Tanzania, where the West Nile perch was artificially introduced into Lake Victoria in the 1950s and 1960s. The processing and export industry that arose as a result created an export market of about US$122 million by 2005 (UNCTAD and WTO 2008). The center for Tanzanian fishing operations and processing is the city of

Mwanza. According to the City Council of Mwanza, the fishing industry of Lake Victoria has created direct employment for more than 8,000 local processing workers and 300,000 indirect jobs. About 52,000 Tanzanian fishermen benefit directly from the West Nile perch (Bofinger 2007a, p. 19). The key logistics element for the timely export of the processed fish is air transportation. Mwanza has an airport with a 3,300-meter long runway and two nonprecision instrument approach procedures. This allows the use of medium-sized cargo aircraft that can transport the fish directly to destinations in Europe for distribution. About 400,000 kilograms of fish pass through the Mwanza airport each month. The declared value of the product is US$3.20 per kilogram and the estimated overall cost of transport to the final destination as value added to the product is about US$1 per kilogram (Bofinger 2007a, p. 20).

The industry for which air transportation has become indispensable is tourism. The tourism industry is probably the largest sector overall if all related services and activities are included. On a worldwide scale, tourism generated US$7 trillion of economic activity (total demand) in 2007 (World Travel and Tourism Council 2007, p. 6). The demand for tourism activity is expected to grow to US$13.2 trillion by 2017. In 2007, tourism accounted for US$1.85 trillion, or 3.6 percent, of global GDP (World Travel and Tourism Council 2007, p. 11). The world's tourism and travel industry directly employed more than 76 million people in 2007, or 2.7 percent of global employment. This global direct employment is expected to grow to more than 87 million jobs by 2017 (World Travel and Tourism Council 2007, p. 12).

With regard to air transportation, a growing proportion of international tourists are traveling to and from their destinations by air. In 2002, more than 45 percent of all international tourists arrived by air, compared with only 35 percent in 1990 (ICAO 2004a, pp. 1–3). The direct effect of spending generated by tourists arriving via air transport was the creation of an estimated 6.7 million jobs in 2004, of which about 675,000 were in Africa (Oxford Economic Forecasting 2005, p. 19). An additional 5.7 million indirect jobs from industries that support the tourism industry were created globally as a result of air travel by tourists. Finally, the induced effect of tourism-related air transportation has generated 3.1 million jobs (Oxford Economic Forecasting 2005, p. 18). The total job creation effect (direct, indirect, and induced) of tourism related air travel is estimated at 15.5 million jobs, which generates an estimated US$300 billion of world GDP (ICAO 2004a, pp. 1–7). However, the importance of spending related to tourists traveling by air varies greatly from region to region. The largest impact of international tourism through the creation of jobs and increased prosperity is observed in several developing countries. For example, in North America, foreign visitors traveling by air only account for about 10 percent of overall tourism spending. By contrast, in Africa, more than 50 percent of tourism spending comes from visitors traveling by air (World Travel and Tourism Council 2007, p. 24). This explains why air transportation to and from developing countries has a proportionally higher economic impact than in the developed world.

Social Impact of Air Transportation
The social impact of air transportation is a significant factor that is quite easy to understand, but difficult to quantify with hard evidence. Air transportation is often the only practical mode of transportation, allowing the integration of remote populations of large countries. In that sense, air transportation plays an important role in shaping the global economy by facilitating the integration of new countries and regions into the global economy (Stevens 1997, p. 33). Travel and tourism are important elements of this international integration, which air transportation facilitates. The resulting increased understanding of different cultures and nationalities is necessary for opening up trade and movement of people, which are helping developing nations in their efforts to integrate into a global world (Air Transport Action Group 2005). Air transportation can even be seen as the key facilitator for creating multicultural societies by facilitating interaction and understanding between people of all races. Finally, a well-developed air transport infrastructure facilitates the delivery of emergency and humanitarian aid, including the timely delivery of medical supplies and organs for transplantation.

The provision of air services to remote areas of large and sparsely populated countries is one of the most significant social benefits of air transportation. A good example is Australia, where the government subsidizes regional air services to remote territories. The government of Australia considers support for air services a community service obligation. The prime argument is that people living in remote regions should have the same level of access to services that metropolitan communities provide and that they "should be able to engage with other Australians" (Standing Committee on Transport and Regional Services of the Parliament of Australia 2003, p. 29). However, developing countries often do not have the necessary funding to support regional air transportation to remote destinations, even though the social benefits are just as important as in developed nations. This is, for example, especially the case in relation to conflict resolution or avoidance, where ongoing interaction between the parties involved is widely recognized as one of the most important factors (Azar and Burton 1986). In Africa, for example, air transport is often the only means of transportation that can quickly support the integration of, and interaction with, remote populations. Thus, fostering social cohesion, facilitating access to services, and maintaining the viability of remote and rural communities are benefits that air services can provide. The provision of air services is therefore a government responsibility that needs to be reflected in public sector policies.

Potential Impact of Liberalizing of Air Transport Services

The current international air transport system has its roots in the Chicago Conference of 1944. The objective of this conference, held during the final stages of World War II, was to lay a liberal foundation that would have allowed all nations unrestricted operating rights up to the fifth freedom for international air traffic, to assure sustainable growth of the air transport industry (Dempsey and Gesell 2004, p. 751). However, several nations resisted this liberal strategy, which was proposed by the United States, because they felt that they would face a serious disadvantage given that their air transport fleets would not have sufficient capacity to compete. As a result, the Chicago Conference did not agree on the multilateral granting of all five freedoms or on market forces as determinants of capacities, frequencies, and fares for scheduled international air traffic. Instead, the conference resulted in the Chicago Convention, which reaffirmed the principle of exclusive sovereignty over each nation's airspace. The result was that international air traffic had to be agreed upon and regulated bilaterally between individual pairs of nations (Dempsey and Gesell 2004, p. 754). This led to numerous bilateral air service agreements, the first one being the so-called Bermuda agreement between the United States and the United Kingdom in 1946.

In 1978, the United States promulgated the Airline Deregulation Act, which called for gradual deregulation in order to create competition among domestic U.S. carriers. The move toward deregulation was driven by the notion that economic regulation of the airline industry had caused the high air fares, the misallocation of funds, the denial of price and service options to consumers, and the excess capacity in the industry. This criticism was voiced by Albert Kahn, who was nominated chair of the U.S. Civil Aeronautics Board in 1977 and who introduced several deregulatory initiates (Dempsey 1987, p. 24). Deregulation of the domestic U.S. air transport market led to intense competition among carriers. On the positive side, tariffs decreased and connectivity grew, mainly because of the newly established hub system. On the negative side, many older, less solid airlines collapsed and a fierce battle ensued between new entrants and established carriers. While lower fares and higher connectivity are often attributed to deregulation, some argue that deregulation actually increased (or reduced decreases in) fares, because as a direct result of deregulation routes became increasingly circuitous, service became poorer, and fewer carriers operated. For example, Dempsey (1990, p. 33) states that 10 years after deregulation, passengers were paying 2.6 percent more for air fares that they would given the observed decline in fares resulting from technology and market improvements prior to deregulation. He argues that the unprecedented level of competition among airlines resulted in the aging of the aircraft fleet, the disappearance of carriers, and a costly hub-and-spoke system that increased distances and time to final destinations. Occasionally, some suggest reregulating the U.S. airline market by noting that with the help of modern information technology, the regulatory tools of price regulation may be performed more efficiently than before deregulation in 1978 (Dempsey 2003, p. 12).

The EU undertook the first significant liberalization of international air services in 1992, when it created an open aviation area within the EU. The so-called Third Package of European Community regulations created a fully open and integrated air transport market for European carriers by removing all restrictions for airlines in relation to frequencies and destinations within the territory of the EU (both domestic and intra-EU international flights), provided that the carrier was majority owned and controlled by EU nationals. Similar open aviation areas were created between Australia and New Zealand, the Caribbean states, and some Latin American countries. However, according to IATA, only 17 percent of international air traffic is currently conducted in a deregulated environment and full liberalization to the eighth freedom has only been achieved within the EU (IATA 2007a, p. 16). IATA is calling for greater liberalization of the air transport sector, which should remove current constraints related to access, frequency, and capacity in existing bilateral air service agreements and constraints arising from ownership restrictions. IATA is also calling for more effective regulation of airports and air navigation service providers, because most of these entities enjoy a natural monopoly and economic regulation could improve efficiency and productivity (IATA 2007a, p. 18).

One approach that has been used to assess the potential economic impact of liberalizing air services was to analyze the effects of operational (for example, product market) and ownership (for example, capital market) liberalization in four different industries: (a) retail banking, (b) energy (gas and electricity), (c) telecommunications, and (d) media (OXERA 2006). Each industry has certain characteristics in common with the airline industry that were addressed when liberalizing these industries. For example, the EU and the United States experienced efforts to reduce regulation in the retail banking sector to allow the creation of a single market and remove restrictions on ownership and control. Similar liberalization occurred in the telecommunications and energy sectors, where markets were liberalized and ownership restrictions were lifted (OXERA 2006, p. 1). The OXERA (2006) study finds three sets of benefits of liberalization for consumers. First, liberalizing energy markets resulted in significantly lower prices. In EU countries, for example, electricity prices were 10 to 20 percent lower than before liberalization and gas prices were 35 percent lower. The effects on the telecommunications sectors of Japan and the Republic of Korea were even more significant: the cost of long-distance telephone calls fell by up to 50 percent. Second, liberalization of the media market has increased output and choices, as demonstrated in India and New Zealand, where television and radio broadcast services increased in quality and in the diversity of channels. Finally, a significant improvement of service quality resulted in the U.S. banking sector following the relaxation of interstate ownership restrictions (OXERA 2006, p. 23).

The study concludes that airline industry consumers could experience great benefits if the air transport markets were further liberalized in terms of access and ownership restrictions. The latter in particular is a key element of liberalization that would allow airlines to improve capacity utilization, for instance, by sharing optimal size aircraft; increase productivity, transfer best practices to associated carriers, and increase investment, including by foreign investors, which would result in improved profitability and market value of the firm. This, in turn, would allow better service at lower cost (OXERA 2006, p. 65). At the firm level, the strategic response in a liberalized industry is typically to focus on expansion into new markets (as occurred in the EU energy market), diversification into new products (as occurred in the Indian media market), specialization in niche products (as occurred in the U.S. banking sector), or market exit in response to stronger competition (as occurred in the German television sector) (OXERA 2006, p. 68). For airlines, the increased flexibility of strategic choices that come with liberalization is important in both a developed competitive environment, such as the U.S. domestic market, and in a less developed market that has not yet reached maturity. The latter is highly relevant in Africa, where air transport sector remains underdeveloped in many regions.

Intervistas (2006) on behalf of IATA, carried out one of the most detailed recent research projects on the impact of liberalization of air services. Intervistas developed a mathematical model of air service liberalization that dealt with a variety of regulatory changes affecting numerous nation pairs and airlines. The model's overall objective was to estimate the effect of liberalizing air services on passenger traffic, air freight movements, employment, GDP, and tourism and the resulting catalytic effects for any country pair (Intervistas 2006, p. 9). The methodology applied in the research included two methods. First, in the time series or case history method, five representative country pairs with multiple destinations were selected: (a) the United States and the United Kingdom, (b) the intra–European Community market, (c) the United Arab Emirates and the United Kingdom and Germany, (d) Malaysia and Thailand, and (e) Australia and New Zealand (Intervistas 2006, p. 20). The study analyzed traffic and economic data and socioeconomic indicators by running various regressions on time series before and after a specific liberalization event.

The second method was the cross-sectional approach, which involved analyzing more than 1,400 country pair aviation relationships at the same point in time (more than 40,000 country pairs could have been included, but relevant and accurate data could only be obtained for about 1,400 pairs) (Intervistas 2006, p. 62). The analysis of these country pairs had to be based on the assumption that a particular relationship between traffic, the extent of liberalization, and socioeconomic conditions applied to every market. The data sample was also individually (per country pair) adjusted for variations in economic activity and other extraneous factors. Intervistas is confident that the large size of the sample as well as its inclusion of all regions of the world yielded an accurate estimate of the impact of liberalization for any arbitrary country pair (Intervistas 2006, p. 61).

The overall conclusion of the Intervistas research was as follows: "This study found extensive and significant evidence that supports the generally accepted 'conventional wisdom' that liberalization of air services between countries generates significant additional opportunities for consumers, shippers, and the numerous direct and indirect entities and individuals affected by such liberalization. Conversely, it is also evident that restrictive bilateral air service agreements between countries stifle air travel, tourism and business, and, consequently, economic growth and job creation" (Intervistas 2006, p. ES-2).

The specific findings of the research include the following:

- The traffic growth after liberalizing air service agreements between countries typically averages 12 to 35 percent, but in several cases has exceeded 50 percent and even 100 percent.
- A simulation run on 320 country pairs that were not liberalized at the time of the study resulted in an estimated potential traffic growth of 63 percent, which is significantly higher than the typical world traffic growth of 6 to 8 percent. The simulation further revealed that liberalization of these 320 bilateral relationships alone could create 24.1 million full-time jobs and generate an additional US$490 billion of GDP, which at the time of the study was almost equivalent to the economy of Brazil.
- The growth rate in the EU nearly doubled from 1990–94 to 1995–2000 following the creation of the single European aviation market in 1993. This alone produced about 1.4 million new jobs.
- The full liberalization of the aviation market between the United States and the United Kingdom would result in an estimated traffic increase of 29 percent, because of lower fares and multiple new destinations in the United States serving London directly. The expected economic impact would be the creation of 117,000 new jobs and an incremental increase in GDP of US$7.8 billion.

The Brattle Group (2002) researched the potential economic impact of an open skies agreement between the EU and the United Sates in a study for the European Commission. The methodology to assess the impact of liberalization on restricted trans-Atlantic routes was based on a regression analysis that estimated changes in the volume of passengers changes based on observations following prior liberalization of certain routes between Europe and the United States, such as the open skies agreement between the Netherlands and the United States. The regression analysis also determined the relationship between passenger volumes and relevant economic factors using data from the period prior to specific open skies agreements, which created the necessary baseline for the entire European aviation area (Brattle Group 2002, p. A21). The assumption of an open EU–United States aviation area would remove a set of market restrictions that would result in

- no restrictions on ownership and control of U.S. airlines by European investors, including European airlines, and no restrictions on ownership and control of European airlines by U.S. investors, including U.S. airlines;

- EU investors or airlines having the right of establishment in the United States and U.S. investors or airlines having the right of establishment in the EU;
- EU and U.S. carriers enjoying up to full fifth and seventh freedom rights, as well as cabotage (based on foreign ownership of a domestic operator), and wet lease operations.[1]

The study concluded that the creation of an open EU-U.S. aviation area would increase trans-Atlantic travel by 4.1 million to 11 million passengers per year, which represented an increase of 9 to 13 percent. The resulting increase on intra-EU routes would result in an additional 13.6 million to 35.7 million passengers, an increase of 5 to 14 percent (Brattle Group 2002, p. 6-1). The liberalization would also create about US$5.2 billion of consumer benefits per year as a result of lower fares and increased travel. The overall estimated increase in economic output of directly related industries was US$3.6 billion to US$8.1 billion per year. Finally, the estimated direct effect on employment ranged from 2,800 to 9,000 new jobs in the EU and 2,000 to 7,300 new jobs in the United States, representing a 1 to 3 percent increase in aviation employment in the EU and the United States (Brattle Group 2002, p. 6-4).

In 2007, the European Commission mandated a new study to update the findings of the 2002 report (Booz Allen Hamilton 2007). The analysis used updated parameters and a revised baseline, with changes such as including the countries of the European Free Trade Association and the new EU member states (Booz Allen Hamilton 2007, table 37). The conclusions of the study included the following:

- The number of traveling passengers would increase for five years following the signing of an open skies agreement. During that period, the liberalization would generate an additional 26 million passengers, an estimated increase in growth of 6.4 percent. At the end of the five-year period, the air transport market between the United States and the EU would be 34 percent larger than it would have been without the open aviation area (Booz Allen Hamilton 2007, p. 159).

- The air cargo market would also experience strong growth following the establishment of the open aviation area. Based on the assumption that the average air cargo per enplaned passenger on combination carriers (cargo transported in the belly of passenger planes) of 38 kilograms remains constant, the study estimated that the volume of cargo would increase from 67,000 to 105,000 tons in 2006 and from 371,000 to 423,000 tons by 2010 (Booz Allen Hamilton 2007, p. 75). However, the liberalization of air services between the United States and the EU would also affect cargo freighter operations even though passenger flights handle most intercontinental cargo traffic. The study found that integrated carriers would benefit because they could improve and optimize their flight networks based on economics rather than on agreed traffic rights.[2] The study estimated that this impact would generate from 1,600 to 3,300 direct and 4,500 to 8,900 indirect jobs. The study estimated a smaller impact—because of the relatively small size of the market—for all-cargo carriers of about 140 direct and 411 indirect new jobs (Booz Allen Hamilton 2007, p. 75).

- Liberalizing air transportation between the United States and the EU will greatly stimulate trade in services and merchandise. In 2005, overall trade between the United States and the EU amounted to US$880 billion, of which 71 percent resulted from merchandise trade and 29 percent from trade in services (Booz Allen Hamilton 2007, table 31). Even though air carriers were handling a relatively low share of import and export shipments in terms of weight, they transported about half of all goods exchanged between the United States and the EU in terms of value. Of the all the services traded between the two markets, 25 percent were essentially dependent on airline services (Booz Allen Hamilton 2007, p. 137). Given the importance of air transportation in the trade of services and merchandise, an increase in passenger and cargo traffic expected to result from the open aviation area will substantially promote trade and act as an economic stimulus on both markets.

Overall, the expected economic benefits of the open aviation area would be the result of three main effects: (a) additional GDP generated by increased demand for passenger and cargo air transportation, (b) increased employment in the air transportation sector and related industries, and (c) higher purchasing power for air transportation by existing and new consumers as a direct result of price reductions (Booz Allen Hamilton 2007, p. 143). The report argues that these effects are primarily generated by the removal of output constraints, such as regulatory restrictions on capacity, frequency, and designation (for example, which airlines may operate in a given market). The removal of such constraints would allow new entrants to serve formerly restricted markets and to compete on the basis of price and/or improved service (for instance, higher frequencies).

Additional cost reductions will result from closer airline relationships ranging from code sharing operations to mergers and acquisitions that will become necessary in a more competitive environment. Finally, the economic benefits of opening the aviation market would include the multiplier effects generated by additional air travel and cargo transportation for a wide range of economic activities (Booz Allen Hamilton 2007, p. 144).

In another recent paper, Micco and Serebrisky (2006, p. 45) conclude that signing an open skies agreement generally reduces air transport costs by 9 percent and increases the share of imports arriving by air by 7 percent. The paper further estimates that open skies agreements could increase trade by 12 percent. However, there are major differences between developed and developing countries. In developed and upper-middle-income countries, air freight rates declined 6.8 percent within three years of the signing of an open skies agreement, but in developing countries this reduction effect has been less than 1 percent (Micco and Serebrisky 2006, p. 40). The authors conclude that the weak effect in low-income developing countries is due to the limited market size and the existence of other barriers to competition that prevent market participants from taking advantage of an open skies regime.

While many experts have recognized that lower airfares and higher productivity of airlines are the key benefits of the liberalization of air transport, others criticize liberalization from several different viewpoints. From the sociopolitical viewpoint, fears exist that a global (or pan-African) push for liberalizing air transport might create asymmetrical pressure on certain states, especially those at a low level of development. The result could be that carriers of the latter countries would be less prepared to adjust their strategies and to make the necessary investments to respond to rising competitive pressures, which require a new business model. Governments tend to raise sovereignty as the key issue when defending their resistance to pressures to liberalize international air services, but in fact the authorities may be simply defending their political standpoint (for example, their view that public opinion favors protecting a national carrier) or may even be shielding relatives or friends who operate national airlines from competition rather than addressing the economic costs of maintaining and often subsidizing noncompetitive domestic carriers.

Nevertheless, Flouris (2003, p. 21) concludes that even if the economic costs of resisting liberalization clearly surpass the political costs, political considerations generally prevail and influence government policy. Governments fear the short-term political costs, which could result in social upheaval, labor action, and/or loss of political power. Politicians in smaller or less developed African nations that operate a dominant but noncompetitive state-owned carrier sometimes cite additional arguments, such as the national pride that comes with "carrying the flag," to resist the liberalization of air services or the privatization of the state carrier. This resistance motivates government officials to continue providing support and subsidies for their carrier, often at the economic costs of higher taxes or reduced government services. This is especially likely in less developed countries where governments have subsidized inefficient flag carriers for many years while providing insufficient support for the health, education, and/or nutrition sectors. A typical case is Cameroon, which supported its state-owned carrier, Cameroon Airlines, for decades. After years of pressure by international organizations to privatize the carrier to reduce the massive subsidies necessary to keep it operating, in 2007, the government finally had to commit to eliminating all budgetary subsidies (Inoni 2007). Soon after, the government had to initiate the process to liquidate the 36-year-old carrier.

According to Flouris (2003), the costs of economic intervention such as liberalizing markets may create public dissatisfaction during their initial stages, but eventually the measures will have positive effects and the political costs will gradually disappear. Flouris (2003, p. 22) concludes that resisting liberalization measures because of their short-term political costs is not a valid argument, given that the economic costs nearly always outweigh the political costs. This conclusion is especially plausible in poor countries, where often only a small minority of the population can afford to travel by air.

Economic Significance of Liberalizing African Air Transport Services

The reports and studies generally suggest that liberalization of air services results in lower costs, increased traffic, and improved efficiency for participating carriers, but most of the studies discussed focus on mature markets, where competition was ready to respond to the new opportunities that arose when certain restrictions were lifted. In terms of the continent's revenue passenger-kilometers, Africa currently has less than 1 percent of the global air service market despite having more than 12 percent of the world's population spread across the second largest continent after Asia (World Bank 2007). Thus, one of the key questions to evaluate is whether liberalization of the thin air traffic in Africa would have the same impact as in developed markets.

As outlined in chapter 5, air traffic grew the most in East and southern Africa, while development in West and Central Africa was much slower. Southern Africa is a good region to examine because of the existence of a variety of bilateral relationships, from extremely restricted to de facto liberalized, as well as cases of domestic liberalization, that provide evidence about the impact of liberalization on the market. One recent study of southern Africa's air transport markets examined the importance of liberalizing air services in the SADC region to stimulate shared economic growth within the region (Myburgh and others 2006).

The study found the following evidence of impact in specific cases (Myburgh and others 2006, pp. 16–19):

- The Nairobi–Johannesburg route was initially liberalized in 2000 by agreeing to multiple designations of carriers and increasing daily flights from 4 to 14. The route was then fully liberalized in 2003. Following liberalization, the effect was a 69-fold increase in passenger volumes.

- The domestic market in South Africa was liberalized in 1990 by allowing new carriers to enter and compete. This led to the establishment of domestic low-cost carriers in early 2000. The overall passenger market grew by 80 percent between 1994 and 2004. One remarkable observation was that traffic on certain routes to remote destinations experienced strong growth even though they served small, low-income communities.

- The liberalization of traffic to destinations in the Eastern Cape region of South Africa was followed not only by passenger growth (52 percent), but also by an increase in tourists (13 percent) because of the entry of a low-cost carrier serving the Eastern Cape in 2004. The increase of tourists is economically significant for this region given that it is one of the poorest provinces in South Africa.

- The Johannesburg–Lusaka route is one where South African Airways enjoyed high ticket prices because it was the only carrier on this route following the liquidation of Zambia Airways in 1995. However, in 2006, newly established Zambian Airways signed a wet lease agreement with the South African low-cost carrier Kulula that allowed Zambian Airways to serve the route on behalf of Zambia. The immediate effect was a 33 percent drop in airfares at the top end (the most expensive full-fare economy class tariff), a 38 percent drop at the bottom end (the least expensive fare), and a 38 percent increase in passengers. Estimates indicate that the outcome translates to an additional 6,300 tourist arrivals per year in Zambia, which has resulted in additional income of about US$8.9 million per year from tourism (Schlumberger 2007, p. 201).

- The case of Mozambique is an example of the protection of a national carrier resulting in high airfares, in effect hindering the development of tourism. Airfares between Johannesburg and Maputo, Mozambique, were 163 percent more expensive in 2006 than the fares for the same distance flown within South Africa (the example examined was Johannesburg–Darwin). While Mozambique has significant potential for tourism, including more than 2,500 km of undeveloped coastline with white beaches and many national parks, game reserves, and hunting areas, high airfares are negatively influencing international tourists who can find cheaper vacation packages in neighboring South Africa.

Based on the examined cases of the observed effects of liberalizing air services in the SADC region, Myburgh and others (2006, pp. 22–24) applied two econometric models to estimate the overall drop in prices and increase in passenger volumes that occurred in the southern Africa region. The result was then used as a basis for calculating tourism expenditures likely to occur as a result of further liberalization.

The first model, a volume analysis, estimated the impact of entering into a liberalized bilateral air service agreement that would result from the large, one-time increase in capacity under the new agreement. Using data from 16 countries in Africa, Asia, and Europe, the study found that the one-time increase in passenger volumes was 12 percent, which eventually led to a 23 percent overall increase in demand for air travel. A second model, a price analysis, examined how much prices of air travel fell once the market was liberalized. It analyzed price changes on 56 routes within SADC by running various regression analyses. The analyses concluded that air fares on liberalized routes declined by an average of 18 percent. In cases where a low-cost carrier entered the market, air fares were generally 40 percent lower than before liberalization. The overall conclusions of the study, taking the findings of the case studies into account and consolidating the results of all the regressions, was that full liberalization throughout the SADC region would increase passenger volumes by 20 percent.

For assessment of the overall potential economic impact that liberalization would have on the region, both the direct and the indirect economic impacts had to be evaluated. The direct impacts result from traveling passengers' expenditures on air fares, accommodation, and local travel. The indirect impacts are derived, for example, from manufacturing, construction, and additional government expenditures. The calculations demonstrated that liberalizing air services within the SADC region would result in a substantial increase in employment and economic activity throughout the region. The study estimated that more than 500,000 additional foreign tourists would arrive by air and would spend more than US$500 million. This spending, taking the multiplier effect on SADC's economy as a whole into account, would increase the region's GDP by about US$1.5 billion, which represents growth of 0.5 percent. In addition, 35,000 jobs in the tourism industry and an additional 35,000 jobs in the overall economy would be created.

The Myburgh and others (2006) study confirms that the conclusions drawn from studies of markets in other regions are also valid for Africa. Another study, which empirically measured the economic effects of progressive air transport liberalization of routes from 20 cities to and from Addis Ababa (effectively analyzing the African route network of Ethiopian Airlines), came to a similar conclusion (Abate 2007). The study found that more benefits can be unlocked in the form of improvements in service quality by abandoning the currently restrictive regulatory regimes in international bilateral air service agreements in Africa. These benefits are derived from a significant increase in departure frequencies. Moreover, there is no evidence that liberalization produced any damaging market dominance by a single carrier.

With regard to some critical considerations, such as Dempsey's (1990) conclusion that passengers are flying 2.6 percent more after deregulation, resulting in higher costs because of the concentration of carriers serving specific hubs, Africa must still be considered an underdeveloped continent, where in many cases inefficient state-owned carriers dominate routes and hinder development. The removal of these carriers and the opening of air traffic to destinations that were not served in the past would have a significant impact even on regions with less developed markets. This was demonstrated by the example of Ethiopian Airlines, which established a large intra-African network that even serviced remote destinations based on seventh freedom rights (see appendix A).

Conclusion

The liberalization of air services in Africa would, in general, have a major impact on the development of the air transport sector, leading to a significant economic impact on various other sectors. The air transport industry itself has a strong direct impact, as it typically employs a large range of personnel, from low-skilled laborers to highly specialized technicians. The industry further affects a wide field of commercial activities that directly (for example, catering) or indirectly (for instance, duty free shops in airports) depend on air transportation. Finally, the financial sector in poor countries typically depends only on a few activities that generate hard currency income. Air transportation provides several sources of hard currency income that can include airport and air traffic fees, fuel sales, maintenance of foreign aircraft, and tax revenues.

Given the large size of the African continent and its mostly low population density, air transportation also has the potential of further substituting for difficult and lengthy road travel by passengers and certain goods. This substitution has already resulted in increased trade, both on an intercontinental and a regional basis. Increased trade will support various sectors, from perishables to high-tech goods. In addition, increased economic exchange is fostering foreign investment in production and infrastructure. The most significant economic impact would be felt in the tourism industry. This is because about 20 percent of all tourism-related jobs in Africa (675,000 in 2004) are supported by international visitors arriving by air, compared with only 4 percent (310,000 jobs) in North America (Oxford Economic Forecasting 2005, p. 19).

Nevertheless, air transportation remains a relatively expensive mode of transportation for many people, especially in Africa, where a large part of the population lives in poverty. Lowering the cost of air transportation to a level where commercial activity would consider its gains in time, reliability, safety, and comfort a genuine alternative to road travel remains the most important element for the successful development of air transport services. Several studies have demonstrated that liberalization of air services, both in Africa and around the world, has resulted in a significant reduction in airfares. The increased competitive environment has nearly always resulted in strong growth of traffic, leading to a reduction in airfares for passengers and cargo. The only exception where liberalization reduced air traffic has typically concerned routes that until liberalization had been subsidized or had enjoyed a monopoly. Ending public subsidies of noncompetitive or unviable carriers in poor countries is itself a viable argument for liberalizing air services in Africa.

Finally, the full liberalization of air services would facilitate the inclusion of remote countries or regions in international trade, including the possibility of becoming low-cost manufacturing sites. This would not only support economic development, but in large countries also facilitate social integration on regional and national levels. However, continued resistance to the liberalization of intra-African air services remains as yet another obstacle in the way of Africa's challenging path out of poverty.

Notes

1. Wet lease operations in this instance are based on a leasing arrangement whereby a domestic airline provides an aircraft, complete crew, maintenance, and insurance to a foreign airline that handles actual operations and pays the domestic airline by the hour for hours operated. (Brattle Group 2002, pp. 1–14).
2. An integrated carrier is an air cargo operator that operates its own flights. Prior to deregulation, freight forwarders were limited to the functions of a common carrier, which had to rely on air carriers to perform the air haul (O'Connor 2000, p. 175). Prominent examples of integrated carriers include Emery and UPS (united parcel service).

CHAPTER 7

Conclusions and Policy Recommendations

The air transport sector has long been one where policy dialogue has been difficult. The strong traditional association between governments, national identities, and often state-owned flag carriers has resulted in subjective arguments sometimes overshadowing rational considerations about economic objectives and public interests. However, many changes have taken place over the past 10 years that have affected governments' perspective and made moving forward easier. The rapid development of air traffic driven by economic globalization and international migration, along with the failure of the traditional business model on which many African legacy carriers were based (that is, the cross-subsidization of unprofitable domestic routes by profits generated on intercontinental routes protected by monopoly-oriented restricted bilateral agreements), the entry of private sector interests in the air transport industry, and the trend toward transborder consolidations, have significantly changed the business climate for air transport. Other ingredients of change have also played an important role, such as stronger concerns for aviation safety and security, volatile fuel prices, and new environmental issues and demands. However, in the African context the most effective single element of change has been the change in the rules of the game brought about by the Yamoussoukro Decision that, despite some shortcomings, has acted as a catalyst for changes triggered by the other factors.

The Yamoussoukro Decision is a relatively ambitious treaty framework that aims to open up air services between all African states. Indeed, it is a relatively progressive and radical move away from regulating air services between states on the basis of restrictive bilaterals. However, implementation of the decision has encountered two quite opposite realities. Implementation in terms of carrying out public policy has seen little progress at the pan-African level: many of the key policy elements are still missing or exist only on paper. At the same time, in terms of operational implementation many examples can be seen of countries opening up by applying the Yamoussoukro Decision at the bilateral level. Given the current structure of the air transport sector in many African countries, we can assume that about two-thirds are willing to apply the Yamoussoukro Decision because they see little value in protecting their own markets from outside competition.

As a result, the decision can also be regarded as a historic opportunity for implementing a pan-African accord, both on a continent-wide and on a regional level, which is key for Africa's regional integration. The Yamoussoukro Decision has a long history of failed or ineffective objectives of integrating Africa, such as the Lagos Plan of Action, but given that the decision is increasingly supported and applied by states that are helping their national carriers obtain traffic rights that are based on the decision, it has good prospects of being applied and implemented in most regions in the future. This is the case even if the implementation of the missing elements by the African Union or the RECs continues to drag on.

From a policy standpoint, the African Union or the RECs must continue with several elements of implementation; however, none of these elements would hinder the continued application of the Yamoussoukro Decision on a bilateral basis between two or more party states. An effective executing agency, and a conflict resolution system, along with competition regulation, are necessary tools that need to be established. Nevertheless, an increasing number of bilateral relationships between states that conform to the Yamoussoukro Decision may provide the motivation to implement these missing elements. In the meantime, operational implementation must continue on a bilateral or multilateral basis, regardless of the progress made in policy implementation.

To continue pan-African implementation of the Yamoussoukro Decision, this report recommends that the 10 countries that are not party states (Djibouti, Equatorial Guinea, Eritrea, Gabon, Madagascar, Mauritania, Morocco, Somalia, South Africa, and Swaziland) review their current status. Some of these countries may not even be aware that they cannot be considered party states because they ratified or deposited their instruments of ratification too late. These countries, as well as those that never signed or ratified the Abuja Treaty, such as Morocco, might consider joining the Yamoussoukro Decision, which provides for a simple procedure for nontreaty states that wish to be parties to the decision (UNECA 1999, annex 1 [a]).

Regional implementation of the decision must be continued, especially in those RECs that have come close to liberalization. The EAC should amend its bilaterals to conform them to the principles of the decision, while COMESA declared the establishment of the Joint Competition Authority to be the last obstacle to full implementation. The strong growth of air transportation in the region that is being driven by two main operators that are increasingly providing air transportation in markets abandoned by failing carriers should be recognized as a strong argument for certain countries to stop supporting their non-viable airlines. Nonviable air carriers are also the major obstacle to implementation of a liberalized market in southern Africa. The argument that South African Airways would destroy weak foreign carriers of the region can be countered with the observation that South Africa's domestic market has prospered since the introduction of a truly competitive environment. Liberalization of the SADC region should therefore be possible, even if it entails the disappearance or integration of certain national carriers, such as in Malawi or Mozambique. The only requirement to assure competition would be a policy of, for example, allowing more than one carrier to serve city pairs within the region, even if both carriers are registered in, for example, South Africa.

On a national level, as well as on the level of the RECs, this report recommends that the states strengthen their policy formulation capabilities. This should be done from an institutional standpoint, in particular, by clarifying the respective roles and responsibilities of policy-making bodies, for example, ministries responsible for transport, the economy, tourism, and land use planning; regulating agencies such as civil aviation authorities; law enforcement agencies, for instance, customs and immigration, whose role in facilitation is crucial for efficient use of airport facilities; and service providers, for example air navigation service providers or agencies, airport operators, safety oversight service providers, and private security organizations, in accordance with the recommendations of ICAO where they apply.

This also requires an improvement of methods of and criteria for policy development. Policy formulation, in particular, should be supported by improved knowledge of the economic background by means of better air traffic statistics and economic statistics; improved dialogue with stakeholders, namely, air carriers, freight forwarders, and the travel and tourism industry; and enhanced understanding of the driving factors of air traffic generation and of the economic benefits of air transport in relation to national development objectives. Safe, secure, reliable, frequent, and cost-effective air transport is a necessary condition for an enabling environment. It has an impact not only in terms of direct and indirect jobs, but more important, on connectivity, competitiveness, reliability, and choices of access. Moreover, effective air transport connectivity is a necessary condition for the emergence of businesses such as new service and production industries where just-in-time features are valuable. It is also a prerequisite for opening the remote communities and regions of a country to enhanced development opportunities.

Also at the national level, several African countries continue to support their failing national carriers. These states should be encouraged to abandon this strategy by privatizing, disposing of, or liquidating their failed carriers. This is especially important when considering the large amounts of public funds used to keep nonviable carriers operating. In addition, most countries in Africa that have abandoned their failing carriers and opened up to foreign operators in applying the principles of the Yamoussoukro Decision have experienced positive development of air services.

Finally, achieving an adequate safety and security oversight regime remains the most urgent measure that must be implemented in relation to the development of air services. The fact that 31 African countries currently have poor safety standards remains the single most important policy measure that must be addressed in the short term. Poor safety oversight results in more expensive insurance premiums and the inability to develop code sharing and other business arrangements. It also scares away potentially high-yield international customers and potential private sector investors. Africa's air transport industry needs private capital, and sensible investors want their investments to be protected by an efficient safety oversight system. Poor safety is also a major hindrance to the consolidation of Africa's air transport industry. Such consolidation is highly desirable to make African air transport more cost-effective. The key tool introduced by the Yamoussoukro Decision to facilitate and encourage consolidation in Africa's air transport industry is the clause authorizing a state party to designate a carrier registered (and regulated) by another state party. This requires building up mutual trust that safety standards are met irrespective of the state of registration. As concerns infrastructure, this report recommends that a definite objective be set for the percentage of infrastructure investment to be dedicated to safety over the next 10 years, that is, 10 percent as recommended by the General Assembly of the United Nations. Failing to meet internationally accepted safety and security standards will not only hinder the development of air services regardless of the progress made in the implementation of the Yamoussoukro Decision, but also continue to push certain African states into isolation by being labeled as countries with poor governance. This report strongly recommends that a definite timeframe be fixed for establishing strong, independent, and technically reliable supervision agencies and that the target date for completing the establishment process should not extend beyond 2012.

APPENDIX A

Ethiopian Air Service Agreements with Other African States

Appendix A

Table A.1 Bilateral Air Service Agreements Concluded by Ethiopia with Other African States as of October 2006

No.	Country	Date signed	Designated carrier, Ethiopia	Designated carrier, counterpart	Routes
1	Algeria	10.Apr.85	Ethiopian Airlines	Air Algeria	Any in each country, 3 intermediate, 3 beyond
2	Angola	20.May.77 and memorandum of understanding 15.Sep.98	Ethiopian Airlines	TAAG	Addis Ababa–any intermediate–LAD–any beyond vice versa
3	Benin	17.Jul.86	Ethiopian Airlines	To be designated	Ethiopia: 8 points (Addis Ababa-NBO-FIH-COO-ACC-MLW-CKY-BJL) and vice versa; Benin: 6 points, of which one is outside Africa (COO-LBV- 2 other points–ABB–BOM) and vice versa
4	Burkina Faso	14.Oct.03	Ethiopian Airlines	Air Burkina	Ethiopia: Any points in Ethiopia–any intermediate points–any point in Burkina Faso–beyond points in Africa, North America, and Europe (except France); Burkina Faso: any points in Burkina Faso–any intermediate points–any points in Ethiopia–points beyond in Africa, Asia, and Middle East (except Saudi Arabia)
5	Burundi	23.Mar.70	Ethiopian Airlines	Air Burundi	Points in Ethiopia–points in 4 intermediate states–Bujumbura and vice versa for both carriers
6	Cameroon	3.Aug.73 and memorandum of understanding 28.Aug.03	Ethiopian Airlines	Cameroon Airlines	Any point in Ethiopia–any intermediate points–any points in Cameroon–any beyond point in Africa and vice versa for both carriers
7	Cape Verde	29.Dec.89	Ethiopian Airlines	Transportes Aéreos de Cabo Verde	Ethiopia: Addis Ababa–any intermediate point–any point in Cape Verde–any point in North and South America; Cape Verde: Sal–any intermediate points–any point in Ethiopia–any points beyond

Ethiopian Air Service Agreements with Other African States 179

Rights	Frequency	Type of aircraft	Yamoussoukro Decision conformity	Routes currently flown[a]
3rd, 4th, 5th	Open	Not specified	Yes, but restricted to only 3 intermediate and beyond points	None
3rd, 4th, 5th	4 PAX, 3 cargo per week	Any type	No, due to limitation of frequency	3rd, 4th freedoms: 157 (113)
3rd, 4th	3 per week for each carrier	B727, B767, AB3, DC10 or similar	No, too restricted	None
3rd, 4th, 5th	Unlimited	Any type	Yes	None
3rd, 4th, 5th	Not stipulated	Not specified	Yes, but restricted to a few intermediate points	3rd, 4th, 5th freedoms: 419 (282)
3rd, 4th, 5th	Unlimited	Any type	Yes	3rd, 4th freedoms: 104 (116); 5th freedom: 98 (52)
3rd, 4th, 5th	Unlimited	Any type	Yes, but commercial agreement for 5th freedom between national carriers	None

(continued)

Table A.1 Bilateral Air Service Agreements Concluded by Ethiopia with Other African States as of October 2006 *(continued)*

No.	Country	Date signed	Designated carrier, Ethiopia	Designated carrier, counterpart	Routes
8	Central African Republic	23.Mar.72 and memorandum of understanding 18.Mar.82	Ethiopian Airlines	Open	Any point in Ethiopia (Central African Republic)–only 2 defined intermediate points–any 3 points to be defined later beyond and vice versa for both carriers
9	Chad	4.Jan.88	Ethiopian Airlines	Air Chad	Any point in Ethiopia (Chad)–3 defined intermediate points–3 defined points beyond and vice versa for both carriers
10	Comoros	27.Mar.84	Ethiopian Airlines	Air Comoros	Any point in Ethiopia (the Comoros)–3 open intermediate points–1 point in the Comoros (Ethiopia)–3 open points beyond and vice versa for both carriers
11	Congo, Rep. of	2.Apr.83 and 22.Jan.05	Ethiopian Airlines	Open	Any point in Ethiopia–any intermediate points–any points in the Republic of Congo–any beyond point in Africa and vice versa for both carriers
12	Congo, Dem. Rep. of	10.Oct.72, revised 21.Oct.05	Ethiopian Airlines	Air Congo/LAC	Any Point in Ethiopia (the Democratic Republic of Congo)–7 defined intermediate points in Africa–12 defined points in Africa (for the Democratic Republic of Congo: 2 African, 3 intercontinental) beyond and vice versa for both carriers
13	Côte d'Ivoire	2.May.62, memorandum of understanding 14.Jul.92	Ethiopian Airlines	Open	Two fixed routes for each carrier stating at the capital city of each country, and 8 points for Ethiopian Airlines, and 6 points for a Côte d'Ivoire carrier
14	Djibouti	12.Jul.79, revised 3.Feb.98 and 23.Nov.98	Ethiopian Airlines	Air Djibouti and Djibouti Airlines	Addis Ababa–DIR–JIB and vice versa and beyond points

Rights	Frequency	Type of aircraft	Yamoussoukro Decision conformity	Routes currently flown[a]
3rd, 4th, 5th	2 per week, DLA only once	Not specified	No, due to restriction to a few intermediate and beyond points and limited frequency	None
3rd, 4th, 5th (limited)	3 per week for each carrier, 4th frequency under commercial cooperation	A300, B727, B757, B767	No, too restricted	None
3rd, 4th, 5th	3 per week for each carrier	B727, B737, B767, or similar	No, too restricted	None
3rd, 4th, 5th	Unlimited	Any type	Yes	3rd, 4th freedoms: 261 (227); 5th freedom: 522 (227)
3rd, 4th, 5th (limited)	Initially 5, then 6, and finally 7 per week	Any type	No, due to limitation of frequency	3rd freedom: 40 (22); 4th freedom: 301 (249)
3rd, 4th, 5th (on limited routes only)	7 per week for Ethiopian Airlines, 1 must be jointly operated	Any type	No	3rd, 4th freedoms: 36 (75); 5th freedom: 238 (323)
3rd, 4th, 5th	ET 4, Djibouti Airlines 3 per week alternating	Any type	No, due to limitation of frequency	3rd, 4th freedoms: 209 (209)

(continued)

Table A.1 Bilateral Air Service Agreements Concluded by Ethiopia with Other African States as of October 2006 *(continued)*

No.	Country	Date signed	Designated carrier, Ethiopia	Designated carrier, counterpart	Routes
15	Egypt, Arab Rep. Of	11.Mar.50, memorandum of understanding 10.Jul.68 and 15.Jun.95	Ethiopian Airlines	Egypt Air	Any points in Ethiopia–several intermediary in Africa (and some in Europe for ET) points–any points in Egypt, several specified 5th freedom points beyond in Africa
16	Equatorial Guinea	19.Dec.05	Ethiopian Airlines	Open	Any points in Ethiopia (for ET) or Addis Ababa–any intermediate points–Malabo and beyond and vice versa
17	Eritrea	27.Sep.93	Ethiopian Airlines	Eritrean	Any points in Ethiopia–any points in Eritrea–any points beyond and vice versa
18	Gabon	23.Mar.06	Ethiopian Airlines	Open	Any points in each country (capital only for counterpart)–any 3 points within Africa–any 5 open points beyond
19	Gambia, The	1.Aug.03, new bilaterals 5.Feb.07	Ethiopian Airlines	Gambia International Airlines	Any points in each country–any intermediate points–points beyond
20	Ghana	9.Jun.60, newbilaterals 18.Nov.05	Ethiopian Airlines	Open	Any points in each country (capital only for counterpart)–any intermediate points–points beyond
21	Guinea	1.Jun.60, revised 9.May.88	Ethiopian Airlines	Open	Two fixed routes for each carrier with any points in each country, and 6 and 10 points for Ethiopian Airlines and 6 and 5 points for a Guinean carrier
22	Kenya	5.Oct.67, memorandum of understanding 13.Mar.05	Ethiopian Airlines	Kenya Airways	Any points in each country–any intermediate points–and points beyond, if COMESA
23	Liberia	25.May.60	Ethiopian Airlines	Open	Any points in each country (capital only for counterpart)–7 defined points (ABJ, ACC, LOS, DLA, BCape Verde, FIH, NBO)–and 3 open points beyond
24	Libya	4.Dec.80	Ethiopian Airlines	Libya Arab Airlines	Any points in each country (capital only for counterpart)–any 2 intermediate points–and 3 points beyond

Rights	Frequency	Type of aircraft	Yamoussoukro Decision conformity	Routes currently flown[a]
3rd, 4th, and limited 5th	5 per week	Any type	No, due to limitation of frequency and restricted 5th freedom	3rd, 4th freedoms: 62 (121); 5th freedom: 199 (178)
3rd, 4th, and 5th	Unlimited	Any type	Yes	None
3rd, 4th, and 5th (with commercial agreement)	Unlimited	Any type	Yes, but commercial agreement for 5th freedom	None
Limited 3rd, 4th, and 5th	3 per week for each designated carrier	Any type	No, due to limitation of frequency and restricted 3rd, 4th, and 5th freedoms	3rd, 4th freedoms: 104 (80); 5th freedom: 104 (0)
3rd, 4th, 5th	Unlimited	Any type	Yes	None
3rd, 4th, 5th	Unlimited	Any type	Yes	3rd, 4th freedoms: 0 (131); 5th freedom: 408 (74)
3rd, 4th, 5th (on limited routes only)	3 per week for each designated carrier, 4th frequency under commercial agreement	Any type	No	None
3rd, 4th, 5th (COMESA only)	Unlimited	Any type	Yes, but 5th freedom COMESA only	3rd, 4th freedoms: 400 (569); 5th freedom: 353 (48)
3rd, 4th, and limited 5th	One daily frequency for each designated carrier	Any type	No, due to limitation of frequency and restricted 3rd, 4th, and 5th freedoms	None
3rd, 4th, and limited 5th	2 per week for each designated carrier	To be agreed by civil aviation authority later	No, due to limitation of frequency and restricted 5th freedom	None

(continued)

184 Appendix A

Table A.1 Bilateral Air Service Agreements Concluded by Ethiopia with Other African States as of October 2006 *(continued)*

No.	Country	Date signed	Designated carrier, Ethiopia	Designated carrier, counterpart	Routes
25	Madagascar	15.Dec.05	Ethiopian Airlines	Open	Two points in each country (capital only for counterpart)–any intermediate points–and points beyond
26	Malawi	15.Jul.70, memorandum of understanding 12.Oct.00	Ethiopian Airlines	Air Malawi	Any points in each country (capital for counterpart)–any intermediate points–and points beyond, except defined points for each carrier (ET not HRE, JNB, LUN, NBO; AM not CAI, KRT, NBO)
27	Mali	22.Jul.81, rev. 25.Apr.95 and memorandum of understanding 13.Jan.05	Ethiopian Airlines	Open	Any points in each country (capital only for counterpart)–any intermediate points–and points beyond
28	Mauritius	6.Nov.02	Ethiopian Airlines	Air Mauritius	Not specified
29	Mozambique	21.Nov.75	Ethiopian Airlines	LAM	Not specified, but for 5th freedom the two carriers must agree and obtain approval from their civil aviation authority
30	Namibia	5.Feb.97	Ethiopian Airlines	Open	Any points in each country (capital only for counterpart)–any intermediate points–and points beyond
31	Niger	28.Jul.81	Ethiopian Airlines	Open	Any points in each country (capital only for counterpart)–1 intermediate points–and any 3 points beyond
32	Nigeria	7.Apr.77, new bilaterals 1.Apr.04	Ethiopian Airlines	Virgin Nigeria	Any points in each country (capital only for counterpart)–any 10 intermediate points–and any 10 points beyond
33	Rwanda	30.Apr.70, new bilaterals 2.Apr.04	Ethiopian Airlines	Rwanda Air Express	Any points in each country (capital only for counterpart)–any intermediate points–and points beyond
34	Senegal	22.Dec.62	Ethiopian Airlines	Air Senegal	Any points in each country (capital only for counterpart)–any intermediate points–and points beyond

Ethiopian Air Service Agreements with Other African States   185

Rights	Frequency	Type of aircraft	Yamoussoukro Decision conformity	Routes currently flown[a]
3rd, 4th, and 5th	Unlimited	Any type	No, due to limitation to two points in each country	None
3rd, 4th, and limited 5th	7 per week for each designated carrier	Any type	No, due to limitation of frequency and restricted 5th freedom	3rd, 4th freedoms: 206 (76); 5th freedom: 412 (130)
3rd, 4th, and 5th	Unlimited	Any type	Yes	3rd, 4th freedoms: 121 (0); 5th freedom: 255 (237)
Not specified	Not agreed, but 1 weekly frequency per carrier proposed	Not specified	No	None
3rd, 4th, and limited 5th	2 per week for each designated carrier	Long- and/or medium-range jet aircraft	No	None
3rd and 4th	3 per week for each designated carrier	To be agreed by the civil aviation authority later	No, due to limitation of frequency	None
3rd, 4th, and limited 5th	3 per week for each designated carrier	Any type	No	None
3rd, 4th, and 5th	Unlimited	Any type	No, due to limitation of 10 intermediate and 10 beyond points	3rd, 4th freedoms: 665 (402); 5th freedom: 300 (37)
3rd, 4th, and 5th	Unlimited	Any type	Yes	3rd, 4th freedoms: 60 (226); 5th freedom: 413 (334)
3rd, 4th, and 5th	Unlimited	Any type	Yes	3rd, 4th freedoms: none; 5th freedom: 191 (178)

(continued)

Table A.1 Bilateral Air Service Agreements Concluded by Ethiopia with Other African States as of October 2006 *(continued)*

No.	Country	Date signed	Designated carrier, Ethiopia	Designated carrier, counterpart	Routes
35	Seychelles	22.Feb.79	Ethiopian Airlines	Open	Any points in each country (capital only for counterpart)–3 intermediate points (NBO, JRO, DAR)–and three (for ET) or 5 points (for Seychelles' carriers) beyond
36	Somaliland	10.Nov.00	Ethiopian Airlines	Daalo	Not defined
37	Somalia	22.Feb.69, memorandum of understanding 3.Dec.88	Ethiopian Airlines	Somalia Airline	Any points in each country (capital only for counterpart)–up to 5 intermediate points to be defined–and points beyond
38	South Africa	4.Mar.93, new bilaterals 14.May97, memorandum of understanding 22.May 00	Ethiopian Airlines	South African Airways	Any international entry points in each country–any intermediate points–points beyond
39	Sudan	6.Sep.56, memorandum of understanding 23.May02, and notification by Sudan 9.Apr.03	Ethiopian Airlines	Sudan Airways	Any points in each country (capital only for counterpart)–any intermediate points–and defined points beyond but for Ethiopia only KRT-BEY
40	Swaziland	6.Aug.81	Ethiopian Airlines	Royal Swazi National Airlines	Addis Ababa–any intermediate–MTS–defined points beyond vice versa
41	Tanzania	19.Sep.67, new bilaterals 17.Dec.04	Ethiopian Airlines	Air Tanzania	Any points in own country and defined points in country of counterpart–any intermediate points–any points beyond
42	Togo	25.Apr.62, revised 10.Aug.89 and 10.Nov.05	Ethiopian Airlines	Open	Any points in each country (capital only for counterpart)–any intermediate points–points beyond
43	Tunisia	17.Jul.02	Ethiopian Airlines	Open	Any points in each country–any intermediate points–points beyond

Rights	Frequency	Type of aircraft	Yamoussoukro Decision conformity	Routes currently flown[a]
3rd and 4th	2 per week for each designated carrier	Any type	No	None
Not defined	Not defined	Not defined	No	None
3rd and 4th (5th pending)	2 frequencies per week	F27, B737, B727, B707, B767, A310	No, due to limitation of frequency and pending 5th freedom	None
3rd, 4th, and 5th	Unlimited	Any type	Yes	3rd, 4th freedoms: 360 (264)
3rd, 4th, and limited 5th	Daily flights of each carrier	Any type	No, due to limitation of frequency and restricted 5th freedom	3rd, 4th freedoms: 405 (347); 5th freedom: 199 (178)
3rd, 4th, and limited 5th	3 per week for each designated carrier	Any type	No, due to limitation of frequency and restricted 5th freedom	None
3rd, 4th, and 5th (with commercial agreement)	Maximum 28 frequencies for each designated carrier	Any type	No, due to limitation of frequency and restricted 5th freedom	3rd, 4th freedoms: 353 (344)
3rd, 4th, and 5th	Unlimited	Any type	Yes	3rd, 4th freedoms: 208 (161); 5th freedom: 208 (197)
3rd, 4th, and 5th (with civil aviation authority agreement)	Unlimited	Any type	Yes	None

(continued)

Table A.1 Bilateral Air Service Agreements Concluded by Ethiopia with Other African States as of October 2006 *(continued)*

No.	Country	Date signed	Designated carrier, Ethiopia	Designated carrier, counterpart	Routes
44	Uganda	25.Sep.67, memorandum of understanding and new bilaterals 8.Apr.05	Ethiopian Airlines	Dario Air Services, East Africa Airlines, Eagle Air, and any other carrier	Any points in each country (capital only for counterpart)–any intermediate points–points beyond
45	Zambia	4.Apr.98, memorandum of understanding 28.May.96 and 6.May05	Ethiopian Airlines	Open	Any points in each country (capital only for counterpart)–any intermediate points–points beyond
46	Zimbabwe	8.May.81, revised 21.Aug.90	Ethiopian Airlines	Air Zimbabwe	Any points in each country–any intermediate points–and points beyond

Source: Strategic Planning Consulting 2006; for flights currently flown: Soars 2007.
Note: COMESA = Common Market for Eastern and Southern Africa. "Intermediate" refers to an additional destination between the two airports and "beyond" refers to an additional destination beyond the two airports.
a. Flights per year in 2007 (2006).

Table A.2 Summary of Intra-African Bilateral Air Service Agreements Concluded by Ethiopia in Conformity with the Yamoussoukro Decision and Actual Routes Flown

Routes flown	Number of bilaterals in conformity with the Yamoussoukro Decision	Number of bilaterals not in conformity with the Yamoussoukro Decision
3rd and 4th freedoms	2	2
3rd, 4th, and 5th freedoms	11	8
None	6	17
Total	19	27

Source: Author's calculations based on table A.1.

Rights	Frequency	Type of aircraft	Yamoussoukro Decision conformity	Routes currently flown[a]
3rd, 4th, and 5th	Unlimited	Any type	Yes	3rd, 4th freedoms: 359 (339); 5th freedom: 359 (219)
3rd, 4th, and 5th (with commercial agreement)	Unlimited	Maximum 400 seats for PAX and 100 tons cargo per frequency per direction	Yes, but commercial agreement for 5th freedom (PAX and cargo limitations no factor)	3rd, 4th freedoms: 362 (167); 5th freedom: 0 (102)
3rd, 4th, and 5th (with commercial agreement)	7 per week for each designated carrier	Any type with maximum capacity of a B767	No, due to limitation in frequency, capacity, and 5th freedom with commercial agreement only	3rd, 4th freedoms: 0 (26); 5th freedom: 312 (167)

APPENDIX B

African Country Overview of Air Transport and the Yamoussoukro Decision

Country	Date Abuja Treaty signed	Date Abuja Treaty ratified	Date Abuja Treaty instruments deposited	Yamoussoukro Declaration member	REC membership	REC Yamoussoukro Declaration membership[a]	National airline[b]	Remarks and observations about implementation of the Yamoussoukro Decision
Algeria	6.Mar.91	21.Jun.95	18.Jul.95	Yes	AMU	No	Yes	One fully state-owned airline and one private carrier; the government is considering opening up, but is still quite restrictive.
Angola	6.Mar.91	11.Apr.92	23.Jun.92	Yes	COMESA, SADC	Pending	Yes	One fully state-owned airline; restrictive bilaterals policy
Benin	27.Feb.92	10.May.99	31.May.99	Yes	WAEMU	Yes	No	Three small operating carriers
Botswana	6.Mar.91	27.Jun.96	3.Jul.96	Yes	SADC	No	Yes	One 100% state-owned carrier
Burkina Faso	6.Mar.91	19.May.92	17.Jun.92	Yes	WAEMU	Yes	No	One privately owned operator
Burundi	6.Mar.91	5.Aug.92	6.Oct.92	Yes	EAC, COMESA	Pending	No	One privately owned operator
Cameroon	6.Mar.91	20.Dec.95	8.Apr.96	Yes	CEMAC	Yes	Yes	Liquidation of national airline in progress
Cape Verde	6.Mar.91	12.Apr.93	11.May.93	Yes	BAG, ECOWAS	No	Yes	Restructuring of national airline in progress
Central African Republic	6.Mar.91	18.Jun.93	22.Jun.93	Yes	CEMAC	Yes	No	No known operator

Country							Notes
Chad	6.Mar.91	26.Jun.93	24.Aug.93	Yes	CEMAC	Yes	No	National carrier Air Chad is 98% state owned, but no longer operating.
Comoros	6.Mar.91	6.Jun.94	20.Jun.94	Yes	COMESA	Pending	Yes	Majority state-owned carrier
Congo, Dem. Rep. of	6.Mar.91	19.Jun.93	21.Jun.93	Yes	COMESA, SADC	Pending	No	Five small operators, all banned in Europe
Congo, Rep. of	6.Mar.91	30.Jul.96	15.Jan.97	Yes	CEMAC	Yes	No	Three small private operators
Côte d'Ivoire	6.Mar.91	22.Feb.93	11.May.93	Yes	WAEMU	Yes	No	Air Ivoire is 49% state owned and 34% owned by Air France.
Djibouti	6.Mar.91	N.A.	N.A.	No	COMESA	Pending	Yes	One small state-owned and one small private operator
Egypt, Arab Rep. of	6.Mar.91	18.Dec.92	26.Jan.93	Yes	COMESA	Pending	Yes	Dominant state-owned carrier and one small private operator
Equatorial Guinea	N.A.	20.Dec.02	19.Feb.03	No	CEMAC	Yes	No	Several small private operators all banned in Europe
Eritrea	6.Mar.91	N.A.	N.A.	No	COMESA	Pending	No	Two private operators
Ethiopia	6.Mar.91	5.Nov.92	6.Nov.92	Yes	COMESA	Pending	Yes	One state-owned operator; government pursues a very open policy; most new bilateral air service agreements conform to the Yamoussoukro Decision.

(continued)

Country	Date Abuja Treaty signed	Date Abuja Treaty ratified	Date Abuja Treaty instruments deposited	Yamoussoukro Declaration member	REC membership	REC Yamoussoukro Declaration membership[a]	National airline[b]	Remarks and observations about implementation of the Yamoussoukro Decision
Gabon	6.Mar.91	N.A.	N.A.	No	CEMAC	Yes	No	Two private operators
Gambia, The	6.Mar.91	20.Apr.93	14.May.93	Yes	BAG, ECOWAS	No	No	Three private operators
Ghana	6.Mar.91	25.Sep.91	25.Oct.91	Yes	BAG, ECOWAS	No	No	State-owned carrier ceased operations in 24; one private operator.
Guinea	6.Mar.91	17.Jul.92	21.Sep.92	Yes	BAG, ECOWAS	No	No	One private operator
Guinea-Bissau	6.Mar.91	24.Jun.92	30.Jun.92	Yes	WAEMU	Yes	No	One private operator
Kenya	6.Mar.91	18.Jun.93	22.Jun.93	Yes	COMESA, EAC	Pending	Yes	Government pursues an open policy toward the Yamoussoukro Decision; it retains only 23% of Kenya Airways, while KLM owns 26%; five other private operators.
Lesotho	6.Mar.91	12.Aug.97	11.Feb.98	Yes	SADC	No	No	No known operators
Liberia	6.Mar.91	23.Jun.93	29.Jun.93	Yes	BAG, ECOWAS	No	No	Two private operators, both banned in Europe
Libya	6.Mar.91	2.Nov.92	28.Jan.93	Yes	COMESA	Pending	Yes	Three state-owned and three private carriers
Madagascar	6.Mar.91	N.A.	N.A.	No	COMESA, SADC	Pending	Yes	One majority state-owned carrier
Malawi	6.Mar.91	26/0693	22.Jul.93	Yes	COMESA, SADC	Pending	Yes	One fully state-owned carrier

Country								Notes
Mali	6.Mar.91	13.Nov.92	27.Jan.93	Yes	WAEMU	Yes	Yes	One majority state-owned carrier and two private carriers
Mauritania	6.Mar.91	20.Nov.01	4.Jul.02	No	AMU	No	Yes	One fully state-owned carrier
Mauritius	6.Mar.91	14.Feb.92	27.Feb.92	Yes	COMESA, SADC	Pending	Yes	Reservations concerning the Yamoussoukro Decision were expressed at the African Union because of missing competition regulation; strong majority state-owned carrier.
Morocco	N.A.	N.A.	N.A.	No	AMU	No	Yes	Not a member of the African Union; strong majority state-owned carrier and one private operator
Mozambique	6.Mar.91	14.May.92	9.Jul.92	Yes	SADC	No	Yes	Majority state-owned carrier and one small private operator
Namibia	6.Mar.91	28.Jun.92	1.Jul.92	Yes	SADC	No	Yes	Fully state-owned carrier
Niger	6.Mar.91	22.Jun.92	22.Jul.92	Yes	WAEMU	Yes	No	No known operators
Nigeria	6.Mar.91	31.Dec.91	9.Jan.92	Yes	BAG, ECOWAS	No	No	Eleven privately owned carries
Rwanda	6.Mar.91	1.Oct.93	15.Nov.93	Yes	COMESA, EAC	Pending	No	One privately owned operator

(continued)

Country	Date Abuja Treaty signed	Date Abuja Treaty ratified	Date Abuja Treaty instruments deposited	Yamoussoukro Declaration member	REC membership	REC Yamoussoukro Declaration membership[a]	National airline[b]	Remarks and observations about implementation of the Yamoussoukro Decision
Saharawi Arab Democratic Republic (Western Sahara)	6.Mar.91	25.Aug.92	23.Oct.92	Yes	N.A.	No	No	No known operators; not an International Civil Aviation Organization contracting state, which renders aircraft registration and international airline operations difficult
São Tomé and Principe	6.Mar.91	2.Jun.93	22.Jun.93	Yes	N.A.	No	No	One 35% state-owned and majority privately owned carrier
Senegal	6.Mar.91	26.Feb.92	18.Mar.92	Yes	WAEMU	Yes	No	One private carrier that is fully owned by Royal Air Maroc
Seychelles	6.Mar.91	11.Oct.91	7.Nov.91	Yes	COMESA	Pending	Yes	Fully state-owned carrier
Sierra Leone	6.Mar.91	15.Mar.94	12.Apr.94	Yes	BAG	No	No	Four privately owned carriers three of which are banned in Europe
Somalia	6.Mar.91	N.A.	N.A.	No	N.A.	No	No	One known private carrier
South Africa	10.Oct.97	31.May.01	25.Jun.01	No	SADC	No	Yes	One majority state-owned carrier and at least twelve private operators; the government has declared an open skies policy and has started to apply the Yamoussoukro Decision in bilaterals.

Sudan	6.Mar.91	8.Feb.93	15.May.93	Yes	COMESA	Pending	Yes	One fully state-owned carrier and three private operators
Swaziland	29.Jun.92	6.Jun.01	22.Jun.04	No	COMESA, SADC	Pending	No	Two private operators of which one is banned in Europe
Tanzania	6.Mar.91	10.Jan.92	3.Feb.92	Yes	EAC, SADC	No	Yes	One fully state-owned carrier and five private operators; the government has displayed a relatively open skies policy, especially within the EAC and the SADC.
Togo	6.Mar.91	5.May.98	18.May.98	Yes	WAEMU	Yes	No	Two private operators of which one is for cargo only
Tunisia	6.Mar.91	3.May.94	10.Jun.94	Yes	AMU	No	Yes	One majority state-owned carrier and two private operators
Uganda	6.Mar.91	31.Dec.91	9.Mar.92	Yes	COMESA, EAC	Pending	No	Two private operators; since its national carrier was liquidated in 2001, the government has been applying an open skies policy within the Yamoussoukro Decision framework.

(continued)

Country	Date Abuja Treaty signed	Date Abuja Treaty ratified	Date Abuja Treaty instruments deposited	Yamoussoukro Declaration member	REC membership	REC Yamoussoukro Declaration membership[a]	National airline[b]	Remarks and observations about implementation of the Yamoussoukro Decision
Zambia	6.Mar.91	26.Oct.92	9.Nov.92	Yes	COMESA, SADC	Pending	No	One private operator; the government protects its market in view of the possible start-up of a new national carrier.
Zimbabwe	6.Mar.91	6.Nov.91	26.Nov.91	Yes	COMESA, SADC	Pending	Yes	One fully state-owned carrier

Source: Author's compilation.

Note: N.A. = not applicable, AMU = Arab Maghreb Union, BAG = Banjul Accord Group, CEMAC = Economic and Monetary Community of Central Africa, COMESA = Common Market for Eastern and Southern Africa, EAC = East African Community, ECOWAS = Economic Community of Western African States, REC = regional economic community, SADC = Southern African Development Community, WAEMU = West African Economic and Monetary Union.

a. Some RECs have implemented the Yamoussoukro Decision with binding regulation within their communities. This column answers the question whether a given state, based on its membership in a REC, is currently bound to the Yamoussoukro Decision.

b. The state owns and controls at least 51 percent of its national carrier.

c. The case of Mauritius is unclear. According to an interview with the African Union's legal counsel, Fafré Camara, on 25 April 2007, in Addis Ababa, the African Union's depository did not receive a letter indicating that Mauritius had withdrawn from the Yamoussoukro Decision in 24. The government of Mauritius is aware that it never submitted a formal notification of withdrawal. Apparently, the situation provided some diplomatic advantages according to an interview with Deputy Prime Minister C. G. Xavier Luc Duval on 17 September 2007, in Montreal. However, this is in contradiction to a recommendation in an African Union report (2005b, p. 13), which clearly mentions that Mauritius withdrew and recommends "necessary action to bring Mauritius to reconsider its position." In the absence of any formal document of withdrawal, Mauritius should still be considered a member of the Yamoussoukro Decision (African Union 2007c).

APPENDIX C

Safety Review and Rating of African States

Country	ICAO Safety Assessment Audit[a]	ICAO safety audit Date	FAA IASA[b]	Number of carriers banned by the EU	IATA IOSA	Number of fatal accidents (events/deaths)[c]	Overall rating[a]	Remarks and special considerations
Algeria	1	29.Jun.04	N.A.	N.A.	N.A.	15/353	2	Despite recent improvements, lack of oversight persists; several past accidents.
Angola	3	12.Dec.04	N.A.	1	N.A.	25/460	3	EU declared a ban on the national carrier TAAG on 4 July 207.
Benin	3	27.Feb.07	N.A.	N.A.	N.A.	1/141	3	Serious lack of oversight reported in the accident report of the Guinea-registered carrier UTA B737 accident, in Cotonou.
Botswana	3	5.Sep.06	N.A.	N.A.	N.A.	2/81	3	None
Burkina Faso	3	23.Jun.03	N.A.	N.A.	N.A.	2/50	3	None
Burundi	N.A.	N.A.	N.A.	N.A.	N.A.	0/0	3	No audits were possible because of the ongoing civil war in recent years.
Cameroon	3	9.Jun.06	N.A.	N.A.	N.A.	18/445	3	Significant deterioration in safety oversight was observed during the 2006 ICAO audit.
Cape Verde	2	10.Feb.03	1	N.A.	N.A.	2/19	1	Significant improvements led to IASA category 1 in 203.
Central African Republic	3	3.Dec.07	N.A.	N.A.	N.A.	4/91	3	None
Chad	3	16.Feb.01	N.A.	N.A.	N.A.	2/10	3	None

Country		Date						Notes
Comoros	2	19.Nov.04	N.A.	1	N.A.	3/34	3	One air carrier certified by the Comoros has been operationally restricted by the EU.
Congo, Dem. Rep. of	3	18.Sep.06	2	51	N.A.	48/656	3	All air carriers certified by the Democratic Republic of Congo are banned by the EU.
Congo, Rep. of	3	27.Jun.01	N.A.	N.A.	N.A.	4/42	3	None
Côte d'Ivoire	2	17.Mar.04	2	N.A.	N.A.	5/260	2	None
Djibouti	3	17.Dec.00	N.A.	N.A.	N.A.	5/93	3	None
Egypt, Arab Rep. of	1	14.Nov.05	1	N.A.	1	33/745	1	EgyptAir is IOSA certified.
Equatorial Guinea	3	14.May.07	N.A.	5	N.A.	3/127	3	All air carriers certified by Equatorial Guinea are banned by the EU.
Eritrea	3	8.Jun.01	N.A.	N.A.	N.A.	3/67	3	None
Ethiopia	2	4.Dec.06	1	N.A.	1	15/217	1	Ethiopian Airlines is IOSA certified.
Gabon	3	2.May.07	N.A.	N.A.	N.A.	7/73	3	None
Gambia, The	2	20.Sep.05	2	N.A.	N.A.	1/24	2	None
Ghana	2	20.Nov.06	2	N.A.	N.A.	2/8	2	Downgraded to IASA category 2 in 205
Guinea	2	29.Jan.03	N.A.	N.A.	N.A.	2/38	3	Serious lack of oversight was reported in the accident report of the Guinea registered carrier UTA B737 accident resulting in 141 deaths in 203.
Guinea-Bissau	3	27.Jan.03	N.A.	N.A.	N.A.	0/0	3	A significant safety concern was issued by the ICAO concerning the system for issuing air operator certificates following the audit in April 208.

(continued)

Country	ICAO safety audit Assessment ICAO Safety Audit[a]	ICAO safety audit Date	FAA IASA[b]	Number of carriers banned by the EU	IATA IOSA	Number of fatal accidents (events/deaths)[c]	Overall rating[a]	Remarks and special considerations
Kenya	2	30.Nov.01	N.A.	N.A.	1	17/183	2	Kenya Airways is IOSA certified.
Lesotho	2	24.Jun.04	N.A.	N.A.	N.A.	1/18	2	None
Liberia	3	15.May.06	N.A.	All	N.A.	6/113	3	All air carriers certified by Liberia are banned by the EU.
Libya	2	26.May.01	N.A.	N.A.	N.A.	20/474	2	None
Madagascar	2	25.Nov.04	N.A.	N.A.	N.A.	8/138	2	None
Malawi	3	1.Dec.04	N.A.	N.A.	N.A.	0/0	3	None
Mali	3	16.Jun.03	N.A.	N.A.	N.A.	6/86	3	A significant safety concern was issued by the ICAO concerning the system for issuing air operator certificates following the audit in January 208.
Mauritania	3	24.Mar.04	N.A.	N.A.	N.A.	4/121	3	None
Mauritius	2	15.Jul.04	N.A.	N.A.	1	0/0	2	Air Mauritius is IOSA certified.
Morocco	2	7.Jul.04	1	N.A.	1	19/792	1	Royal Air Maroc is IOSA certified.
Mozambique	2	12.Dec.03	N.A.	N.A.	N.A.	7/74	2	None
Namibia	2	25.Apr.06	N.A.	N.A.	N.A.	2/127	2	None
Niger	3	15.Jan.04	N.A.	N.A.	N.A.	2/16	3	None
Nigeria	2	7.Nov.06	N.A.	N.A.	N.A.	42/1,319	2	Several serious accidents in the recent past reveal a serious lack of oversight, but the situation has begun to improve.

Country							Notes
Rwanda	3	10.Jul.01	N.A.	1	0/0	3	One air carrier is banned by the EU. A significant safety concern was issued by the ICAO concerning the system for issuing air operator certificates following the audit in November 207.
Saharawi Arab Democratic Republic (Western Sahara)	N.A.	N.A.	N.A.	N.A.	N.A.	N.A.	No database or any authority other than the African Union lists the country. It therefore cannot be rated.
São Tomé and Principe	3	25.May.01	N.A.	N.A.	2/27	3	None
Senegal	2	12.Apr.06	N.A.	N.A.	7/141	2	None
Seychelles	2	21.Aug.07	N.A.	N.A.	0/0	2	A significant safety concern was issued by the ICAO concerning the system for issuing air operator certificates following the audit in August 207.
Sierra Leone	3	05.Aug.06	N.A.	8	1/1	3	All air carriers certified by Sierra Leone are banned by the EU.
Somalia	N.A.	N.A.	N.A.	N.A.	5/101	3	None
South Africa	1	5.Jul.07	1	N.A.	19/146	1	Comair Limited, Nationwide Airlines, and South African Airways are IOSA certified.

(continued)

Country	ICAO safety audit		FAA IASA[b]	Number of carriers banned by the EU	IATA IOSA	Number of fatal accidents (events/ deaths)[c]	Overall rating[a]	Remarks and special considerations
	Assessment ICAO Safety Audit[a]	Date Date						
Sudan	2	21.Nov.06	N.A.	1	N.A.	26/476	3	One air carrier is banned by the EU. Several serious accidents have occurred.
Swaziland	3	12.Mar.99	N.A.	6	N.A.	1/2	3	All air carriers certified by Swaziland are banned by the EU.
Tanzania	2	18.Dec.03	N.A.	N.A.	1	7/51	2	Recent improvements were observed during World Bank missions in October 2005 and June 206. Precision Air is IOSA certified.
Togo	3	19.Feb.07	N.A.	N.A.	N.A.	0/0	3	None
Tunisia	1	2.Jul.04	N.A.	N.A.	N.A.	2/29	1	None
Uganda	3	5.Dec.01	N.A.	N.A.	N.A.	3/13	3	None

Zambia	3	5.Feb.04	N.A.	N.A.	6/77	3	World Bank missions in April 2006 and March 2007 confirmed poor safety oversight.
Zimbabwe	2	21.Jul.04	N.A.	2	6/13	2	Little information is available other than ICAO audit results.

Summary:

- ICAO audit report: 4 states rated 1 (good), 21 states rated 2 (marginal), 26 states rated 3 (poor).
- FAA IASA: 5 states certified as category 1 (compliant with ICAO SARP), and 5 states certified as category 2 (noncompliant with ICAO SARP).
- EU list of banned carriers: 9 states have one or more banned carriers.
- IAUA IOSA: 7 states have IATA certified carriers.
- Overall rating: 6 states rated good, 16 states rated marginal, 31 states rated poor.

Source: ICAO audits: ICAO Universal Safety Audit Oversight Audit Reports; FAA IASA: FAA 2007; carriers banned in the EU: European Commission 2007b; IATA IOSA: IATA 2007; accidents; Flight Safety Foundation 2007.

Note: N.A. = not applicable, EU = European Union, FAA IASA = U.S. Federal Aviation Administration International Aviation Safety Assessment Program, IATA IOSA = International Air Transport Association Operational Safety Audit, ICAO = International Civil Aviation Organization, SARP = standards and recommended practices.

a. Overall assessment ratings as follows: 1 = good, 2 = marginal, 3 = poor.
b. Ratings are as follows: 1 = compliant with ICAO standards, certified by the FAA; 2 = noncompliant, not certified by the FAA.
c. Accidents and deaths are for air transport category aircraft registered in the given state.

APPENDIX D

Aviation Laws and Regulations Adopted and Enacted by the West African Economic and Monetary Union

Name of regulation	Adoption	Summary of major provisions
Regulation No. 06/2002 on air carrier certification within WAEMU	27 June 2002, in Dakar, Senegal, by the Council of Ministers	Article 4: Conditions for carrier certification include (a) place of business in member state, (b) main activity is air transport, and (c) member states or member states nationals represent the majority in relation to the carrier's capital and control. Article 5: Carrier must be able to (a) cover liabilities within a 24-hour period, and (b) finance the fixed and operating cost of the first three months of operations in accordance with its stated business plan. Article 6: Management must be appropriately trained and of good moral standing. Article 7: Liability insurance requirement exists for air carriers. Article 9: Registration of aircraft is to occur in member state, but exceptions may be granted for leased aircraft. Article 10/13: Issuance of air operator certificates will have a validity of initially one year, thereafter three years. Article 12: Certification is to be published in official bulletin by the state and WAEMU.
Regulation No. 07/2002 on tariffs for air service for passengers, freight, and mail within WAEMU	27 June 2002, in Dakar, Senegal, by the Council of Ministers	Article 3: WAEMU carriers shall freely fix tariffs for passenger, freight, and mail transportation. Article 4: Tariffs for transportation of passengers under service public regulations may be regulated in accordance with WAEMU Regulation No. 24/202. Article 5: Tariffs must be filed with member states concerned at least 24 hours in advance, except in the case of alignment of an existing tariff. Article 7: A member state may suspend a tariff if considered excessively high or abnormally low. The WAEMU Commission and any other member state concerned must be notified of the suspension. The commission and the other state may approve or disapprove the proposed tariff. In the case of disapproval, consultations between all parties shall seek a conclusion. If no conclusive settlement is reached, the matter shall be submitted to the Council of Ministers for a final decision by rule making. Article 9/10: The commission shall consult once a year with air carriers and users on air fares and rates and every two years submit a report on enforcement of this regulation that shall be published in the union's official bulletin.

Directive No. 05/2002 on investigation of aviation accidents and incidents within WAEMU	27 June 2002, in Dakar, Senegal, by the Council of Ministers	Article 3/4: Accidents or serious incidents that occur in the union's territory or involving an aircraft registered in a member state must be investigated. Article 6: Each member state much enact national legislation for the creation of a permanent or ad hoc accident investigation entity in accordance with the relevant provisions of annex 13 of the Chicago Convention. Article 7/8: Accident and incident investigation is subject to a report that shall incorporate relevant air safety recommendations.
Regulation No. 24/2002 on conditions for market access by air carriers within WAEMU	18 November 2002, in Ouagadougou, Burkina Faso, by the Council of Ministers	Article 3: WAEMU air carriers are entitled by their member states to operate any intracommunity traffic (cabotage). Article 4: Public service obligations may be issued by one or several member states by decision based on general interest in territorial development. Restrictions or obligations imposed on carriers must be notified to the commission for publication in the union's official bulletin. Article 5: Traffic rights to nonmember states of the union shall be granted based on international agreements; however, a third party state that operates to the territory of a member state of the union must grant the same treatment (access) to the union's carriers. Article 6: The exercise of traffic rights is subject to competition legislation, as well as to respective national or union regulation on safety, security, environmental protection, and slot allocation. Article 8: Member states may suspend the granting of cabotage rights during a transitional period until 31 December 2005, at the latest. Article 9: Necessary enforcement action may be taken by the commission.
Regulation No. 02/2003 on air carriers' liability in case of an accident	20 March 2003, in Ouagadougou, Burkina Faso, by the Council of Ministers	Article 3: Air carriers cannot limit liability except for damages above SDR 100,000 provided that the carrier proves that the damage is not caused by negligence or other wrongful acts or omission by the carrier or its servants or agents, or the damage is solely due to the negligence of a third party. Article 5: Advance payment shall be for at least SDR 15,000 within 15 days in case of death of a person entitled to compensation.

(continued)

Name of regulation	Adoption	Summary of major provisions
		Article 6: Travelers must be informed about a carrier's liability.
		Article 7: Jurisdiction is according to the plaintiff's choice in any union member state, carrier's domicile or place of establishment, or a court of the final destination.
Regulation No. 03/2003 on compensation due to denial of embarkation, flight cancellation, or mayor flight delays	20 March 2003, in Ouagadougou, Burkina Faso, by the Council of Ministers	Article 3: Carrier must determine and communicate its embarkation rules.
		Article 4: Passenger has several choices when embarkation is denied and is entitled to minimum compensation according to class and distance of the leg of the journey.
		Article 6: Several choices exist, including full refund for paid ticket in case of cancelled flight.
		Article 7/8: Compensation is for major delays, defined as more than three hours on trips less than 2,000 kilometers, and more than five hours for longer trips.
Regulation No. 04/2003 on common rules for slot allocation at WAEMU airports	20 March 2003, in Ouagadougou, Burkina Faso, by the Council of Ministers	Article 3: Definition of a "coordinated airport" is when carriers represent majority of traffic and/or capacity considered insufficient by authorities.
		Article 4: Designation of an airport coordinator shall be by a member state that shall act in a transparent, neutral, and nondiscriminatory way.
		Article 5: Coordinating committee shall be established involving different users and operators, as well as the authorities.
		Article 6: Airport capacity must be determined twice a year by the relevant authorities of the concerned member state.
Regulation No. 01/2003 on ground handling market access at WAEMU airports	20 March 2003, in Ouagadougou, Burkina Faso, by the Council of Ministers	Article 4: Member states must grant free access to ground handling market, provided the service provided meets certain financial and operational criteria.
		Article 5: Centralized infrastructure may be exempt from ground handling operations of a device provider (for example, joint fuel distribution system).
		Article 7/8: A user and an advisory committee are to be created for implementation.
		Article 10: Member states must define the selection process for the provider.

| Regulation No. 01/2004 on the legal status of civil aviation authorities of member states | 17 September 2004, in Lomé, Togo, by the Council of Ministers | Article 11: Number of service providers may be limited when justified by a low level of activity, space constraints, or safety and security considerations. The state must inform the commission, which approves or rejects the limitation.
Article 15: Member states must implement the directive by issuing the necessary legislation, as well as making regulatory and administrative provisions for enforcement.
Article 3: The civil aviation authority must be a public legal entity with financial autonomy and must report to the ministry in charge of civil aviation.
Article 4: The mission of the civil aviation authority includes implementing the government's civil aviation policy, undertaking negotiations of bilaterals, developing technical regulations according to standards and recommended practices, engaging in regulatory and operational supervision of civil aviation with respect to safety and security, supervising airport and air navigation services, and ensuring training and development within the sector.
Article 5: The minimal organizational structure includes a board of directors and a directorate general.
Article 9: Financial resources of the civil aviation authority are provided by policy sector budgetary allocation or come from air navigation services, fees for services rendered, concession income, loans, subsidies, and/or grants.
Article 16: An appropriate compensation system must be implemented in order to recruit and retain qualified personnel that demonstrate professional integrity. |
| Regulation No. 06/2005 on licensing, training, and supervision of aeronautical personnel | 16 September 2005, in Ouagadougou, Burkina Faso, by the Council of Ministers | Article 2: The licensing of aeronautical personnel, the requirements for the certification of flight training centers, and the certification of instructors and examiners are outlined in the regulation and its annex.
Article 3: The regulation is applicable to licensing, training, authorizations, and certifications by WAEMU civil aviation authorities.
Article 4: Member states, the commission, and the union's supervisory entity are to cooperate to implement this regulation. |

(continued)

Name of regulation	Adoption	Summary of major provisions
		Article 7: National regulations on licensing, training, and supervision of aeronautical personnel that are not contradictory to the specification in the annex of this regulation remain valid.
Regulation No. 07/2005 on aircraft airworthiness certification	16 September 2005, in Ouagadougou, Burkina Faso, by the Council of Ministers	Article 2: Certificates of aircraft airworthiness are delivered according to the joint technical regulations. Article 3: The regulation applies to all aircraft registered in a member state. Article 4: Member states, the commission, and the union's supervisory entity are to cooperate to implement this regulation. Article 7: National regulations of airworthiness that are not contradictory to the technical specification in the annex of this regulation remain valid.
Regulation No. 08/2005 on medical requirements for licensing of aeronautical personnel	16 September 2005, in Ouagadougou, Burkina Faso, by the Council of Ministers	Article 2: The medical requirements for the licensing of aeronautical personnel in member states are outlined in the regulation and its annex. Article 3: The regulation applies to all licensing of aeronautical personnel by WAEMU civil aviation authorities. Article 4: Member states, the commission, and the union's supervisory entity are cooperating for the implementation of this regulation. Article 7: National regulations on medical requirements for licensing of aeronautical personnel, which are not contradictory to the specifications in the annex of this regulation, remain valid.
Regulation No. 09/2005 on operational requirements for commercial operators and air carrier certification	16 September 2005, in Ouagadougou, Burkina Faso, by the Council of Ministers	Article 2: The certification of commercial operators and air carriers is done according to the joint requirements of the present regulation and its annex. Article 3: The regulation does not apply to state aircraft of member states. Article 4: Member states, the commission, and the union's supervisory entity are to cooperate to implement this regulation. Article 7: National regulations on operational requirements for commercial operators and air carrier certification that are not contradictory to the requirements in the annex of this regulation remain valid.

Regulation No. 10/2005 on certification of aircraft maintenance and repair organizations	16 September 2005, in Ouagadougou, Burkina Faso, by the Council of Ministers	Article 2: The requirements for certification of aircraft maintenance and repair organizations are set forth in the regulation and its annex. Article 3: The regulation applies to all aircraft maintenance and repair organizations that are domiciled in the union or that maintain an aircraft registered in the union. Article 4: Member states, the commission, and the union's supervisory entity are to cooperate to implement this regulation. Article 7: National regulations on certification of aircraft maintenance and repair organizations that are not contradictory to the requirements in the annex of this regulation remain valid.
Regulation No. 11/2005 on security of civil aviation in member states	16 September 2005, in Ouagadougou, Burkina Faso, by the Council of Ministers	Article 2: The purpose of the regulation is to assure the security of passengers, crew, ground personnel, and the public, against unlawful interference with the civil aviation of member states. The regulation also provides a common basis for interpretation and applicability of annex 17 of the Chicago Convention. Article 3: The provisions of the regulation are applicable to all international airports of the union. Article 5: The joint norms for security are issued as an executing regulation by the commission on the basis of annex 17 of the Chicago Convention. Article 6: Member states may apply rules or regulations that are stricter than those set forth in this regulation. Article 7: Each member state establishes a national organization for civil aviation security and develops a national program of aviation security that is headed by a national aviation security committee. Article 8: Each member state establishes a coordination unit that implements the security measures at all airports to which this regulation applies. Article 12: A consultative committee for aviation security is established by the union. The committee is headed by the commission.

(continued)

Name of regulation	Adoption	Summary of major provisions
		Article 15: The commission will initiate inspections of member states on the implementation of and conformity with the national security programs six months after the regulation comes into force.
Regulation No. 13/2005 on a regional mechanism for the supervision of aviation safety	16 September 2005, in Ouagadougou, Burkina Faso, by the Council of Ministers	Article 2: A regional mechanism for the supervision of aviation safety is to be developed to assist member states in their regulatory oversight of the civil aviation sector. The Cooperative Development of Operational Safety and Continued Airworthiness Program builds these objectives by establishing a regional safety oversight entity.
		Article 3: The commission of the union coordinates the activities of the Cooperative Development of Operational Safety and Continued Airworthiness Program during the transitory period of two years starting in July 2005, after which the regional safety oversight entity should become operational.
		Article 4: The coordination activities of the commission are carried out in accordance to the memorandum of understanding between the International Civil Aviation Organization and WAEMU.
		Article 7: Participation in the regional safety oversight mechanism is open to any International Civil Aviation Organization contracting state.
Regulation No. 01/2007 on the adoption of a WAEMU Civil Aviation Code	6 April 2007, in Lomé, Togo, by the Council of Ministers	Article 1: The WAEMU Civil Aviation Code, as outlined in the annex of the present regulation, is hereby adopted.
		Article 2: The regulation is rendered into force upon its signature and publication in the official bulletin of the WAEMU.

Source: WAEMU 2007.
Note: WAEMU = West African Economic and Monetary Union.

References

Abate, Megersa Abera. 2007. "The Economic Effects of Progressive Air Transport Liberalization in Africa." Unpublished manuscript, Addis Ababa University, School of Graduate Studies, Addis Ababa.

Abbey, Douglas. 2008. *Detailed Analysis of African Air Services Schedules.* Washington, DC: Velocity Group.

Adedeji, Adebayo. 2004. "ECOWAS: A Retrospective Journey." In *West Africa's Security Challenges*, ed. Adebajo Adedeji and Ismail Rashid. Boulder, CO: Lynne Rienner.

AFCAC (African Civil Aviation Commission). 1969. *AFCAC Constitution.* CAB/LEG/23.1. Dakar: AFCAC.

AFRAA (African Airlines Association). 2006. *Final Resolutions Adopted by the 38th Annual General Assembly.* Resolution 38/5. Cairo: AFRAA.

African Union. 2000. *Constitutive Act of the African Union.* Lomé: African Union.

———. 2002. "Rules of Procedure of the Assembly of the Union." Rules determined at the Assembly of the African Union, First Ordinary Session, Durban, South Africa, July 9–10.

———. 2005a. "The 4th Meeting of the Monitoring Body for the Implementation of the Yamoussoukro Decision." Report of the Meeting of African Ministers Responsible for Air Transport, First Ordinary Session, Addis Ababa, March 3–4.

———. 2005b. "Report of the Meeting of Experts on Air Transport in Sun City, South Africa 2005." Report of the Second Meeting of African Ministers Responsible for Air Transport, Sun City, South Africa, 18–19 May.

———. 2006a. "Decisions of the 6th Ordinary Session of the Assembly of Heads of State and Government." Decisions taken at the Sixth African Union Summit, Khartoum, 16–24 January.

———. 2006b. *List of Countries Which Have Signed, Ratified/Acceded to the African Union Convention on Treaty Establishing the African Economic Community*. Addis Ababa: African Union.

———. 2006c. "Report of the Experts Meeting in Libreville Gabon 2006." Report of the Conference of African Ministers Responsible for Air Transport. Libreville, Gabon, 15–17 May.

———. 2007a. "Addis Ababa Resolution on Entrusting the Functions of the Executing Agency of the Yamoussoukro Decision to the African Civil Aviation Commission." Resolution arrived at during the Third African Union Conference of Ministers Responsible for Air Transport, Addis Ababa, 7–11 May.

———. 2007b. *Projet de Décision portant Règles Communes sur la concurrence et Project de Décision fixant les Exemptions aux Règles de Concurrence en Matière de Transport Aérien*. Addis Ababa: African Union.

———. 2007c. "Report of the Meeting of Experts." Report from the Third African Union Conference for Air Transport, Addis Ababa, 10–11 May.

Aghrout, Ahmed, and Keith Sutton. 1990. "Regional Economic Union in the Maghreb." *Journal of Modern African Studies* 28 (1): 115–39.

Air Transport Action Group. 2005. *The Economic and Social Benefits of Air Transport*. Geneva: Air Transport Action Group.

Air Transport Agreement between the United States of America and Singapore. 31 March 1978. Reprinted in CCH *Aviation Law Reporter* 3 (26495a), article 6 (2) (1981).

Akanle, O., ed. 1993. *The Legal and Institutional Framework of the African Economic Community*. Lagos: Nigerian Institute of Advanced Legal Studies.

Akintan, S. A. 1977. *The Law of International Economic Institutions in Africa*. Leyden, Netherlands: Springer.

Arab Civil Aviation Commission. 2004a. *Agreement on the Liberalisation of Air Transport between the Arab States*. Damascus: Arab Civil Aviation Commission.

———. 2004b. *Agreement on the Mechanism for Arab Collective Negotiations with Regional and Sub-Regional Groupings*. Rabat: Arab Civil Aviation Commission.

Arab League. 1981. *Agreement of Arab Free Trade Area*. Tunis: Arab League.

Aradhyula, Satheesh, Tauhidur Rahman, and Kumaran Seeivasan. 2007. *Impact of International Trade on Income and Income Inequality*. Tucson, AZ: University of Arizona.

Atiba, Aduke. 2007. "Taking the Bold Step." *Aviation and Allied Business* (June): 15.

Azar, Edward, and John Burton, eds. 1986. *International Conflict Resolution: Theory and Practice.* Boulder, CO: Lynne Rienner.

BAG (Banjul Accord Group). 1997. *Banjul Accord for the Accelerated Implementation of the Yamoussoukro Declaration of 3 April 1997.* Memorandum of understanding of the Second Consultative Meeting of the Group of Directors of Civil Aviation and Airline Executives of the Banjul Accord Member States. Banjul: BAG.

———. 2004a. *Agreement to Establish the Banjul Accord Group and Implement the Banjul Accord for the Accelerated Implementation of the Yamoussoukro Declaration.* Banjul: BAG.

———. 2004b. *Memorandum of Understanding for the Implementation of a Co-operative Development of Operational Safety and Continuing Airworthiness Project for the Banjul Accord Group.* Banjul: BAG.

———. 2004c. *Multilateral Air Service Agreement for the Banjul Accord Group.* Banjul: BAG.

Bernard Krief Consultants. 2008. *Country Profile Madagascar.* Addis Ababa: ICT Africa Market Place.

Blackwell Synergy. 2007. "LIBERIA: Charles Taylor on Trial." *Africa Research Bulletin: Political, Social and Cultural Series* 44 (6): 17107B –17108A.

Boeing Company. 2006. *Current Market Outlook.* Seattle: Boeing Company.

Bofinger, Heinrich C. 2007a. *Description and Assessment of a Sample of Export Markets with Dependence on Air Cargo in Developing Countries.* Washington, DC: World Bank.

———. 2007b. *Note on the Air Transport Sector of the Republic of Malawi.* Washington, DC: World Bank.

Booz Allen Hamilton. 2007. *The Economic Impacts of an Open Aviation Area between the EU and the US.* Report for the Directorate General Energy and Transport of the European Commission, London.

Brattle Group. 2002. "The Economic Impact of an EU-US Open Aviation Area." Report for the European Commission, Washington, DC, and London.

Brownlie, Ian. 2003. *Principles of Public International Law.* 6th ed. Oxford, U.K.: Oxford University Press.

Bureau d'Enquêtes et d'Analyses pour la Sécurité de l'Aviation Civile. 2002. *Accident which Occurred on 30 January 2000 in the Sea Near Abidjan Airport to the Airbus 310-304 Registered 5Y-BEN Operated by Kenya Airways.* Paris: Bureau d'Enquêtes et d'Analyses pour la Sécurité de l'Aviation Civile.

———. 2004. *Accident survenu le 25 décembre 2003 sur l'aérodrome de Cotonou Cadjèhoun (Benin) au Boeing 727-223 immatriculé 3X-GDO exploité par l'Union des Transports Africains.* Paris: Bureau d'Enquêtes et d'Analyses pour la Sécurité de l'Aviation Civile.

Cameroon Civil Aviation Authority. 2010 (28 April). "Technical Investigation into the Accident of the B737-800 Registration 5Y-KYA Operated by Kenya Airways that Occurred the 5th of May 2007 in Douala." Yaoundé, Cameroon.

CEMAC (Economic and Monetary Community of Central Africa). 1994. *Traité instituant la Communauté Économique et Monétaire de l'Afrique Centrale*. N'Djaména, Chad: CEMAC.

———. 1999a. *Réglementation des pratiques commerciales anticoncurrentielles*. Douala: CEMAC.

———. 1999b. *Règlement portant adoption de l'Accord relatif au Transport Aérien entre les Etats membres de la CEMAC*. Bangui: CEMAC.

———. 2000a. *Code de l'Aviation Civile de la CEMAC*. Bangui: CEMAC.

———. 2000b. *Règlement portant adoption du Code de l'Aviation Civile de la CEMAC*. Bangui: CEMAC.

Charrier, Guy, and Abou Saïb Coulibaly. 2007. *Voluntary Peer Review of Competition Policy: West African Economic and Monetary Union, Benin and Senegal*. New York and Geneva: United Nations.

Charter of the Organization of African Unity. 13 September 1963. *United Nations Treaty Series* 479 (II): 69–88.

Chérif, Taïeb. 2006. "Address by the Secretary General of the ICAO to the Opening Session of the 38th Annual General Assembly of the African Airlines Association." Cairo, 6–7 November.

COMESA (Common Market for Eastern and Southern Africa) Secretariat. 1994. *Agreement Establishing the Common Market for Eastern and Southern Africa (COMESA)*. Lilongwe: COMESA Secretariat.

———. 1999. "Legal Notice No. 2." *Official Gazette of the Common Market for Eastern and Southern Africa* 5 (2).

———. 2003a. "Draft COMESA Competition Regulations." COMESA, Lusaka.

———. 2003b. "The COMESA Air Transport Liberalization Experience." Paper presented at the seminar prior to the International Civil Aviation Organization Worldwide Air Transport Conference on the Challenges and Opportunities of Liberalization, Montreal, 22–23 March.

———. 2004. *Report and Decisions*. Decisions taken at the 17th Meeting of the COMESA Council of Ministers, Kampala, Uganda.

———. 2005. *The Development and Implementation of Competition Regulations in Eastern and Southern Africa*. Meeting of African Ministers Responsible for Air Transport, Sun City, South Africa.

———. 2007. *COMESA in Brief*. 3rd ed. Lusaka: COMESA Secretariat.

Committee on Foreign Relations. 1981. "Air Transport Agreement between the United States of America and Singapore." *CCH Aviation Law Reporter* 3 (26495a), article 6 (2).

Convention on International Civil Aviation. 7 December 1944. *United Nations Treaty Series* 15 (II): 295–374.

Council of Ministers for the Implementation of the Yamoussoukro Decision on Air Transport Liberalization in West and Central Africa. 2003. "Resolution of the Second Ordinary Session." Resolution taken at the Second Meeting of the Council of Ministers, Lomé, 28 February.

Council of Ministers of COMESA and EAC Responsible for Civil Aviation and the Committee of Ministers of Transport and Communications of SADC. 2004. *Regulations for Competition in Air Transport Services within COMESA, EAC and SADC*. Gaborone: Southern African Development Community Secretariat.

Dempsey, Paul Stephen. 1987. *Law and Foreign Policy in International Aviation*. Ardsley-on-Hudson, NY: Transnational Publishers.

———. 1990. *Flying Blind: The Failure of Airline Deregulation*. Washington, DC: Economic Policy Institute.

———. 2003. "The Cyclical Crisis in Aviation: Causes and Potential Cures." Paper presented at a seminar prior to the International Civil Aviation Organization Worldwide Air Transport Conference on the Challenges and Opportunities of Liberalization, Montreal, 22–23 March.

———. 2004. "Compliance and Enforcement in International Law: Achieving Global Uniformity in Aviation Safety." *North Carolina Journal of International Law and Commercial Regulation* 30 (1): 1–74.

———. 2006. *Public International Air Law*. Montreal: McGill University.

Dempsey, Paul Stephen, and Laurence E. Gesell. 2004. *Air Commerce and the Law*. Chandler, AZ: Coast Aire Publications.

Deutsche Lufthansa AG. 2007. *Lufthansa Annual Report 2007*. Cologne, Germany: Deutsche Lufthansa AG.

Doganis, Rigas. 2001. *The Airline Business in the 21st Century*. London and New York: Routledge.

EAC (East African Community). 1999. *East Africa Community Treaty*. Arusha: EAC.

EAC (East African Community) Secretariat. 2006. *Report of the Meeting of the 11th Meeting of the Council of Ministers*. Arusha: EAC Secretariat.

———. 2007. "Protocol on the Establishment of the East African Community Civil Aviation Safety and Security Oversight Agency." Decisions taken at the Extra Ordinary Meeting of the Council of Ministers, Arusha, 18 April.

———. 2008. *Report of the Meeting of the Heads of Civil Aviation and Airport Authorities*. Arusha: EAC Secretariat.

ECOWAS (Economic Community of West African States). 1993 (24 July). *Revised Treaty*. Cotonou: ECOWAS.

———. 2007. "Air Transport Policy in Economic Community of West African States." Policy paper presented at the 36th Session of the Assembly of the International Civil Aviation Organization, Montreal, 26 September.

ECOWAS and CEMAC Project Secretariats. 2004. "Implementation of the Yamoussoukro Decision on the Liberalisation of Air Transport Markets in Africa: Report of Activities Jan 2001–Nov 2004." Report presented at the Third Meeting of the Coordination and Monitoring Committee for the Implementation of the Yamoussoukro Decision in West and Central Africa, Libreville, 29–30 November.

East African Business Week. 2009. "Africa: Air Tanzania Debts to South Africa Airways Stand at $13 Million." 7 February.

El Alj, Mohamed. 2007. *Liste des pays ayant ratifié la Convention sur la Liberalisation du Transport Aerien*. Rabat: Arab Civil Aviation Commission.

El-Ayouty, Yassin, and William I. Zartman, eds. 1984. *The OAU after Twenty Years*. New York: Praeger.

Euromed Transport Project. 2005. "Ministerial Conclusions." Conclusions of the Euro-Mediterranean Ministerial Conference on Transport, Marrakesh, Morocco, 15 December.

European Commission. 2005a. *Developing the Agenda for the Community's External Aviation Policy*. COM(2005) 75 final. Brussels: European Commission.

———. 2005b. "Information Note: EU-Morocco Euro-Mediterranean Air Transport Agreement." http://ec.europa.eu/transport/air_portal/international/pillars/common_aviation_area/morocco_en.htm.

———. 2007a. "European Neighbourhood Policy: Who Participates? http://ec.europa.eu/world/enp/partners/index_en.htm (accessed 8 August 2007).

———. 2007b. "List of Air Carriers Banned within the EU." http://ec.europa.eu/transport/air-ban/list_en.htm (accessed 6 July 2007).

European Conference of Ministers of Transport. 1995. "Towards the Development of Coordinated and Harmonised Transport Systems in the Western Mediterranean Region." Paper presented at the Meeting of Ministers of Transport of Western Mediterranean Countries, Paris, 20 January.

European Court of Justice. 2002. "Judgment of the Court." *Official Journal of the European Communities* C Series 323: 2–8.

European Parliament and the European Council. 2004. "Regulation 261/2004 of the European Parliament and of the Council Establishing Common Rules on Compensation and Assistance to Passengers in the Event of Denied Boarding and of Cancellation or Long Delay of Flights, and Repealing Regulation (EEC) No 295/91." *Official Journal of the European Union* L Series 46: 1–7.

EU (European Union). 2002. "Treaty Establishing the European Union." *Official Journal of the European Communities* C Series 325: 33–184.

FAA (Federal Aviation Administration). 2007. "International Aviation Safety Assessment (IASA) Results by Country." http://www.faa.gov/safety/programs _initiatives/oversight/iasa/ (accessed 5 July 2007).

Feige, Irene. 2007. *Transport, Trade and Economic Growth: Coupled or Decoupled?* Berlin: Springer-Verlage Berlin.

FlightSafe Consultants. 2007. Countries in the FlightSafe Database. http://www .flightsafe.co.uk/.

Flight Safety Foundation. 2007. "Air Safety Network: Aviation Safety Database." http://aviation-safety.net/index.php (accessed 29 June 2007, 28 September 2007).

Flouris, Triant G. 2003. "A Theoretical Justification of Global Air Transport Liberalization: The False Dilemma of Political Versus Economic Cost." *Business Briefing: Aviation Strategies: Challenges and Opportunities of Liberalization* (March): 20–22.

Ford, Neil. 2007. "Rwanda, Burundi to Join East African Community." *African Business* 1 (April). http://www.thefreelibrary.com/Rwanda%2c+Burundi+to +join+East+African+Community%3a+Rwanda+and+Burundi...- a0162237549.

Frankel, Jeffrey A., and David Romer. 1999. "Does Trade Cause Growth?" *American Economic Review* 89 (3): 379–99.

Geddes, Charles L. 1991. *A Documentary History of the Arab-Israeli Conflict*. New York: Praeger.

Gibbs, David. 1984. "The Politics of Economic Development: The Case of the Mauritanian Fishing Industry." *African Studies Review* 27 (4): 79–93.

Government of Uganda. 2006. *The Uganda Gazette*, vol. XCVIX, Statutory Instruments Supplement No. 27. Kampala: Uganda Printing and Publishing Corporation.

Guttery, Ben R. 1998. *Encyclopedia of African Airlines*. Jefferson, NC: McFarland & Company.

Gwet, Henri, and Christophe Rizet. 1998. *An International Comparison of Road Haulage Prices: Africa, South-East Asia, Central America*. Paris: Elsevier.

Gwilliam, Ken. 2007. *Roads in Africa*. Washington, DC: World Bank.

Henshaw, Amber. 2008. "Sudan Crash Airline Is Grounded." BBC News. http://news.bbc.co.uk/2/hi/africa/7467423.stm (accessed 23 June 2008).

IATA (International Air Transport Association). 2004. *Safety Report: 2004 Edition*. Montreal and Geneva: IATA.

———. 2006. *Safety Report: 2006 Edition*. Montreal and Geneva: IATA.

———. 2007a. *Airline Liberalisation* Geneva: IATA.

———. 2007b. *IATA Operational Safety Audit (IOSA)*. Montreal and Geneva: IATA. http://www.iata.org/ps/certification/iosa (accessed 5 July 2007).

ICAO (International Civil Aviation Organization). 1944. *International Air Services Transit Agreement*. Chicago: ICAO.

———. 1999. *Convention for the Unification of Certain Rules for International Carriage by Air*. Document 9740. Montreal: ICAO.

———. 2000. *Safety Oversight Audit Manual*. Document 9735, AN/960. Montreal: ICAO.

———. 2001. *Annex 13 to the Convention on International Civil Aviation: Aircraft Accident and Incident Investigation*. Montreal: ICAO.

———. 2003a. *ICAO Universal Safety Oversight Audit Programme*. 18 E/CAR DCA - IP/03. Montreal: ICAO.

———. 2003b. "Instituting Mechanisms for Fair Competition." Working Paper 87, ICAO, Montreal.

———. 2004a. *Economic Contribution of Civil Aviation*. Circular 292-AT/124. Montreal: ICAO.

———. 2004b. *Manual on the Regulation of International Air Transport*. Document 9626. Montreal: ICAO.

———. 2006. Regionalization of Safety." Working Paper 31, ICAO, Montreal.

———. 2007. "Developments in the Statistics and Forecasting Programmes." Report presented at the 36th Assembly of the ICAO, Montreal, 7 March.

———. 2008. *Significant Safety Concerns on Djibouti*. Montreal: ICAO.

Inoni, Ephraim. 2007. Letter of Intent from the Prime Minister of Cameroon to the International Monetary Fund. http://www.spm.gov.cm/detail_artbg.php?iddocument=459&lang=en&tpl=1&type=docbg.

Institute for Security Studies. 2007a. *History and Background of the Organisation of African Unity, the African Economic Community, and the African Union*. Pretoria: Institute for Security Studies.

———. 2007b. *Profile: Arab Maghreb Union*. Pretoria: Institute for Security Studies.

Institute of Air Transport. 1990. "Africa and the Liberalization of the Air Transport Regulatory System." In *20 ITA Studies and Reports*. Paris: Institute of Air Transport.

Interstate Aviation Committee. 2006. *The State of Flight Safety of the Aircraft Designed and Manufactured in the Former USSR for the 30 Years of Operation*. Montreal: Interstate Aviation Committee.

Intervistas. 2006. *The Economic Impact of Air Service Liberalization*. Washington, DC: Intervistas.

Kaminski, Bart. 2007. "Morocco's Integration into the European Common Aviation Area: Should Tunisia Follow?" In *Tunisia Global Integration Study: Further Integration Services and Manufacturing Sectors to Boost Growth.* Washington, DC: World Bank.

Kamtoh, Pierre. 2002. "La Mise en Œuvre du Droit Communautaire dans les Etats Membres de la CEMAC." Paper prepared for the Institut international de droit d'expression et d'inspiration françaises, Paris.

Kayizzi-Mugerwa, Steve, ed. 1999. *The African Economy: Policy, Institutions and the Future.* London: Routledge.

Klee, Ulrich, ed. 1997, 2001, 2004, 2007. *JP Airline-Fleets International.* Zurich: Bucher.

Kofele-Kale, Ndiva. 1981. "Cameroon and Its Foreign Relations." *African Affairs* 80 (319): 197–217.

Kotaite, Assad. 2006. "Address to the Eighth Session of the General Assembly of the Arab Civil Aviation Commission." Marrakech, 15 May.

Langewiesche, William. 2007. "Congo from the Cockpit." *Vanity Fair*, July.

League of Arab States. 1992. "Pact of the League of Arab States." *Arab Law Quarterly* 7 (2): 148–52.

———. 2007. "About the Arab League: Member States." http://www.arableagueonline.org/las/english/level2_en.jsp?level_id=11 (accessed 9 August 2007).

Leinbach, Thomas R., and John T. Bowen, Jr. 2004. "Air Cargo Services and the Electronics Industry in Southeast Asia." *Journal of Economic Geography* 4 (3): 299–321.

Macdonald, Donald. 2006. *Yamoussoukro Decision: Kill or Cure?* Montreal: International Civil Aviation Organization, World Bank, and Air Transport Action Group Air Transport Development Forum.

Mandaza, Ibbo, and Arne Tostensen. 1994. *In Search of a Common Future: From the Conference to the Community.* Gaborone: Southern African Development Community.

Matthews, Jacqueline. 1984. "Economic Integration in Southern Africa: Progress or Decline?" *South African Journal of Economics* 52 (3): 171–76.

M'buyinga, Elenga. 1982. *Pan Africanism or Neo-Colonialism: The Bankruptcy of the O.A.U.* London: Zed Press.

Mead, Donald C. 1969. "Economic Co-Operation in East Africa." *Journal of Modern African Studies* 7 (2): 277–87.

Micco, Alejandro, and Tomás Serebrisky. 2006. "Competition Regimes and Air Transport Cost: The Effects of Open Skies Agreements." *Journal of International Economics* 70: 25–51.

Middle East Online. 2007. "Maghreb Countries Plan Open Skies Deal." http://www.middle-east-online.com/English/mauritania/?id=20194 (accessed 6 August 2007).

Ministry of Aviation. 2006. *Final Report on the Accident to Sosoliso Airlines DC9-32 Aircraft Registered 5N-BFD at Port Harcourt International Airport on 10 December 2005*. Abuja: Government of Nigeria.

Ministry of Civil Aviation. 2005. *Factual Report of Investigation of Accident: Flash Airlines Flight 604, January 3, 2004, Boeing 737-300 SU-ZCF, Red Sea off Sharm El-Sheikh, Egypt*. Cairo: Government of the Arab Republic of Egypt.

Ministry of Transport Department of Air Accident Investigation. 2003. *Accident Report CAV/ACC/8/2003*. Nairobi: Government of Kenya.

Mugomba, Agrippah T. 1978. "Regional Organisations and African Underdevelopment: The Collapse of the East African Community." *Journal of Modern African Studies* 16 (2): 261–72.

Munyagi, Margaret T. 2006. *Existing Bi-lateral Air Service Agreements of Tanzania as of 30 November 2006*. Dar-es-Salaam: Tanzania Civil Aviation Authority.

Myburgh, Andrew, Fathima Sheik, Fatima Fiandeiro, and James Hodge. 2006. *Clear Skies over Southern Africa*. Woodmead, South Africa: ComMark Trust.

National Commission of Inquiry. 2004. *Report on the Accident on 6 March 2003 at Tamanrasset to the Boeing 737-200 Registered 7T-VEZ Operated by Air Algérie*. Algiers: Ministry of Transport, Government of Algeria.

National Transportation Safety Board. 2002. *Aircraft Accident Brief: EgyptAir Flight 990, Boeing 767-366ER, SU-GAP, 60 Miles South of Nantucket, Massachusetts, October 31, 1999*. Washington, DC: National Transportation Safety Board.

OAU (Organisation of African Unity). 1973. *10th Summit Anniversary*. Addis Ababa: OAU Secretariat.

———. 1980. *Lagos Plan of Action for the Economic Development of Africa, 1980–2000*. Lagos: OAU. http://www.uneca.org/itca/ariportal/docs/lagos_plan.PDF.

———. 2000. *Profile: The Organization of African Unity*. Addis Ababa: OAU Directorate of Foreign Affairs.

Obuah, Emmanuel. 1997. *The Context of Development through a Regional Cooperation Strategy: The Case Study of ECOWAS*. Brighton, U.K.: University of Sussex.

O'Connor, William E. 2000. *An Introduction to Airline Economics*. London: Greenwood.

Official Airline Guide. 2007, available at http://www.oag.com.

OXERA. 2006. "What Are the Economic Impacts of Relaxing Product and Capital Market Restrictions?" Report for the International Air Transport Association, Oxford, U.K.

Oxford Economic Forecasting. 2005. *The Economic and Social Benefits of Air Transport.* Geneva: Air Transport Action Group.

Peaslee, Amos Jenkins. 1974. *International Governmental Organizations.* The Hague: Martinus Nijoff.

Peaslee, Amos Jenkins, and Dorothy Peaslee Xydis. 1976. *International Governmental Organizations: Constitutional Documents,* revised 3rd ed. The Hague: M. Nijhoff.

Petersen, Tina Loevom. 2005. *The EAC: The Fast Guide.* Copenhagen: MsActionaid.

Radhi, Hassan. 1996. "The Arab Organisation for Civil Aviation." *Arab Law Quarterly* 11 (3): 285–93.

Rother, Philipp C. 1999. "Money Demand in the West African Economic and Monetary Union: The Problems of Aggregation." *Journal of African Economies* 8 (3): 442–47.

Rowlands, Ian H. 1998. "Mapping the Prospects for Regional Co-operation in Southern Africa." *Third World Quarterly* 19 (5): 917–34.

Sabooni, Amin. 2007. "Maghreb Countries Plan Open Skies." *Iran Daily,* April 4, p. 11. 2 http://irandaily.ir/1386/2808/html/ieconomy.htm.

SADC (Southern Africa Development Community). 1992. *Treaty of the Southern African Development Community.* Windhoek, South Africa: SADC.

———. 1996. *Protocol on Transport, Communications and Meteorology in the Southern African Development Regions.* Maseru, Lesotho: SADC.

———. 2005. *Major Achievements and Challenges.* Gaborone: SADC Secretariat.

———. 2006. *Annotated Record for the Ninth Meeting of the SADC Civil Aviation Committee.* Manzini, Swaziland: SADC.

———. 2007. *Status of the Implementation of the YD in SADC and EAC as of 4 May 2007.* SADC.

Schlumberger, Charles E. 2007. "Air Transport: Revitalizing Yamoussoukro." In *Services Trade and Development: The Experience of Zambia,* ed. Aaditya Mattoo and Lucy Payton, 191–209. Washington, DC: World Bank.

Schmeling, Ursula. 2007. "Royal Air Maroc (RAM): Competition on the Upswing." *International Transport Journal* (special edition on North Africa, ITZ 27–28): 12. http://www.transportjournal.ch/e/itz/itz/artikel.php?id =14182.

SH&E Ltd. and Ernst and Young. 2005. *Formation of a National Airline in Zambia.* Report prepared for the Government of Zambia.

Soars, Jonathan, ed. 2007. "Back Aviation Solutions OAG Schedules Database." In *Published and Unpublished Non-Stop Passenger Departures.* Report prepared for the World Bank.

Standing Committee on Transport and Regional Services of the Parliament of Australia. 2003. *Commercial Regional Aviation Services in Australia and*

Transport Links to Major Populated Islands. Canberra: Government of Australia.

Sterling Merchant Finance, Ltd. 2007. *Privatization of TACV: Market Research and Strategic Options*. Washington, DC: Sterling Merchant Finance, Ltd.

Stevens, Barrie. 1997. "The Impact of Air Transport." *OECD Observer* (Special Edition on Sustainable Development).

Strategic Planning Consulting. 2006. *Digest of Bilateral Air Service Agreements Concluded by Ethiopia*. Addis Ababa: Strategic Planning Consulting.

Thomas, Geoffrey, and Christine Forbes Smith. 2003. *Flightpaths*. Perth, Australia: Aerospace Technical Publications International.

Treaty Creating the Arab Union of the Maghreb. 1992. *Arab Law Quarterly* 7 (3): 205–8.

Tsie, Balefi. 1996. "States and Markets in the Southern African Development Community (SADC): Beyond the Neo-Liberal Paradigm." *Journal of Southern African Studies* 22 (1): 75–98.

UNCTAD (United Nations Conference on Trade and Development) and WTO (World Trade Organization). 2008. *International Trade Statistics 2001–2005*. International Trade Centre. http://www.intracen.org/tradstat/sitc3-3d/er834.htm (accessed 5 February 2008).

UNECA (United Nations Economic Commission for Africa). 1988. *Declaration of Yamoussoukro on a New African Air Transport Policy*. Yamoussoukro, Côte d'Ivoire: UNECA.

———. 1999. *Decision Relating to the Implementation of the Yamoussoukro Declaration Concerning the Liberalization of Access to Air Transport Markets in Africa*. Lagos: UNECA, Regional Cooperation and Integration Division.

———. 2000. *Report of the First Meeting of the Monitoring Body of the Yamoussoukro Decision*. Addis Ababa: UNECA.

———. 2002. *Decision Relating to the Implementation of the Yamoussoukro Declaration Concerning the Liberalization of Access to Air Transport Markets in Africa*. Addis Ababa: UNECA.

———. 2004. *La Décision de Yamoussoukro et le transport aérien en Afrique*. Paris: Servedit.

United Nations Information Organization. 1944. *Report of the Chicago Convention on International Civil Aviation*. New York: United Nations Information Organization (now the United Nations Secretariat Department of Public Information).

Usim, Uche. 2007. "How Poor Business Models Ruined African Carriers: Interview with Christian Folly-Kossi, Secretary General, African Airlines Association." *Daily Sun* (Lagos), October 1. http://www.sunnewsonline.com/webpages/features/ceomagazine/2007/oct/01/ceomagazine-01-10-2007-001.htm.

Van den Boogaerde, Pierre, and Charalambos Tsangarides. 2005. "Ten Years after the CFA Franc Devaluation: Progress toward Regional Integration in the WAEMU." Working Paper WP/05/145, International Monetary Fund, Washington, DC.

Vienna Convention on the Law of Treaties. 23 May 1969 (entered into force Jan, 27, 1980). *United Nations Treaty Series* 1155: 331.

WAEMU (West Africa Economic and Monetary Union). 1994. *Traité portant création de l'Union Economique et Monétaire Ouest Africaine (UEMOA)*. Dakar: WAEMU.

———. 2002a. *Décision portant adoption du programme commun du transport aérien des Etats membres de l'UEMOA*. Bulletins officiels de l'UEMOA 08/2002:CM/UEMOA. Dakar: WAEMU.

———. 2002b. *Programme Commun du Transport Aérien des Etats Membres de l'UEMOA*. Ouagadougou: WAEMU.

———. 2002c. *Règlement relatif aux pratiques anticoncurrentielles à l'intérieur de l'UEMOA*. Bulletins officiels de l'UEMOA 02/2002:CM/UEMOA. Ouagadougou: WAEMU.

———. 2003a. *Protocole d'Accord entre L'Union Économique et Monétaire Ouest Africaine et l'Organisation de l'Aviation Civile Internationale (OACI) relatif à la mise en oeuvre du Projet "COSCAP" pour la Supervision de la Sécurité Aérienne dans les États Membres de l'UEMOA*. Ouagadougou: WAEMU.

———. 2003b. *Traité modifié de l'Union Economique et Monétaire Ouest Africaine (UEMOA)*. Dakar: WAEMU.

———. 2007. "Bulletins officiels de l'Union Économique et Monétaire Ouest Africaine." http://www.uemoa.int/actes/Default.htm (accessed 23 August 2007).

World Bank. 1998. *Air Transport Trends and Economics in Western and Central Africa*. Washington, DC: World Bank.

———. 2000. "Grant for the Implementation of Air Transport Agenda in West and Central Africa: IDF Grant No. TF027394." In *Economic Community of West African States*. Washington, DC: World Bank.

———. 2002. "Grant for Building Capacity for Implementing a Program for Liberalization of Air Transport Services in West and Central Africa: IDF Grant No. TF051220." In *Economic Community of West African States*. Washington, DC: World Bank.

———. 2005. *République Démocratique et Populaire Algérienne: La Reforme du Sector des Transports*. Washington, DC: World Bank.

———. 2007. *World Development Indicators*. Washington, DC: World Bank.

World Travel and Tourism Council. 2007. *The 2007 Travel & Tourism Economic Research*. London: World Travel and Tourism Council.

Index

Note: b, f, t, and n. indicate box, figure, table, and note, respectively.

A

African Airlines Association
  commitment to liberalization, 5, 41
  in Yamoussoukro Decision monitoring body, 14
African Air Transport agency, 30
African Civil Aviation Commission
  accomplishments, 36–37
  as executing agency of Yamoussoukro Decision, 34, 36, 37, 55
  member states, 37, 58n. 4
  mission, 36
  shortcomings, 37
  in Yamoussoukro Decision monitoring body, 14
African Economic Community
  adoption of Yamoussoukro Decision, 11
  establishment of, 16
  implementation schedule, 18
  itemization of actions, 18
  Organisation of African Unity and, 18–19
  organizational structure, 19
  significance of, 18

African Union
  binding nature of decisions of, 24–26
  competition rules, 33–34
  establishment of, 21
  mission, 21
  organizational structure, 21–22
  Treaty of Abuja and, 20, 22, 23
  Yamoussoukro Decision and, 22, 24, 27, 32
air force, 48–51
airline industry
  benefits of liberalization, 159–60
  consolidation, 3, 7, 121, 125, 136, 140, 147, 174
  data sources, 116–19
  economic benefits, 152–56
  employment, 152
  evolution, 1–2, 150–51
  failing carriers, rationale for abandoning, 174
  liberalization goals, 5
  nonviable carriers as obstacles to liberalization, 173
  perishable goods transport, 153–55

229

social impact of air transportation, 156–57
structure and scope, 151–52
tourism industry, 155–56, 169
see also African Airlines Association
Algeria, 41, 62, 64, 71, 127–28, 192*t*, 200*t*
Angola, 92, 93, 100, 101, 192*t*, 200*t*
Arab Civil Aviation Commission, 67
Arab Maghreb Union, 62–65, 127
Arab Organization for Civil Aviation, 67
arbitration provisions of Yamoussoukro Decision
Articles, 14, 32
as implementation of Yamoussoukro Decision, 34, 55
see also dispute resolution
Australia, 156

B

Bahrain, 67, 68, 71
Bamako Action Plan, 74
Banjul Accord Group, 72, 74, 82–86, 111, 119–21, 124, 127, 130
banking sector, 159
Benhima, Dress, 65
Benin, 72, 76, 130, 136, 192*t*, 200*t*
bilateral air service agreements
competition regulation in, 55
development in Africa, 2
Ethiopia's, 39–40, 178–89*t*
historical evolution, 157–59
implementation of Yamoussoukro Decision through implementation of, 31, 40, 172
protectionist policies of Zambia, 38
Botswana, 37, 41, 100, 101, 143, 192*t*, 200*t*
Burkina Faso, 37, 72, 76, 130–32, 192*t*, 200*t*
Burundi, 37, 92, 93, 105, 139–40, 192*t*, 200*t*

C

Cameroon, 41, 86–87, 165, 192*t*, 200*t*
capacity. *see* traffic, frequency and capacity
Cape Verde, 37, 41, 72, 82, 132, 192*t*, 200*t*
cargo transport
expected benefits of U.S.–EU open skies agreement, 162–63
perishable goods trade, 153–55

Central African Economic and Monetary Community, 86–92, 111, 121–24, 127, 134, 136
Central African Republic, 42, 87, 136, 192*t*, 200*t*
Chad, 37, 87, 136, 193*t*, 200*t*
Chicago Conference/Convention, 46, 57, 85, 94–95, 108, 157
Civil Aviation Council of the Arab States, 66–67
Common Market for Eastern and Southern Africa, 33, 34, 92, 93–100, 111, 130, 137, 173
Communauté française d'Afrique, 76, 113n. 6
Comoros, 37, 41, 93, 144, 193*t*, 201*t*
competition
African Union rules for, 33–34
airline regulation in U.S., 157–58
Central African Economic and Monetary Community agreement, 91–92
Common Market for Eastern and Southern Africa agreement, 97, 98–99
goals of Yamoussoukro Declaration, 10
historical development of air transport in Africa, 2
implementation of Yamoussoukro Decision, 32–34, 54–55
international, pressure for liberalization and, 146
League of Arab States open skies agreement, 69–70
liberalization outcomes, 125, 127
problems of state-owned carriers, 5–6, 174
provisions of Yamoussoukro Decision, 13–14, 31–32
regulation in bilateral agreements, 55
resistance to deregulation, 2–3
West African Economic and Monetary Union agreement, 80, 113n. 7
Conference of African Ministers Responsible for Transport and Communication, 11
Congo, Democratic Republic of, 37, 48, 92, 93, 101, 134, 193*t*, 201*t*
Congo, Republic of, 37, 87, 136, 193*t*, 201*t*
consolidation of airline industry, 3, 7, 121, 125, 136, 140, 147, 174
consumer protection, 36, 70, 81, 113n. 8
Côte d'Ivoire, 41, 72, 76, 132, 133, 193*t*, 201*t*

customs administration, 173
Customs and Economic Union of Central
    Africa, 87

D

Dahomey, 76
Declaration of Mbabane, 3
dispute resolution
    Banjul Accord Group agreement, 86
    League of Arab States open skies
        agreement, 70
    see also arbitration provisions of
        Yamoussoukro Decision
Djibouti, 37, 41, 93, 111, 139–40,
    172–73, 193t, 201t

E

East African Community, 33, 34, 92,
    103–10, 111, 137, 173
East African High Commission, 103–4
Economic Commission for Africa, 3
Economic Community of West African
    States, 72–76, 111, 112n. 4
economic performance
    benefits of air transport sector for other
        industries, 152–56, 159, 167–69
    deregulation outcomes, 158
    economy-wide benefits of air transport
        sector, 152, 168–69, 174
    evolution of air transport sector,
        150–51
    expected benefits of air services
        liberalization in developed markets,
        159–64
    importance of trade, 149–50
    subsidized air routes, 169
    tourism, 155
    transportation costs and, 150, 153
economic policy
    goals of African Economic
        Community, 18
    Lagos Plan of Action, 17
    role of Organisation of African Unity,
        16–17
    see also liberalization of air services,
        generally; liberalization of air services
        in Africa; Yamoussoukro Decision
Egypt, 41, 66, 68, 71, 93, 130,
    193t, 201t
eighth freedom right, 4–5b, 158
electronics industry, 153

energy markets, 159
enforcement
    binding nature of African Union
        decisions, 24–26
    Central African Economic and Monetary
        Community agreement, 92
    Common Market for Eastern and
        Southern Africa agreement, 99
    safety and security assessments,
        42–44, 51–52
    Southern African Development
        Community agreement, 101
    Yamoussoukro Decision
        implementation, 14–15
    see also monitoring body of
        Yamoussoukro Decision
Equatorial Guinea, 24, 27, 37, 41, 87,
    111, 136, 172–73, 193t, 201t
Eritrea, 41, 93, 111, 139–40, 172–73,
    193t, 201t
Ethiopia, 41, 93, 136, 148, 168, 193t
    air safety performance, 201t
    bilateral agreements, 39–40, 178–89t
    market characteristics, 126, 137–39
European Union
    agreements with North African
        countries, 63–64
    airline regulation, 158
    benefits of open skies agreement with
        U.S., 161–63
    blacklisted carriers, 43–44, 59n. 10
    open skies agreements, 112n. 1
executing agency of Yamoussoukro
    Decision
    African Civil Aviation Commission
        designation as, 36, 37, 55
    African Union recommendations for
        implementation, 52–54
    arbitration procedures, 34
    implementation of Yamoussoukro
        Decision indicated by, 36–37
    responsibilities, 32, 36
    Yamoussoukro Decision Articles and
        provisions, 14–15

F

failing carriers, 148
    as obstacles to liberalization, 173
    policy recommendations, 174
    rationale for abandoning, 174
fares, passenger, 166–67, 169

fifth freedom right
  definition, 4b
  development in Western countries, 157
  in East Africa, 140
  goals of Yamoussoukro Decision,
    11, 28n. 3
  goals of Yamoussoukro Declaration,
    10, 28n. 2
  protectionist policy case examples,
    38–39
  trends, 124, 126–27, 127t, 128t, 147
  see also freedoms of the air
first freedom right
  definition, 4b
  see also freedoms of the air
fleet characteristics
  accidents involving Eastern-built
    aircraft, 48, 49t, 50t, 51
  data sources, 118–19, 124
  impact of liberalization, 124–25
  patterns and trends in Africa, 121–24,
    123t, 125, 125t
  safety performance of Western-built
    aircraft operating in Africa, 45t
  see also traffic, frequency and capacity
fourth freedom right
  definition, 4b
  see also freedoms of the air
freedoms of the air
  African Airlines Association's
    proposal, 5
  Banjul Accord Group agreement, 84
  Central African Economic and Monetary
    Community agreement, 89
  Common Market for Eastern and
    Southern Africa and, 95
  Declaration of Mbabane, 3
  definition and scope, 4–5b
  League of Arab States open skies
    agreement, 68–69
  Yamoussoukro Decision and, 6, 11, 147
  Yamoussoukro Declaration, 10
frequency of flights. see traffic, frequency
  and capacity

G

Gabon, 41, 87, 111, 172–73, 194t, 201t
Gambia, 41, 72, 82, 132, 194t, 201t
gateway airports, 9
Ghana, 41, 72, 82, 132, 133, 194t, 201t
Ghellab, Karim, 65

governance capacity for liberalization,
  173–74
gross domestic product, trade share of,
  149–50, 153
Guinea, 41, 82, 130, 194t, 201t
Guinea-Bissau, 41, 72, 76, 130, 194t, 201t

I

implementation of Yamoussoukro Decision
  as administrative action by specialized
    body, 30
  African Union recommendations for,
    52–54
  as application of operational principles,
    30–31
  arbitration procedures as indication
    of, 34
  by club of ready and willing states,
    41, 42
  competition rules as indication of,
    32–34, 54–55
  contract law principles of precedent and
    subsequent conditions, 54–57
  current state, 41–42, 111–12, 119, 120t,
    192–98t
  entry into force, 20–21, 23
  establishment of executing agency as
    indication of, 36–37
  future prospects, 172
  harmonization of liberalizing rules, 33
  as implementation of bilateral
    agreement compatible with Decision,
    31, 40, 172
  interpretations of meaning of, 29–31
  main elements, 31–32
  monitoring body activities as indication
    of, 35, 55, 56–57
  obstacles to, 6, 13, 15, 33, 52, 57, 171,
    172, 173, 174, 175
  operational level, 37–38, 40, 41–42, 172
  policy formulation capabilities for,
    173–74
  recommendations for uncommitted
    states, 172–73
  safety and security concerns, 52, 57,
    174–75
  uncommitted states, 111–12
  see also regional implementation of
    Yamoussoukro Decision
Indian Ocean island countries, 144–46
informal carriers, 118

infrastructure
  recommendations for policymakers, 174–75
  road, 150
insurance
  eligibility for operational permit, 13
  provisions of Yamoussoukro Declaration, 9–10
intercontinental air service
  Arab Maghreb Union agreements, 63–64
  development in Africa, 2–3
  Lagos Plan of Action, 3
  safety record, 44
  sixth freedom services, 147
Intergovernmental Agency on Development, 58n. 3
International Air Transport Association, 43, 158
International Aviation Safety Assessment Program, 43
International Civil Aviation Organization
  data collection, 116
  safety and security oversight, 42–43, 51–52, 112n. 5
  Yamoussoukro Decision reference to, 13
Interstate Aviation Committee, 51
intra-African air services
  goals of Yamoussoukro Decision, 11
  historical development, 2–3
  Lagos Plan of Action, 3
  traffic patterns and trends, 119–21
  Yamoussoukro Declaration, 3–5, 9–10
  see also bilateral air service agreements; Yamoussoukro Decision
Iraq, 68
Israel, 66

J

Jordan, 67, 68, 70

K

Kahn, Albert, 157–58
Kenya, 41, 92, 93, 103, 104–5, 109, 113–14n. 10, 126, 137, 148, 154, 194t, 202t

L

Lagos Plan of Action, 3, 17–18
League of Arab States
  founding, 65
  membership, 66, 112n. 3
  open skies agreement, 67–71, 111
  purpose, 65–66
  tensions within, 66
  transport market agreements, 66–67
Lebanon, 66, 67, 68, 70
legal system
  African Economic Community provisions, 19
  carrier liability, 81, 113n. 8
  Central African Economic and Monetary Community, 87–88
  governance capacity for liberalization, 173
  West African Economic and Monetary Union, 77–78
Lesotho, 42, 100, 101, 194t, 202t
liability of carriers, 81, 113n. 8
liberalization of air services, generally
  definition, 115
  expected economic benefits in developed markets, 159–64
  historical evolution, 157–58
  negative effects, 164
  political costs, 164–65
  see also liberalization of air services in Africa
liberalization of air services in Africa
  Arab Maghreb Union, 63–65
  causes, 146
  Central African Economic and Monetary Community, 88–92
  commitment to, in Africa, 2–3, 5, 41
  Common Market for Eastern and Southern Africa, 94–100
  current state, 2, 6–7, 37–38, 111–12, 119, 120t
  domestic political environment and reform for, 171
  East African Community, 106–10
  Economic Community of West African States, 73–76
  Economic Community of West African States agreements, 73–76
  future prospects, 147–48, 171, 172
  goals of Yamoussoukro Decision, 11, 29
  harmonization, 33
  League of Arab States agreement, 67–71, 111
  outcomes. see outcomes of air services liberalization

Southern African Development Community agreement, 102–3
state-owned carriers as obstacles to, 5–6
state support for, 38
West African Economic and Monetary Union agreement, 78–82
Yamoussoukro Declaration, 3–5, 6
see also Yamoussoukro Decision
Liberia, 37, 41, 72, 82, 132, 194*t*, 202*t*
Libya, 37, 62, 71, 93, 128, 136, 194*t*, 202*t*
licensing and certification
   safety and security provisions of Yamoussoukro Decision, 13, 42
   see also operator designation and authorization
Lusaka Declaration, 100

M

Madagascar, 37, 92, 93, 101, 111, 144–46, 172–73, 194*t*, 202*t*
maintenance, aircraft, 9–10
Malawi, 37, 92, 93, 100, 101, 143, 194*t*, 202*t*
Malaysia, 153
Mali, 37, 72, 76, 130, 195*t*, 202*t*
Marawa, Amos, 99
market characteristics, Africa air transport
   bilateral trade agreements, 2
   data sources, 116–19
   fleet analysis, 118–19
   global share, 1, 165
   impact of liberalization, 124–46
   informal carriers, 118
   methodology for performance analysis of, 115–16, 118
   potential, 1
   see also outcomes of air services liberalization
Mauritania, 24, 26, 37, 62, 71, 72, 76, 111, 130, 154, 172–73, 195*t*, 202*t*
Mauritius, 37, 92, 93, 101, 144, 195*t*, 202*t*
media sector, 159
Ministers Responsible for Air Transport, 33, 34, 52–54
monitoring body of Yamoussoukro Decision
   arbitration procedures, 14
   Articles and annexes pertaining to, 14, 30
   Central African Economic and Monetary Community monitoring body and, 92
   current status, 55–56
   implementation of Yamoussoukro Decision indicated by, 35, 56–57
   meeting schedule, 59n. 15
   meetings to date, 35, 59n. 15
   membership, 14, 32, 34–35
   principal responsibility, 14, 34
   responsibilities, 56*b*
   special considerations in limiting capacity or frequency, 12
   statement of views on competitive and predatory practices, 14
Montreal Convention, 81
Morocco, 21, 41, 62, 63–64, 65, 67, 71, 111, 128, 172–73, 195*t*, 202*t*
Mozambique, 37, 100, 101, 143, 167, 195*t*, 202*t*
Multilateral Air Services Agreement, 83–86

N

Namibia, 37, 143, 195*t*, 202*t*
national and state-owned carriers, 2, 5–6, 37–38, 41, 42, 71, 127, 164, 165, 167, 168, 171, 173, 174
Niger, 42, 72, 76, 130, 195*t*, 202*t*
Nigeria, 41, 72, 82, 132–33, 136, 195*t*, 202*t*
ninth freedom right, 5*b*
notification of designation and authorization of airline, 12
number of air carriers and aircraft, 124–25, 125*t*

O

Official Airline Guide, 117
Oman, 67, 68, 71
open skies
   definition, 6, 58n. 4
   see also liberalization of air services, generally; liberalization of air services in Africa
Operational Safety Audit Program, 43
operator designation and authorization
   Central African Economic and Monetary Community agreement, 88, 91
   Common Market for Eastern and Southern Africa agreement, 96
   eligibility criteria, 12–13
   notification to other states of issuance of, 12

revocation based on safety concerns, 57
state authority, 12
suspension or revocation, 13
Yamoussoukro Decision provisions, 12–13
Organisation of African Unity
African Economic Community and, 18–19
economic and social mission, 16–17
founding purpose, 16
origins, 16
political mission, 16
Yamoussoukro Decision endorsement, 6
in Yamoussoukro Decision monitoring body, 14
outcomes of air services liberalization
across Africa, 124–27
airfares, 166–67, 169
benefits for other economic sectors, 159, 167–69, 174
in Central Africa, 134–37
in East Africa, 137–40
expansion of African carriers in domestic markets, 127, 168
fifth freedom flights, 126–27
increased tourism, 166, 168, 169
increased trade, 169
in Indian Ocean island countries, 144–46
mechanisms of economic growth derived from, 163–64
in North Africa, 127–30
political costs, 164–65
reduced traffic, 169
in Southern Africa, 140–44, 166–68
traffic and fleet characteristics, 124–48, 166, 167
in West Africa, 130–33, 131*t*

P

Palestine, 68, 70
policy formulation capabilities for liberalization reforms, 173–74
population patterns, 149
poverty patterns, 149
Preferential Trade Area for Eastern and Southern Africa, 93

Q

Qatar, 67, 71

R

regional air services
access of remote areas to trade, 169–70
development in Africa, 2
traffic patterns and trends, 119–21, 127
regional economic communities
air fleet characteristics, 121–24, 123*t*
air safety oversight, 52, 53*t*
air traffic patterns and trends, 119–21, 126*t*
binding nature of African Union decisions, 24–25
Central Africa, 86, 119–21, 134–37, 147. *see also* Central African Economic and Monetary Community
East Africa, 92–93, 119–21, 137–40, 148. *see also specific community*
fifth freedom flights, 126–27, 127*t*, 128*t*
future prospects, 147–48
impact of air services liberalization, 124, 127–46, 166–68
Indian Ocean island countries, 144–46
North Africa, 62, 127–30. *see also specific community*
Southern Africa, 92, 140–44. *see also specific community*
West Africa, 72, 119–21, 130–33, 147. *see also specific community*
see also regional implementation of Yamoussoukro Decision
regional implementation of Yamoussoukro Decision
Arab Maghreb Union and, 62–65
Banjul Accord Group and, 83–86, 111, 130
Central African Economic and Monetary Community and, 88–92, 111, 136–37, 147
Common Market for Eastern and Southern Africa and, 94–100, 111, 130
diversity of approaches and outcomes, 111
East African Community and, 106–10, 111
Economic Community of West African States agreements and, 73–76, 111
future prospects, 172
League of Arab States and, 67–72, 111
obstacles to, 15
possible groupings, 61–62

rationale, 110
recommendations for, 173
significance of, 61
Southern African Development
  Community and, 103
West African Economic and Monetary
  Union and, 78–82, 111, 130, 147
reservations systems, 9–10
La Réunion Island, 146
revenue passenger-kilometers flown,
  1, 115–16, 165
road transport
  costs, 150
  inadequacies, 2, 150
  trade growth in airline substitution
    for, 169
rural–urban population distribution, 149
Rwanda, 41, 92, 93, 105, 139–40,
  195t, 203t

S

safety and security
  accidents involving air force flights,
    48–51
  accidents involving Eastern-built aircraft,
    48, 49t, 50t, 51
  accidents involving older aircraft, 48,
    49–50t
  Banjul Accord Group agreement, 85–86
  causes of accidents among African
    carriers, 46–48
  comparison of African states, 51–52,
    200–205t
  international assessments, 42–44, 51–52
  obstacles to Yamoussoukro Decision
    implementation, 52, 57
  performance of African carriers,
    44–46, 57
  performance of Western-built aircraft
    operating in Africa, 45t
  recommendations for policymakers,
    174–75
  regional oversight, 52, 53t
  revocation of permits or limitation of
    operations because of, 57
  West African Economic and Monetary
    Union agreement, 78–79, 81
  Yamoussoukro Decision provisions,
    13, 42
Saharawi Arab Democratic Republic,
  37, 42, 63, 196t, 203t

São Tomé and Principe, 42, 134, 196t, 203t
Saudi Arabia, 66
Seabury Group, 117
second freedom right
  definition, 4b
  see also freedoms of the air
Senegal, 42, 72, 76, 132, 203t
September 11 terrorist attacks, 119
seventh freedom right, 4b
Seychelles, 37, 92, 93, 101, 144, 196t, 203t
Sierra Leone, 42, 72, 82, 132, 196t, 203t
sixth freedom right
  definition, 4b
  trends, 4b
  see also freedoms of the air
social impact of air transportation, 156–57
Somalia, 42, 68, 111, 139–40, 172–73,
  196t, 203t
South Africa, 24, 26, 38–39, 41, 100, 101,
  111, 140, 142–43, 142t, 166, 172–73,
  173, 196t, 203t
Southern African Development
  Community, 33, 34, 92, 100–103,
  140, 143–44, 166–67, 173
Sudan, 37, 68, 93, 139, 197t, 204t
Swaziland, 24, 26, 42, 92, 93, 100, 101,
  111, 172–73, 197t, 204t
Syria, 67, 68, 70

T

Tanganyika, 103, 104
Tanzania, 37, 92, 93, 100, 101, 103, 104–5,
  109, 139, 148n. 4, 154–55, 197t, 204t
tariffs
  Banjul Accord Group agreement, 84
  Central African Economic and Monetary
    Community agreement, 89, 91
  Common Market for Eastern and
    Southern Africa agreement, 96
  League of Arab States open skies
    agreement, 69–70
  provisions of Yamoussoukro Decision, 11
  West African Economic and Monetary
    Union agreement, 80
telecommunications sector, 159
third freedom right
  definition, 4b
  see also freedoms of the air
Togo, 42, 72, 76, 130, 197t, 204t
tourism
  benefits of air services liberalization, 169

economic significance, 155–56
liberalization outcomes in Southern Africa, 166, 168
trade
  access of remote areas to international markets, 169–70
  air transport sector share, 152
  current patterns in Africa, 149–50
  economic growth and, 150, 153–54, 169–70
  expected benefits of open skies agreements, 162–63, 164, 169
  perishable goods, 153–55
  transportation costs and, 150, 153
traffic, frequency and capacity
  Banjul Accord Group agreement, 84
  cargo transport on passenger aircraft, 154
  Central Africa, 134–37, 135*t*
  Central African Economic and Monetary Community, 89, 91
  city pair combinations, 11, 38, 119–20, 122*t*
  Common Market for Eastern and Southern Africa, 96
  data sources, 116–18, 148n. 1–2
  East Africa, 137–40, 138*t*
  goals of Yamoussoukro Declaration, 9
  Indian Ocean island countries, 144–46
  liberalization outcomes, 124, 127–46, 160–61, 166, 167, 169
  limitations based on safety concerns, 57
  methodology for analysis of, 115–16, 118
  North Africa, 127–30, 129*t*
  patterns and trends, 119–21, 121*t*, 126–27, 126*t*, 127*t*
  Southern Africa, 140–44, 141*t*
  special considerations for limiting, 11–12
  West Africa, 130–33, 131*t*
  Yamoussoukro Decision impacts, 125, 126, 130, 133, 136–37, 146–48
  Yamoussoukro Decision provisions, 11–12
training provisions of Yamoussoukro Declaration, 9–10
Treaty of Abuja
  African Union and, 22, 23
  Articles and provisions, 18–19
  as basis for Yamoussoukro Decision, 20–21, 23, 27
  legal system, 19
  nontreaty states, 23–27
  origins, 16
  ratification and entry into force, 19–20, 23
  signatories, 20, 23–24
Treaty of Lagos, 72, 73
Tunisia, 37, 62, 64, 68, 71, 128–30, 197*t*, 204*t*

U

Uganda, 40, 42, 92, 93, 103, 104–5, 109, 139–40, 197*t*, 204*t*
United Arab Emirates, 67–68, 70
United Nations Economic and Social Council, 3, 10, 14
United States
  airline regulation, 157–59
  benefits of open skies agreement with European Union, 161–63
  Federal Aviation Administration, 43
  global deregulation movement and, 2–3
  Universal Safety Oversight Audit Programme, 42–43
Upper Volta, 76

W

West African Economic and Monetary Union, 72, 74, 76–82, 111, 113n. 7, 124, 127, 130–32
  aviation laws and regulations, 207–14*t*
Western Sahara. *see* Saharawi Arab Democratic Republic
wet leasing, 162, 170n. 1

Y

Yamoussoukro Decision
  African Union and, 22, 24, 27
  annexes, 14
  arbitration provisions, 14, 32
  Articles and provisions, 11–16
  commercial issues, 15
  on competition, 13–14, 31–32
  consultations for interpretation and application, 15–16
  consumer protection provisions, 36
  executing agency. *see* executing agency of Yamoussoukro Decision
  expansion of African carriers in domestic markets, 127
  goals, 6, 11, 29, 172
  implementation. *see* implementation of Yamoussoukro Decision

industry support, 41
monitoring body. *see* monitoring body of Yamoussoukro Decision
operational issues, 15
origins, 6, 10–11, 20
parties to, 24–27, 27
procedure for designating and authorizing carriers, 12–13, 30–31
regional implementation. *see* regional implementation of Yamoussoukro Decision
safety and security compliance assessment, 42–43
safety and security provisions, 13, 42
significance of, 29, 171, 172
tariff rules, 11
traffic and fleet characteristic outcomes, 125, 126, 130, 133, 136–37, 146–48
transitional measures, 15
Treaty of Abuja as basis for, 20–21, 23, 27

Yamoussoukro Declaration and, 9, 29, 30
see also liberalization of air services in Africa
Yamoussoukro Declaration
core provisions, 6, 9
Declaration of Mbabane and, 3–5
implementation schedule, 9–10
objectives, 9–10
obstacles to implementation, 6
origins, 9
outcomes, 6, 10
signing, 6
Yamoussoukro Decision and, 9, 29, 30
Yemen, Republic of, 68, 70

Z

Zambia, 38–39, 42, 92, 93, 100, 101, 143, 166–67, 198*t*, 205*t*
Zimbabwe, 37, 92, 93, 100, 101, 143, 198*t*, 205*t*

ECO-AUDIT
Environmental Benefits Statement

The World Bank is committed to preserving endangered forests and natural resources. ***Open Skies for Africa: Implementing the Yamoussoukro Decision*** is printed on a recycled paper made with 50-percent post-consumer waste. The Office of the Publisher follows the recommended standards for paper usage set by the Green Press Initiative, a nonprofit program supporting publishers in using fiber that is not sourced from endangered forests. For more information, visit www.greenpressinitiative.org.

Saved:
- 9 trees
- 3 million BTUs of total energy
- 819 pounds of net greenhouse gases
- 3,945 gallons of waste water
- 240 pounds of solid waste

www.ingramcontent.com/pod-product-compliance
Lightning Source LLC
Chambersburg PA
CBHW050349230426

43663CB00010B/2044